HOW THE COMMUNIST PRESS WORKS

★ ★ ★ ★

Antony Buzek: HOW THE COMMUNIST PRESS WORKS

Frederick A. Praeger, *Publisher*
New York · London

FREDERICK A. PRAEGER, *Publisher*
111 Fourth Avenue, New York 3, NY, USA
77-79 Charlotte Street, London, W1, England

Published in the United States of America in 1964
by Frederick A. Praeger, Inc., Publisher

© Antony Buzek 1964
Library of Congress Catalog Card Number: 64–21843

This book is Number 147 in the series of
Praeger Publications in Russian History and World Communism

PRINTED IN GREAT BRITAIN

CONTENTS

1
INTRODUCTION
THE PRESS AS A POLITICAL INSTRUMENT

EVEN THE BRIEFEST encounter with the communist press will convince the detached observer that it is something different from the press of the rest of the world. The communist press, and especially the newspapers, retains only a few characteristics of the traditional press. Contents, treatment of events of everyday life, objectivity and truthfulness, methods of reporting and writing, and sometimes even the layout, strike a quite different note from the press and newspapers familiar to readers in the democratic countries.

This different character and face of the press is typical for all countries under communist rule, not only for the Soviet Union. Even the press of countries previously known for their high journalistic standards and traditions, such as Czechoslovakia, Hungary or East Germany, was transformed within a short period after the establishment of the communist regime into a tool of party propaganda and agitation.

Political and economic propaganda and agitation colour every published item, picture, story and even crossword puzzle. The reader becomes immediately aware that the communist newspaper, as the most typical representative of the press, has the prime object of making propaganda, that it is a 'political institution which for purposes of efficiency (only) bears the character of a newspaper', as a former editor-in-chief of the East German communist organ admitted.[1]

The predominance of political and economic propaganda and agitation is one of the main characteristics of the communist press. Another is its total subjection to the communist party. The party alone decides what papers are to be published and exercises control through appointing the editors and journalists and through the allocation of funds and newsprint. This subjection to the party and to the communist ideology restricts the press's freedom not only in publishing news and views, but even in its efforts to entertain the reader.

The press takes a prominent place in the communist system of propaganda and agitation as a means of maintaining the rule of the party. Theoreticians of marxism-leninism and present leaders of the Communist Party of the Soviet Union

(CPSU) invariably call it the most important tool, the sharpest weapon of the party in the battle for the minds of the people. Yet, the press is a rather neglected subject in western literature on the problems of communism. It is dealt with in the few published works on the propaganda system only as a minor part of it, or a few specialised studies, mostly by West German authors, are concerned with the press of one country only, namely that of East Germany.

Thus Alex Inkeles included a chapter on the press in his pioneering work on the methods of communist propaganda and agitation, *Public Opinion in Soviet Russia* (1950), as did also Bruno Kalnins in his book *Der Sowjetische Propagandastaat* (The Soviet Propaganda State, 1956). In the German literature there is one detailed study from 1951 by A. W. Just, *Die Presse der Sowjet Union* (The Soviet Press). Another German work, that of Ernst Richert, *Agitation und Propaganda* (1958), deals with the East German press in the framework of the country's agitational and propagandist system. Mrs E. M. Herrmann was concerned exclusively with the East German press in her work *Die Presse in der Sowjetischen Besatzungszone* (The Press in the Soviet Occupation Zone), published in 1957.

Otherwise a mass of interesting articles, studies and facts about the communist press in general and in particular countries is scattered through journals and reviews over many years. These are usually inaccessible to the ordinary reader interested in communist affairs and, especially communist journalistic publications, are difficult of access even for the serious student.

A very good and useful review of the contemporary position of the press in various communist countries was published in 1959 by the International Press Institute in its *Survey* series under the title *The Press in Authoritarian Countries*. Due to its practical character, the study however concentrated on the latest developments and very general characteristics and did not investigate deeply into the ideological foundations, organisations, methods and contents of the communist press as a whole.

The aim of this book is to fill the undoubted gap and to attempt a balanced account of the theory and practice of the communist press as a whole and in the Soviet Union and east European countries separately whenever and wherever there are differences, without however trying to give a detailed historical and factual review or comparison with the western press.

The stress will be on the application of marxist-leninist doctrine to the contemporary communist press and the re-action of journalists to political and ideological subjection to the party dictate. Countries where there is evidence of an independent national approach to the problems of the press, or from which there is more information available on some specific problems, are dealt with separately in individual chapters. Countries such as Rumania, Bulgaria or Albania, which do not show any specific features and are still retaining the old, pre-1953 pattern with little change, are not discussed in detail.

This inquiry concentrates on the press in its generally accepted meaning—that is newspapers and periodicals—and includes also news agencies which, in the communist press system, are not only practically the only source of news for the newspapers and radio, but also an important tool in the direction of the press. Problems of book publishing and also of radio and television have had to be omitted even where they have common ground with the press. In many aspects these media call for a different approach. To deal with their problems and with those of writers and literature generally would lead into a quite different sphere of propagandist consideration.

An inquiry into the communist press cannot be conducted on the purely practical level. If the reader were to start the inquiry or comparison with the standards of a free society, he would fail to understand the essence of the communist press, its transformation into a fully subordinated tool of propaganda, its place and functions within the larger framework of communist society. Communist society is based upon different philosophical conceptions of social development, of the role of individuals and political or public organisations and institutions within it. It interprets differently such values as truth, freedom, objectivity, and so on.

It is therefore necessary to start in the first place with a brief introduction to those parts of communist ideology which shape the functions, character and contents of the press. Those parts are dialectical and historical materialism, the theory of the dictatorship of the proletariat and from them derives teaching on the communist party justifying the totalitarian grip on all aspects of social life.

Propaganda and agitation together with coercion are the most important tools in maintaining the communist dictatorship. Their theoretical justification and their elaborate system within the party apparatus must be also briefly investigated to enable the reader to understand better the functions and characteristic features of the communist press which are dealt with in the next two chapters. These chapters show how the doctrine prescribes that the press must fulfil the functions of a mass propagandist, agitator, organiser and critic. It also demands from the press that it should approach and treat all problems from the class and party standpoint. These demands have shaped the contents and methods of the press and sub-ordinated it to the supervision and direction by the party.

Further chapters show how all the doctrinal requirements are applied in practice. The results can be seen in the horizontal and vertical structure of the Soviet press adapted to the territorial-administrative levels of the party and state apparatus and to the groupings of the bodies which alone are allowed to publish: the party, the government and public organisations such as trade unions.

This differentiation was supposed to give facilities for the differentiation of the contents of the press best suited to trans-mit in proper form and language the party's propaganda and instructions to different strata of population. Yet the rigid application of dogma and doctrinal requirements led to uni-formity, dullness and drabness of the press in the stalinist period, thereby defeating its own purpose.

Important changes and developments, known generally as 'the thaw', 'liberalisation' or 'destalinisation', have occurred in the communist orbit since 1953 and especially 1956 following the reappraisal of some dogmas and practices. Convulsions in Hungary and Poland, greater independence of satellites from the Soviet Union, ideological splits within the apparently mono-lithic communist movement caused by Peking's aspirations—all these had their effect.

The press, together with other propagandist media, was adapted to the new tasks and in the new communist drive it was considerably expanded. This adaptation and the admission of the possibility of different national roads to communism have led to greater differentiation in the contents of the communist press as a whole and also to a differentiation within the Soviet bloc. Today, it is no longer true to say that the whole com-munist press is uniform. Although the differences between the press of particular communist countries only affect—to use

a marxist formula—the form, not the substance, they are nevertheless noticeable in some important aspects of the treatment of
news and information and the extent of entertainment and
indoctrination of the reader.

Apart from the Soviet press, which still remains the most
important representative of the communist press, there are
differences between, say, the press of Yugoslavia, Poland and
Hungary as one group, and that of Rumania, Bulgaria, Albania
and East Germany as another group. The differences lie between orthodox and rigid or more liberal and supple attitudes
to the demands of the readers. The former group relaxed its
controls over the press, gave more freedom for journalists to
work within a broader party line, while the latter, representing
the old school, tries to retain as long as possible the stalinist
concept of strict party rule over the press.

These changes are shown in the two chapters on the
differentiation in the contents of the Soviet and east European
press (chapters 6 and 7).

Reappraisal of some dogmas and practices had its effect
also on other aspects of the communist press such as direction,
supervision, censorship, the image of life presented in the
newspapers and the conception of news. Separate chapters on
each of these aspects incorporate all the changes after 1953
and, together with the previous chapters on the differentiation
in the contents, thus give a fairly comprehensive picture of the
state of the press today against the background of ideological
principles and their practical adjustments to the changing
conditions of communist society.

A work of this kind which attempts a balanced view of the
communist press as a whole must inevitably contain a large
amount of factual details and be descriptive. In many chapters
it is impossible to avoid reiteration of observations or ideological
concepts when dealing with the theoretical and practical side of
the same problem or when the problems overlap from chapter
to chapter. In some instances the repetition is intentional in
order to emphasise to the reader the need for continually
bearing in mind the over-riding role of doctrine or to facilitate
any future references.

Thus the problems of worker and peasant correspondents
or the problem of criticism in the press are broached in chapters
on the characteristic features of the press and on the changes in
the contents, but their practical application is fully shown in the

chapter on the work of the newspapers. Similarly, the questions of circulation, of advertising or of methods of circulation promotion, touched upon in different places, are explained in greater detail in the context of the work of the newspapers.

Reading through these pages the reader may be intrigued by the question of how the journalists are conditioned and educated, what is their status or their attitude to the subordination of their press to the party's dictate. These questions, broached or partly answered throughout the book, are again summed up in the final chapter on the communist journalists.

The events of recent years have shown that the communist parties, despite all their means of supervision and discipline and despite the fact that the editors are themselves high party functionaries, cannot exert full control over the journalists. In the campaign for brightening the dull, ineffective press of the stalinist period, communist parties in the Soviet Union and in east Europe have had to allow journalists greater freedom albeit of only marginal dimensions. Yet even these marginal freedoms had some undesired effects. Journalists and writers began to probe—with an intensity varying according to the conditions in their countries—into numerous problems of political, economic and cultural life. These activities reflected in their final impact on the position of the communist party itself.

Here communism comes up against one of its inner contradictions which is difficult to resolve. Without permitting more freedom for the journalists and writers, the regime cannot improve the readability of the press and effectiveness of its propaganda. But this freedom breeds ideological and spiritual ferment which could erode the very foundations of the regime. In Poland and Czechoslovakia, therefore, the parties have tried to pull in the reins, to restore a tighter control and reinstate some of the old suppressive practices. This however curtails efficiency and creates dissatisfaction and open opposition as events in Czechoslovakia in 1962 and 1963 have confirmed.

It remains yet to be seen what will be the outcome of this continuous clash between the rigid doctrine and dictate of the party's leadership on the one side and the aspirations of journalists on the other. Many journalists after bitter experiences of the last years are aware that a free press responsible to the people is a precondition for the liberalisation and humanisation of communist society. Their attitude in the recent past shows they are determined to continue their struggle.

2

MARXISM-LENINISM, PROPAGANDA
AND THE PRESS

MARXISM-LENINISM, as the communists claim, provides not only theoretical and philosophical foundations for their movement and society but also practical guidance for the long-term strategy and short-term tactics of their policy and for the day-to-day activities in practically every sphere of social life.

Marxism-leninism is generally defined as 'the science of the laws of nature's and society's development, of the revolution by the oppressed and exploited masses, of the victory of socialism in all countries, of the construction of the communist society'.[1] Communist theoreticians claim that it is a comprehensive, complete, systematic and scientific theory, world outlook, or *Weltanschauung*. Its basic and integral parts—organically tied together—are dialectical and historical materialism, the economic teaching and the theory of scientific communism. The most important part of the latter is the teaching on the dictatorship of the proletariat without which communism could not be built.

It is important to note that communist theoreticians always stress that marxism-leninism is a science, a scientific system. From this 'scientific' character follows its claimed monopoly of historic truthfulness, correctness. And by this they justify all means, including violence, in the pursuit of the final aim: the establishment of the communist society. This society is, as they assert without realising the implied contradiction, bound to be established by an inevitable historic process of evolution, yet cannot be established without revolution, without the use of violence and coercion, without the dictatorship of the prole-tariat.* From the 'scientific' analysis of social processes on the basis of dialectical and historic materialism follows, in the communist view, also the only right approach to the function of the press and manipulation of news and objectivity.

* Khrushchev revised this principle at the Twenty and Twenty-second Congress of the CPSU in 1956 and 1961. He maintained that, under changed conditions, the transition from bourgeois to socialist society could be effected in certain countries even without revolution, through the skilful use of parliamentary democracy. This view was incorporated into official congress documents. The Chinese communists strongly object to this modification as 'revisionist' and a 'betrayal of fundamentals of marxism-leninism'. (See also footnote on p. 17.)

THE PARTY AND THE DICTATORSHIP OF THE PROLETARIAT

The decisive factor in shaping the functions and character of the present-day communist press was, however, the theory of the dictatorship of the proletariat and from it derived the teaching on the revolutionary party. The model and embodiment of its ideals was the Russian Bolshevik Party, the present Communist Party of the Soviet Union. The theoretical foundations of this revolutionary party were laid by Marx and Engels. They claimed in their theory of historic materialism that the laws of human society's evolution designated the proletariat, the working class, led by its politically organised vanguard, the communist party, as the future ruler.

Vague and sketchy ideas of Marx and Engels were developed further by Lenin. He elaborated a comprehensive theory of the party as the leading, directing organisation of the proletariat and set out in great detail its ideological principles (long-term strategy) and political and organisational principles (short-term tactics). But Lenin did something even more important: he translated his theory into practice and founded a truly revolutionary party which under his leadership finally triumphed in the October Revolution and began to build communism.

Lenin pointed out two essentials for the successful fight: a correct ideology and firm organisation. The revolutionary movement—and of course its spearhead, the party—must be first guided by a revolutionary theory because, as he said, 'without the revolutionary theory there is no revolutionary movement'.[2] Then comes the need for a firm organisation because organisation is the basis of any political success.

The paramount need for these two essentials was explained by Lenin in his pamphlet *What is to be Done?*:

> The proletariat can become, and inevitably will become, the victorious force only thanks to the fact that its ideological unity on the basis of the principles of marxism-leninism will be strengthened by the material unity of organisation rallying millions of workers into the army of the working class.[3]

As the leader and guide of the proletarian masses, the party must according to its theory set out the goals, determine the strategy and tactics of the class struggle, must stand at the head of the working class movement. It must never succumb to the moods and vacillations of the masses whose instincts in class matters are basically sound but whose political consciousness is very weak or often non-existent. The party must give due heed to their views and sentiments but must not let itself be drawn by them, to be at the masses' tail. To do this would mean to commit a very serious political error, *khvostism* (from *khvost*—a tail).

Marx, Engels and Lenin agreed on two means which should be applied in the fight for the establishment of the classless communist society. One was violence, coercion with the dictatorship of the proletariat as its outward symbol. It should be applied not only in the struggle for political power but also later for its retention and consolidation. The second means, running parallel to the first, was to convince the masses of the correctness of its policy by explaining the strategy and tactics to them, by winning them over by *persuasion*. This explanatory, persuasive activity forms the basis of communist propaganda and agitation, one of the most important functions of every communist party.

Though the dictatorship of the proletariat and its use of violence and coercion are not directly connected with the press and propaganda, it is necessary to show both foundations of communist power—coercion and persuasion—in proper balance. By understanding the teaching on the use of violence both in the theory and in the practice of communism, the reader will come to understand the militant and sometimes violent character of communist propaganda and agitation even in the most peaceful times, not only towards the 'inner, class enemy', but also towards the outside 'imperialist', 'warmongering' forces.

The dictatorship of the proletariat is the hard core of the theory and practice of communism. Marx had pointed out already in his *Critique of the Gotha Programme* that this dictatorship is an inevitable stage in the transition from the capitalist to the communist society. Lenin again elaborated this basic idea, formulating in several works the role and scope of the dictatorship, and translated it into practice. Stalin condensed Lenin's teaching in the stark definition: 'The dictatorship of the proletariat is the rule of the proletariat unrestricted by law and based on violence.'[4]

Though primarily aimed against the bourgeoisie, the dictatorship of the proletariat was nevertheless meant to be applied even against the proletarian masses themselves. Stalin, again condensing Lenin's ideas, said that the dictatorship had to fulfil three basic tasks:

1   To defeat and overthrow the bourgeoisie and to establish the rule of the proletariat.
2   To detach definitely the workers and the exploited masses from the bourgeoisie; to consolidate them into the union of the proletariat; to draw them into the process of building socialism; to govern them.
3   To organise socialism, to liquidate the classes, to effect the transition into the classless socialist society.

Only these three sides or functions taken together fully constitute, in Stalin's words, the concept of the proletariat's dictatorship.[5]

It must, however, be noted that Lenin and Stalin always stressed the peaceful, educational or persuasive side of the dictatorship in relation to the working masses. Application of violence, coercion of the masses into supporting or just meekly following the policy of the communists could, in their view, alienate them from the party and result in distrust and apathy. (But the practice of communist rule since the 'twenties until the death of Stalin was marked prominently by the use of violence and mass terror and not by persuasion.)

Elucidation of problems, education, persuasion must come first, said Lenin, but in certain circumstances, in emergencies, the party must act without prior persuasion, without winning over the entire working class for its cause. And in such cases the masses must be coerced by force and administrative methods to follow the line. Thus violence must be always kept in reserve, even against the proletariat itself.

The dictatorship of the proletariat, though one of the fundamentals of marxism-leninism, is not a permanent part of communist teaching and rule. It has its roots in the class society and according to theory it will become superfluous with the liquidation of classes.

The Twenty-second Congress of the CPSU declared in 1961 that classes ceased to exist in the Soviet Union after the construction of socialism had been completed and foundations to the communist society had been laid. Thus the dictatorship allegedly outlived its justification.[6] Yet no outward changes have been made. All the institutions and methods used for the oppression and coercion of adversaries or the reluctant population have been retained and the 'disappearance' of the dictatorship of the proletariat is purely of academic character.*

In all other communist states it is still officially, according to party programs and rules, the basis of communist power. In practice it is being pushed into the background and, in preference, an elaborate system of social pressures is used to secure the obedience of the masses.

PROPAGANDA AND AGITATION

Marx, and Lenin yet more emphatically, recognised that even the best organised movement or party cannot achieve its goal without willing co-operation from the masses. To secure this co-operation the party must wage a constant campaign to acquaint the masses with its program and policy, and convince them that their interest lies with the party. Lenin again elaborated this persuasive side of communist activities into a detailed system of propaganda and agitation and made it one of the main features of his bolshevik party.

In Lenin's conception, propaganda and agitation have a general and permanent role to spread the ideas of marxism-leninism, to explain to the masses the policy of the party and to influence them emotionally to support this policy actively. But the contents of propaganda and agitation are not constant or permanent; they change in accordance with the historical

* The dictatorship of the proletariat is one of the main points in the Sino-Soviet ideological dispute. The Chinese communists attack Khrushchev for allegedly giving it up, and brand this as retreat from true marxist-leninist positions. Khrushchev did not, however, renounce the dictatorship and the use of violence. He maintains that they should be always applied during the transition period even in countries where the transition from the bourgeois to the socialist system could be effected without revolution. The Italian Communist Party has gone even further in 'revising' marxist-leninist theory by stating on several occasions in 1963–4 that transition from capitalism to socialism can be effected in some industrially and politically highly developed countries through a multi-party system and not necessarily through rule by communist parties alone. This would imply the abandonment not only of the doctrine of the necessity of revolution but also of the principle of the dictatorship of the proletariat in the transitional period. Against this Chinese communists strongly object. Yet in fact the Italian party is only putting a new slant to the policy pursued since 1947–8 in Czechoslovakia, Hungary and East Germany, where former 'bourgeois' political parties have been formally retained but deprived of all political power by communist parties which have assumed complete supremacy.

B

circumstances and tasks which the party has to face in various phases of its political struggle and the construction of socialism or communism.

The masses, in Lenin's views, had to be guided not only in the pre-revolutionary period or in the short time of the establishment of the proletariat's dictatorship, but in the long period of building the new society. In fact, the guiding role of party propaganda increases in this period. Much broader masses have to be attracted into the process of construction and much more complex problems are to be solved. The need to 'educate' the masses becomes more important and the party then fully assumes the role of the *teacher*. Propaganda and agitation are given new and wider contents, and demands upon their resources increase.

For our understanding of the character of the communist press and propaganda, it is important to bear in mind the already mentioned feature of marxist-leninist theory, namely, that it regards the masses as politically not conscious, not ripe or mature enough. Allegedly they cannot recognise the full truth or understand the situation. Only the party, or better to say its leadership, can correctly analyse the given situation, find the way and the proper methods.

In practice, the bolshevik leaders soon realised that they could direct the masses effectively only when their propaganda and agitation used simplified, schematic concepts, ideas and slogans. These can be easily remembered by the masses and repeated again and again by agitators without danger of misinterpretation or ideological distortion.

The interpretation of events and facts by party propaganda was not sufficient in itself. The free flow of information often flatly contradicted the party images and slogans and hindered indoctrination. The party found it imperative to regulate the flow of information, to restrict and adapt or slant the news and all materials influencing the mind of the masses, in such a way that not only did it not clash with the party propaganda line but supported and supplemented it.

These two characteristics—simplified, preconceived, schematic images and selection and slanting of all information to suit the needs of the party line—have become the backbone of communist propaganda and the press.

In their practical conduct of propagandist and agitational activities, the communist parties in the Soviet Union and east

Europe are guided by the division between the party and non-party apparatus. In this division the party is the *leading, guiding force*, but not the executive organ. It guides and directs the activities of governmental and public organisations and organs through communists appointed to their management. Their duty is to apply in the work of the organs the directives of the party and the principles of marxism-leninism. Party organs and functionaries must not assume the functions of these organs of government and public organisations. They are supposed to exercise their powers indirectly, unobtrusively, and whenever they try to take into their hands the formal executive powers, they are sharply rebuked by the leadership.

In practice, the lower party organs and functionaries often assume these executive powers. The dividing line between the leading and guiding role of the party and the formal executive power is very slender and the inclination to overstep it or confuse the two roles is very much inherent in the system.

Yet the distinction between the party and non-party apparatus is an important fact and enables the party with its numerically limited, selective membership to direct the entire sphere of social life more effectively. In the field of propaganda and agitation and of the press, it gives a wide differentiation of media and better prospects for influencing the masses of non-communists who are less accessible to the direct propaganda conducted by the party apparatus. Such people are more inclined to listen to somewhat subdued 'non-communist' propaganda spread by the public organisations. This is the case even today, after forty-seven years of communist rule in the Soviet Union and especially in the new socialist countries of east Europe.

CONCEPTS OF PROPAGANDA AND AGITATION

The terms 'propaganda' and 'agitation' are today widely used in communist and non-communist societies. Yet their interpretation and the attitude to them differs considerably. In communist society, propaganda and agitation are an integral part and one of the most important aspects of the official activities of the state and the party. They embrace the entire social life and activities—from the sciences through education, press and entertainment to sport—using a much wider range of media than merely the media of mass communication in the western conception. Different also is their place among the social institutions and the significance attached to them.

It is therefore not possible to deal with them in western terms and values; they must be treated as phenomena specific to the communist society. But a brief comparison of terms and definitions of propaganda and agitation in democratic countries and in the communist orbit may be instructive.

THE WESTERN CONCEPT

Having regard to the comparatively minor use of propaganda and agitation in western countries generally and to the popular dislike towards them, it is not surprising that they are a good deal neglected in scholarly literature and that there is a general lack of proper distinction between them. Some western authors have pointed out this shortcoming in their works on communist propaganda.[7] They stress also the fact that western definitions of propaganda or agitation considerably differ from the usage in communist countries.

Changes in social development throughout the world, the rise and fall of nazism in Germany and the fascist episodes in Italy and elsewhere, together with the increased use of propaganda by the west itself during the last war and in the post-war years of the cold war and especially by the expansion of communist propaganda outside the communist orbit render conceptions and comparisons based on the usage in the 'thirties or even 'forties obsolete. More relevant are the latest definitions and views.

The 1961 edition of *The Encyclopaedia Britannica* defines propaganda in the following way:

Propaganda is the making of deliberately one-sided statements to a mass audience. It is an act of advocacy in mass communication. . . . Propaganda as an act of advocacy is distinguished from such closely allied uses of communication as instruction, information and inquiry. It is advocacy to editorialise or to select the content of channels of communication for the purpose of influencing attitudes on controversial issues. It is inquiry, not propaganda, to analyse controversial doctrines for the sake of sharing enlightenment.[8]

Some aspects of totalitarian or communist propaganda are dealt with within the framework of the entry as a whole, but communist propaganda is not treated separately. As for *agitation* there is no entry or reference to it.

The German encyclopaedia *Der Grosse Brockhaus* has only two lines on *agitation* saying that 'agitation is incitement, winning over for definite aims, mostly on behalf of a political group'.[9] A very short entry on *propaganda* describes it as, 'an undersection of *Werbung* (advertising, winning over) which is used especially for definite spiritual goals and ideas. These ideas can be political, religious, or economic. Propaganda is conducted mostly by a movement, party or state in order to win adherents and to influence them permanently.'[10]

The Encyclopaedia Americana has no entry on *agitation*; on the other hand, propaganda is discussed fully. The entry says among other things:

The definition of the term *propaganda* as it has been used in the political democracies, especially in the US, since World War I, differs both from the historic meaning of the word and from the use of this term under the authoritarian regimes. The disrepute into which the word propaganda has fallen in popular usage is reflected in the avoidance of the term propaganda by groups of special pleaders in the democracies. . . . In the democracies, the current popular condemnation of propaganda arises out of the ethical abhorrence for selected, partial information disseminated in the interests of the cause of the disseminators. . . . In contemporary democracies propaganda has become a derogatory epithet hurled accusingly at opposing views and groups. . . . Thus, in its simplest and most inclusive meaning, the propaganda process is an attempt to convince with a conscious, definite interest in the inculcation of a particular content in the attitudes and opinions of as yet unconvinced individuals and groups, rather than an attempt to convince through objectivity and discussion.[11]

The entry is further subdivided into sections: History; World War I, II; USSR Propaganda; Summary. It also has a cross-reference to the section *Soviet Propaganda* in the entry for *The USSR*.

THE COMMUNIST CONCEPT

Turning to communist sources, the importance attached to propaganda and agitation is fully reflected in the vast amount of literature—mostly practical—published on these subjects and in the theoretical and practical distinction between them.

The treatment of entries on agitation and propaganda in the *Large Soviet Encyclopaedia* speaks for itself. The article on *agitation* is spread over seven pages and that on *party propaganda* over five.[12] The encyclopaedia distinguishes, in accord with marxist-leninist theory, between propaganda in the general sense and party, i.e. communist, propaganda. Moreover it has special entries on propaganda on agriculture, on industry and propaganda spread through lectures.

Party propaganda is described as 'oral and press explanation and dissemination of the ideas of marxism-leninism, the policy of the communist party. It is an inseparable, integral part of the work of communist parties in the ideological and political education of party masses and all workers in the spirit of marxism-leninism.'

Agitation is defined as 'political activities with the aim of influencing the political consciousness and mood of the broad masses', and as 'an important instrument of political struggle of classes and parties'.

Though, since Lenin, communist terminology has always been speaking of, and distinguishing between, propaganda and agitation as two different terms and political activities, the dividing line is not always so clear as might be expected.

The basic distinction is based on Lenin's polemic with Martynov, an early Russian marxist. Lenin's definition, or rather a rough attempt to define the terms, is in its turn based on the concept of Plekhanov, another prominent Russian marxist.

But even if Lenin's definition of the functions of propaganda and agitation were correct at that time, that is in 1901–2, the development of these activities and changed social and political conditions in the Soviet Union, in east Europe and in the west have certainly influenced also their usage and meaning. Yet, Soviet theoretical literature on propaganda and agitation published in recent years does not make any attempt to point out such changed conditions, distinctions and meanings. The main cause for this is that the author of such an attempt would have to come to the conclusion that Lenin's definition of who is an agitator, what is agitation, and who is a propagandist or what is propaganda, is at variance with the practice.

Lenin distinguished three forms in the ideological and political work of the bolshevik party:

1 theoretical activity
2 propaganda
3 agitation

One of the distinctions was the number of people conducting these activities or affected by them. Theoretical activity is the domain of only a few individuals, party ideologists or theoreticians, Lenin said. They affect with their work, which is difficult to understand, only a handful of politically educated and conscious people who become propagandists. They again teach or influence only a limited, though much larger circle of people—agitators. It is up to these to spread the ideas and theories in suitable form among the broadest masses.

The task of the theoretician, propagandist and agitator, Lenin maintained, is the same: to educate the masses in the spirit of marxism. But they must approach the problem differently. And here lies the other distinctiom, especially between propaganda and agitation, propagandist and agitator.

Analysing the activities of propagandists and agitators in tsarist Russia and in western Europe, Lenin wrote in his pamphlet *What is to be Done?* in 1901–2:

A propagandist dealing with, say, that same question of unemployment, must explain the capitalistic nature of crises, the reasons why they are inevitable in contemporary society, describe the need for its transformation into socialist society, etc. In a word, he must present 'many ideas', so many indeed that they will be understood as an integral whole only by a (comparatively) few persons. An agitator, however, speaking on the same subject, will take as an illustration a fact that is most glaring and most widely known to his audience, say, the death from starvation of the family of an unemployed worker, the growing impoverishment, etc., and utilising this fact, which is known to all and sundry, will direct all his efforts to presenting *a simple idea* to the 'masses', i.e., the idea of the senselessness of the contradiction between the increase of wealth and increase of poverty; he will strive *to rouse* discontent and indignation among the masses, against this crying injustice, and leave a more complete explanation of this contradiction to the propagandist.[13]

Here the quotation from Lenin ends in current communist reference works because his further conclusions contradict the practice and notions of propaganda and agitation in contemporary communist society and confirm the correctness of the abused Martynov terminology. Lenin went on to say:

Consequently the propagandist operates chiefly by means of the *printed* word; the agitator by means of the *living* word. The propagandist must possess different qualities from the agitator. Kautsky and Lafargue, for example, we call propagandists; Bebel and Guesde we call agitators. To single out a third sphere, or third function, of practical activity and to include in this function 'calling the masses to certain concrete actions' is sheer nonsense because the 'call', as a single act, either naturally or inevitably supplements the theoretical tract, propagandist pamphlet or agitational speech, or represents a purely executive function. Take for example the struggle now being carried on by the German social democrats against the grain duties. The theoreticians write research works on tariff policy and 'call', say, for fight for commercial treaties and for free trade. The propagandist does the same thing in the periodical press, and the agitators in public speeches. At the present time, the 'correct action' of the masses takes the form of signing petitions to the Reichstag against the raising of grain duties. The call for this action comes indirectly from the theoreticians, the propagandists and the agitators, and directly from those workers who carry the petition lists to the factories and to private homes soliciting signatures. According to the 'Martynov terminology', Kautsky and Bebel are both propagandists, while those who solicit the signatures are agitators; is it not so?[14]

Communists today would say those who canvass signatures or engage in similar door-to-door pre-election or other campaigns are agitators. And those who give lectures and public speeches to larger audiences on topical political themes or theoretical problems today are always called, and call themselves, propagandists. Kautsky, Bebel and Guesde alike would today be called propagandists and even theoreticians, never agitators. It is therefore not surprising that the latter part of the quotation from Lenin is today ignored.

The present usage of the terms 'propaganda' and 'agitation' is also at variance with Lenin's distinction as far as the number of people affected by their activities is concerned. There is, of course, mass agitation conducted mainly through the mass media of communication—the press, radio and television—and also through mass meetings organised on various occasions. The greater part of communist agitation today consists, however, of the work of individual agitators.

They still single out one fact, one simple idea, but they speak mostly to a very limited circle of persons working with them in their groups, workshops or offices or living in their neighbourhood. The same is the case also with the agitation through wall newsheets and 'flashes', special leaflets exhorting the workers of a particular workshop or farm to fulfil their specific production targets. This type of work represents nowadays the bulk of agitational activities in communist society.

While it is true that ultimately agitation reaches the widest masses, the same can be said of propaganda. Party propaganda today has undoubtedly a mass character; its task is to reach the masses, too. Views spread even today in some western works on this subject, that communist propaganda is only the schooling of leaders, are outdated by developments. Such views reflect the situation at the beginning of the century or to a lesser degree in the 'twenties and 'thirties when the general level of education in the Soviet Union and consequently among party members was very low. At the end of the 'forties and in the 'fifties the situation changed and now, in the 'sixties, propaganda has long ceased to be the schooling of a few. It can now reach much broader masses.

The party sets out, in fact, as the main task of its propaganda efforts, to reach all the masses in the Soviet Union. Thus, in the decision of January 1960, 'On the task of party propaganda in contemporary conditions', the Central Committee criticised the state of propaganda because 'its sphere of influence, its mass character are narrow', and instructed the party organs and organisations on all levels to spread the ideas of marxism-leninism 'among the entire population of the Soviet Union'.[15]

Outdated also, is Lenin's assertion that 'a propagandist

presents many ideas to one or a few persons'. A propagandist may today elaborate on one idea or present a complex of ideas but he presents them mostly through his lectures or press articles to a wider circle of persons, more diversified and more stratified socially.

Of little importance in practice are some other, doubtful, features which could or could not serve as a guide in distinguishing more exactly between propaganda and agitation. Among them are: the use of media (printed or living word), presence or absence of 'call to action' etc. Both agitation and propaganda make ample use of them.

What then is the exact difference between propaganda and agitation in communist usage?

Propaganda activities, to sum up the present practice in communist countries, are concerned in general with the theoretical aspects of marxism-leninism, with the application of theory in the day-to-day practice and with the political education of the entire population. As such, it can be said, propaganda is based on the rational approach, it *appeals to the intellect*.

Agitation on the other hand activates the masses for the fulfilment of the over-riding task of construction in general and in particular in factories, workshops, farms and *kolkhozes*, and tries to inspire them with the ideals of communism. In this, agitation *appeals to sentiment*, to class origin, to communist patriotism. It tries to arouse hatred towards the 'class enemy', towards 'enemies' of the Soviet Union and other communist states. Agitation uses simple ideas and slogans while propaganda has a 'scientific' character and approach.

In principle, practice confirms this dividing line. Yet it often also shows overlapping and confusion of both activities. Party leaders and theoreticians were aware of the difficulty in some cases of differentiating very exactly and tried to explain it away by saying that there were no firm walls dividing propaganda and agitation. A propagandist who can imbue his audience with the fire of his enthusiasm, it was argued, is at the same time also an agitator. And an agitator who convinces his group, not only through his enthusiasm but through his skilful presentation of the fact or idea, is acting as a propagandist by educating his listeners.[16]

Despite such lesser problems, propaganda and agitation are in communist theory and practice fairly well differentiated and this division is a necessary and useful prerequisite for the smooth functioning of the vast apparatus. It enables the party to divide the tasks among the parts of the apparatus and to carry out more efficiently the political work of indoctrination and attraction of the masses for the communist goals.

THE POPULAR ATTITUDE TOWARDS PROPAGANDA AND AGITATION

Further light on propaganda and agitation, their real evaluation and place in society is thrown by the attitude of the masses —and of party members, too—towards them.

Agitation is generally considered inferior to propaganda, and communist parties both in the Soviet Union and in east Europe experience difficulty in finding volunteers for agitation. Agitators usually must be appointed by bureaucratic methods by the committees of primary organisations because there are few members willing to take up the duties of this function, associated as it is with unpopularity, derision and sometimes even open hatred. This negative attitude to agitators stems from their main tasks: to induce fellow workers to increase output or production norms (which means lower earnings), to attend numerous meetings and rallies, to participate in their spare time in 'voluntary' brigades, to subscribe to the party and communist press etc.

Propagandist work is, on the other hand, considered to be on a higher intellectual level and thus it carries higher status in the popular estimation. The work does not entail the constant and direct urging of fellow-workers to achieve higher and higher output. Most of it consists of lecturing, and volunteers are more willing to engage in work (as part of their obligatory communist activities) which does not involve enforcing upon others the unpleasant duties of 'active participation in political life'.

But this higher esteem for propaganda in comparison with agitation does not mean that propaganda itself is taken at its face value as the communists would like to see. In countries such as Hungary, Poland, Czechoslovakia, East Germany, etc., communist propaganda is discredited. By the masses the propaganda effort of the respective communist parties is regarded in the same light as in the democracies, namely as 'the making of deliberately one-sided statements' or 'partial information disseminated in the interests of the disseminator' (in this case the communists). In these countries, as events in 1956 and subsequent retractions and confessions among writers and journalists—the chief propagandists—have proved, 'propaganda' has become the same 'derogatory epithet hurled accusingly' at communists as is hurled in western countries at opposing groups and their views. Undoubtedly, the masses' experiences of nazi or local fascist propaganda during the war contributed to this negative attitude to agitation and propaganda alike.

It is more difficult to assess to what extent the population of the Soviet Union shares such views and attitudes. Almost the entire present population has grown up under the conditions of communist rule, has been exposed only to communist indoctrination and has had no chance to acquaint itself with other views, teachings and values than those enforced by the party. Yet there is a good pointer to the disrepute into which the words propaganda and agitation had fallen in the stalinist period even among the Soviet people. After the Twenty-second Congress the CPSU, followed by other satellite countries, tried to replace whenever possible these words with the term 'ideological work', and the departments of propaganda and agitation at the party secretariats were renamed 'ideological' departments.

THE PLACE OF PROPAGANDA AND AGITATION IN THE PARTY SYSTEM

Lenin's conception of communism was that of an enormous school for the entire population. Propaganda and agitation were to be the methods of teaching and learning; marxist-leninist theory, the program of the party and its policy the subjects. The end product should have been an entirely new man, the Soviet man, the man of communist society. Every member of the party was supposed to attend this school as a pupil and teacher at the same time. A communist was expected, in Lenin's words, to use every hour of his spare time for ardent propagation of communism, imparting both knowledge and enthusiasm to his fellow citizens. He was also expected to be a model of the future communist man.

This task of total propaganda and agitation was imposed upon members as their principal duty by the party rules from the very beginning of the establishment of the Soviet regime in Russia and accepted also by all communist parties, united in the Comintern. Each succeeding edition of rules in the Soviet Union was more and more explicit on this point. The latest rules of the CPSU, adopted at the Twenty-second Congress in October 1961, reflect the general stress which is now being put on the need for intensified propaganda and agitation to take the place of coercion, which is supposed to disappear with the abolition of the dictatorship of the proletariat.

Every member of the party must, according to paragraph 1 of the rules,[17] 'firmly and unflinchingly translate into life the decisions of the party, explain to the masses the policy of the party . . . actively participate in political life of the country . . . master marxist-leninist theory, increase his ideological level, assist in the formation and education of communist society . . . '

Party organs and organisations below the level of the Central Committee have their duties described in paragraphs 42 and 58, and the latter defines the propagandist and agitational duties at the lowest level, that of the primary organisations. They are to 'educate communists in the spirit of dedication to the cause of the party, in the spirit of firm ideological conviction and communist morals; to organise the study of marxist-leninist theory by communists; to conduct agitational and propagandist work among the masses in the spirit of communism'.[18]

CHANGING CONTENT

Unlike the dictatorship of the proletariat, propaganda and agitation will remain, according to the theory, a permanent and constant foundation of communism, even after the communist party has ceased to exist. In the view of some contemporary communist theoreticians they will always be necessary because the need to educate the people in the spirit of communism, to maintain their political and social consciousness and responsibility, will persist.

The contents and correspondingly also the methods are not, however, constant. They change with the prevailing general tasks and program of the party, as will be apparent from a brief summary of changes since the earliest days of the bolshevik party.

It was again Lenin who laid the foundations of an organised and efficient propaganda system. He personally worked with or led illegal marxist circles in tsarist Russia. In 1903 the Second Congress of the Russian Social Democratic Party adopted at his recommendation a resolution 'On the Situation in Propaganda'. In the pre-revolutionary period propaganda was conducted in Russia through illegal study of marxism in groups and individually and through the spreading of marxist literature and of the bolshevik press. Already in 1911 Lenin considered the training of propagandists as urgent and important, and organised a special school for this purpose at Longjumeau, near Paris.

The tasks of bolshevik propaganda and agitation in that period were to prepare the ground for the revolution by spreading the knowledge of theory among the (comparatively) few future leaders (propaganda) and influencing the revolutionary mood and class consciousness of the masses (agitation).

After the overthrow of tsarist rule, the bolshevik party concentrated on agitation for the socialist revolution. Later, in the years of the Civil War, propagandist and agitational work grew to an enormous extent. Mass meetings and rallies were organised frequently in towns and villages, trains (*agitpoyezds*) and ships were used as mobile offices in the massive campaign to discredit the counter-revolutionaries and consolidate bolshevik rule. Agitation prevailed over propaganda and contributed significantly to the final victory of the communists.

After the Civil War, the main tasks and content of propaganda and agitation were to support the reconstruction of the disrupted national economy and later to explain the New Economic Policy (NEP). After this short period of ideological retreat, the apparatus of propaganda and agitation was fully geared to explain the party's plans for electrification, industrialisation and collectivisation, to 'mobilise and organise' the masses. In this period communist propaganda had not yet a mass character; it was rather the ideological training of selected party cadres for work in the party apparatus, state administration, industry and agriculture. Later, in the 'thirties, the sphere of propagandist 'educational' work was extended also to the non-party technical and economic cadres, the so-called non-party bolsheviks.

Parallel with these political tasks on the home front, propaganda and agitation had also to 'enlighten' the population on the situation outside the Soviet Union. The lot of workers in the capitalist countries, international relations, the foreign policy of the Soviet Union and that of 'imperialist' powers had to be properly explained. This aspect will be discussed later, but it is well to observe here that the relevant general line in the field of propaganda was laid down mainly in the early 1930s and has been followed practically unchanged until now. At that time appeared the familiar division of the world into two opposite, hostile camps: the socialist and the capitalist or imperialist. The socialist camp was depicted as a paradise for workers, as a camp of progress and peace, while the opposite camp was characterised by exploitation and low living standards and preparations for war.

The advantages of a highly organised system of propaganda and agitation totally subordinated to the party and therefore to state control were demonstrated in the war years 1941–5. The enormous strain of effort and sacrifices demanded of the whole of Soviet society to hold the nazi attacks on the country while military and industrial forces were hurriedly stepped up to meet the total nature of modern warfare, needed as much boosting on the home front as in the fighting line.

The theme of socialist or Soviet patriotism, which had not been entirely neglected before, now became the mainstay of all propaganda and agitation. Great figures from Russian and Ukrainian history who had fought against foreign invaders, high moments of national history, formerly derided military traditions, and even the role of the Orthodox Church, were now vividly recalled as glorious examples to be emulated. The personality of Stalin was built up to the stature of a giant Father figure, the epitome of patriotic leadership. Under the spell of this enormously efficient and effective propaganda and agitation, Soviet troops went into battle crying: 'For Stalin—For Fatherland!'

The inflated stature of Stalin during the war helped to intensify another aspect of Soviet propaganda which began slowly to emerge in the late 'thirties and culminated in the late 'forties in intolerable excesses. With the absolute consolidation of Stalin's personal rule over the entire party and state apparatus, propaganda and agitation were turned more and more into a tool for glorifying Stalin or spreading the 'cult of personality', as it is termed by the present leadership of the CPSU.

Rigid schematic simplification and distortion of the image of life at home and abroad during the stalinist period, together with the application of mass terror and enforced conformity, became a hindrance in the effectiveness of propaganda and agitation both in the Soviet Union and east Europe. Stalin's successors realised that these institutions, and the entire regime with them were becoming seriously discredited and that some of their methods had to be changed if they were to fulfil their tasks efficiently. They realised also that with the abolition of the use of terror and coercion, propaganda and agitation would gain in importance as methods of persuasion.

Thus propaganda and agitation were freed from some rigid, outdated conceptions and controls. Their exponents were ordered and encouraged to scrap worn-out clichés and to approach the problems of everyday life more realistically, in an effort to present the people a new image of the party and its policies. The introduction of the concept of peaceful co-existence allowed a slight modification in the presentation of the international situation and of life in foreign countries. The Central Committee and party congresses of 1956, 1959 and 1961 passed numerous resolutions and decisions affecting propaganda and agitation, all with the aim of bringing them effectively in line with the new situation.

This short review shows that propaganda and agitation, although they may undergo important transformation and changes in methods and objectives in order to keep pace with the evolution of the communist idea and society, not only retain but even increase their major role in the general scheme of communist party activity.

THE APPARATUS OF PROPAGANDA AND AGITATION

The elaborate system of communist propaganda and agitation which embraces the press, radio, television, political, artistic and scientific literature, even belles lettres, and theatre and film, evidently requires an equally elaborate system of direction and administration. This apparatus was created in the early stages of the bolshevik rule in Russia and has been perfected since then by numerous party decisions and party rules which, as has been shown, assign a definite place within it for every party organ and organisation.

To see how this object is pursued, a brief outline of the party structure from top to bottom and of the main organisa-tional principles will be helpful in understanding later the structure of the press and the echelons of its direction and supervision.

The organisation and structure of the CPSU and also that of other communist parties in east Europe is based on the prin-ciple of *democratic centralism* and *territorial-production structure*.

Democratic centralism, according to the rules,[18] means:

1 All party organs from top to bottom are eligible.
2 All party organs must periodically account for their activities to their organisations and to the higher organs of the party.
3 All members, organs and organisations must observe strict party discipline, and the minority must submit to the majority.
4 All decisions of the higher organs are unconditionally binding for the lower organs.

From this principle follows also the rule that any discussion within the party organisation is possible only before a decision has been taken by an appropriate party organ. After the decision has been taken further discussion on the subject is forbidden and members who would try to revive it would face expulsion.

The principle of the *territorial-production structure* means that primary organisations are established at the production centres and grouped into higher level organisations in accordance with the administrative territorial division of the Soviet Union.* In 1962 the principle was strengthened in the Soviet Union by the introduction of an element of division based on production even into party organisations higher than the primary level.†

The basic unit of the party, the *primary organisation*, is established on the principle of production units in factories, *sovkhozes*, *kolkhozes*, offices etc. Only members not involved in the production process, such as housewives and pensioners, are organised in street or village organisations. The primary organisation is divided into (party) groups and also, in large

---

* Administratively the Soviet Union is divided into constituent union republics; these are subdivided into *oblasts* or regions (the Russian Federal Republic has several *krays* virtually equivalent to *oblasts*). Within the *oblast* are *rayons*, cities (which can have several *rayons*), and villages. In addition the union republics are sometimes subdivided into autonomous republics. In the Russian Republic (RSFSR) alone there are national *okrugs* of minorities subordinated to *oblasts*.

† The new structure, after reorganisation during 1963, is as follows: in *krays* and *oblasts*, the existing (unified) party organisations have been split into two: one for industry, building and transport, and one for agriculture. At the centre, two bureaux have been created and attached to the CC of the CPSU: one for guiding industry, the other agriculture, throughout the Soviet Union. Such bureaux have also been attached to the central committees of the union republics.

C

factories, *sovkhozes* etc., into sectional organisations, always strictly according to production units such as workshops, farms, departments and so forth. The executive organ is the party committee elected by all members at the annual plenary meeting. Elections of organs at all levels are now conducted in the Soviet Union by secret ballot.

Higher levels in the party structure are:

> *Rayon* or city organisations
> *Okrug* organisations
> *Oblast* or *kray* organisations
> The organisations of the federal republics.

The highest organs of these are conferences below the republican level and congresses of the republican organisations. At these the delegates representing the corresponding lower unit elect the committees or bureaux.

The highest organ of the entire Communist Party of the Soviet Union is its Congress which should be convened by the Central Committee at least once in four years. The Congress decides the party line on home and foreign policy matters and elects its executive organ, the Central Committee which directs, between congresses, all activities of the party.

The leadership of the CPSU since Stalin's death has been trying to raise the role of the congresses and of the Central Committee whose sessions previously only put a rubber stamp on the dictator's decisions. But the Central Committee is a cumbersome body; its members live far from the centre of power and daily political decisions; and thus, despite all genuine efforts, the real power is still in the hands of a small group of party leaders, members of the presidium (formerly the politburo) of the Central Committee. They conduct the highest affairs of the party and state and they are the real masters of the vast party and state apparatus.

All party committees, from the city or *rayon* level upwards, have a special apparatus: the so-called secretariats. These carry out the administrative, directing and controlling duties within their sphere. Each secretariat has—according to its level and size—a certain number of secretaries; one of them is appointed First Secretary. Administratively the secretariat is subdivided into numerous departments responsible for organisation, propaganda and agitation, industry, education and so on.

Into this tightly knit party structure is fitted the system

of propaganda and agitation. The primary organisation is basically entrusted with agitation and propaganda work among the masses. Direct, personal agitation—as opposed to indirect agitation by the press, radio, television—is practically conducted only by these organisations. Agitational activities are the personal responsibility of the secretary of the primary organisation. He is assisted by the propaganda and agitation commission (renamed the Ideological Commission in 1962) elected by the annual meeting which also elects, or should elect, agitators and propagandists. In practice the former are more or less bureaucratically appointed by the committee since there are only a few volunteers. For easier direction and control the agitators are grouped into *agitkollektivs*.

Propagandist work, with its wider ramification, larger range of accessible audience and higher demands on the intellectual qualities of its exponents, requires and makes possible the use of propagandists outside the primary organisations, in the sphere of city or *rayon*. The committees of party organisations in these administrative units form therefore special groups or 'propagandist collectives' of qualified persons who are sent as lecturers to various meetings of primary organisations, public organisations, political schools etc.

THE ORGANISATION OF AGITPROP

Each secretariat, starting with the city or *rayon* level, has a department specially entrusted with propagandist and agitational activities within its radius. The size of this propaganda and agitation department* or *Agitprop* as it is generally called increases with each higher echelon. The latest development in Soviet practice, followed by the satellite parties, is the formation of ideological commissions attached to these departments. They consist of rank-and-file members who are not on the staff of the party apparatus and assist the department's head and staff in every aspect of their work. They are the result of efforts to activate propaganda and to attract for this purpose the widest strata of party membership and at the same time to democratise the party system.

The principle of democratic centralism leads to the con-

* The propaganda and agitation department was renamed the 'ideological' department following the Twenty-second Congress of the CPSU. But the old name and its abbreviated form still prevail in communist practice and we have retained it in this book.

centration of all decisive, directing and controlling functions in the ideological sphere into the Agitprop of the Central Committee's secretariat. The Agitprop elaborates in detail the party propagandist line on internal political and economic problems, and on international affairs according to directives from the presidium and the general party line decided by the Congress. The department transmits the detailed tasks to the lower levels of the party's Agitprop apparatus. The channels between the individual levels enable the central department to reach, when necessary, subordinated organs at every level within the shortest time. They also facilitate the transmission of information on the mood and views of the masses in general or in particular places to the higher and highest levels. The central Agitprop can thus adjust easily the tone, themes and intensity of the activities as the situation requires.

Apart from this vertical structure of channels, the Agitprop of the Central Committee is organised to embrace the vast horizontal sphere of activities in the entire social life of communist society. For this purpose, the department is subdivided into numerous sections. This horizontal structure of Agitprop has never been published in full. It is often adjusted to meet the demands of a given period, with one section taking up several activities and duties or splitting into two or three new, more specialised sections. But basically the sections of Agitprop in Moscow cover the following fields:[19]

> Party propaganda
> Mass propaganda
> Agitation
> Culture
> Central press
> Republic, *kray* and
>   *rayon* press
> Local press
> Radio
> Television
> Schools
> Sciences
> Publishing
> Belles lettres
> Arts
> Film
> Sport and gymnastics

Broadly speaking, the Agitprop at the central secretariats of east European communist countries are similarly subdivided except that local problems may call for additional specialised sections such as propaganda and agitation for the unification of Germany in East Germany, collectivisation of agriculture, or the press of 'bourgeois' parties, and so on.

The work of the central Agitprop is directed by its head who is often also a secretary of the central secretariat. The responsibility for propaganda and agitation is usually entrusted to the most able men at the top of the party leadership, as in the case of A. Zhdanov and M. Suslov in the past, and now of L. Ilyichov.

3

THE FUNCTIONS OF THE COMMUNIST PRESS

IN THE MARXIST-LENINIST concept the press stands at the very top of the hierarchy of the means of propaganda and agitation.

The marxist-leninist theory sees the press as a channel through which the party can influence the masses, communicate with them and direct them in the process of constructing the classless society; it sees the press as a 'tool of education and organisation of the society on the principles of scientific socialism'.[1]

This basic function of the press was elaborated by Lenin, later put in practice with characteristic thoroughness in the years of Stalin's rule, and is continued by his successors. From Lenin and Stalin originate the two fundamental definitions of the tasks of the press and its place in the communist system. Lenin dealt with the problem of utilising the press in the struggle for power and later in establishing and strengthening the party's rule over the masses, both physically and psychologically, in his work *What is to be Done?* in the chapter 'Can a newspaper be a collective organiser?' There he defined the tasks of a communist newspaper as follows:

> A newspaper is not only a collective propagandist and collective agitator, but also a collective organiser. In this respect *it can be compared to the scaffolding* erected around a building under construction; it marks the contours of the structure and facilitates communication between the builders, permitting them to distribute the work and to view the common results achieved by their organised labour.[2]

With time, the word collective has been changed into *mass*, and communist terminology now speaks not of collective propaganda or collective agitation, but of mass propaganda and mass agitation. Nevertheless, the terms *collective propagandist* and *collective agitator* are still used when speaking about the functions of the communist press, and though Lenin coined them in the conditions of the illegal fight for power, their originally prescribed functions are basically valid today, and

communist society will go on using the press as a tool for conducting mass propaganda and agitation and for 'organising and
mobilising' the masses as far into the future as one can visualise.

Some twenty years after Lenin's definition of these
functions, Stalin wrote the second well-known definition of the
place of the press in the hierarchy of propaganda media. He
said: 'The press is the strongest instrument with which, day by
day, hour by hour, the party speaks to the masses in their own
essential language. There is no other means so flexible for
establishing spiritual links between the party and the working
class.'[3]

Contemporary communist textbooks on journalism continually quote Lenin's words, and on them and on the formulation of Stalin (though now they discreetly omit his name),
they base their list of the tasks of the press. The generally
accepted summary of these is as follows:

To propagate the ideas of marxism-leninism;
To agitate for the principles of the party;
To organise the workers in the fight for the application of
    these principles to everyday life;
To forge a lasting link with the popular masses;
To educate them in the spirit of communism;
To explain the policy of the party and government;
To foster vigorously a habit of criticism and self-criticism;
To organise socialist emulation;
To fight for peace;
To expose the warmongers.[4]

This lengthy, though incomplete list of tasks is laid upon
the press by the communist party which insists on strict and
systematic fulfilment of the given party line and tasks. The
Czechoslovak journalists' review described the press's dependence on, and subordination to, the party as follows:

The socialist press, which according to leninist principles
is a collective propagandist, agitator and organiser . . .
bases its work on the general line of the communist party,
helps to realise the party's decisions, and is guided by its
instructions and advice. The party, at the same time,
makes sure that the press fulfils its mission, that it does not
deviate, that it serves the interests of the working class. . . .[5]

The press's tasks can be reduced to the three basic functions assigned to the press by Lenin, with the exception of fostering the habit of criticism and self-criticism. This task was assigned to the communist press after the October Revolution of 1917 when the party leadership realised that the socialist society, under the tendency towards dictatorship and bureaucracy, deprived of the outlets for airing discontent and criticism afforded under democracy by the existence of opposition parties, parliament and an independent press, would soon suffocate or grind to a standstill.

Starting from Marx's premise that the proletarian revolution criticises itself and thereby strengthens itself, Lenin made self-criticism one of the fundamental principles of the bolshevik party. After 1917, he developed an even larger conception of the role of criticism and self-criticism in the new social order. Since then criticism and self-criticism, the 'ability to expose and resolutely to correct one's shortcomings and faults', has been regarded as a fundamental feature of leninism, a 'law of the communist party's development'.[6] Stalin declared 'without self-criticism there is no correct education of the party, working class or masses. . . .'[7] According to the leninist conception, criticism and self-criticism should become the working method of every communist, and should be exercised both by the party and government organisations, and by the workers acting as politically conscious citizens. As ideally conceived, it was intended to function as a two-way control system.

The press, being a two-way channel of communication between the party and the masses, and having to fulfil all basic functions of the party, had also to take over this new role of transmitting official criticism to the masses and the masses' criticism or self-criticism to the appropriate party or government organs. To a considerable degree, and within the communist meaning of the word, the press is now fulfilling this additional function. Summing up the functions assigned to the press by marxist-leninist theory, it must be:

> Mass propagandist,
> Mass agitator,
> Mass organiser,
> Mass critic and controller.

These four basic functions determine the contents of the

communist press. Each of them must be fulfilled by a news-paper every day, in every issue, on every page. They are the criteria for the selection of material, for deciding what, how and where it should be printed.

PROPAGANDIST FUNCTIONS OF THE PRESS

Newspapers

The all-important role of the press in the spreading and elucidation of marxist-leninist theory, and in the communist education of the masses has been repeatedly stressed by Soviet party leaders and various party decisions. In one instance the Central Committee stated: 'In the propagation of marxism-leninism the fundamental, decisive weapon must be the press—periodicals, newspapers, brochures—and the oral propaganda must take the subordinate, ancillary place. The press provides the opportunity for making this or that truth immediately accessible to all and sundry; it is therefore stronger than oral propaganda.'[8]

Even in the early 'twenties, the party decreed that ideological propaganda must take first place in the newspapers, and instructed the republican and central press (later also the *oblast* newspapers) to carry a special column on 'Party Life' with ideological material written by members at the special department of the same name. The press, however, tended to neglect propaganda work and was often criticised for this by the party. A decree of the Central Committee issued in 1938 again ordered the party and *komsomol* newspapers at the central, republican and *oblast* levels to establish departments of propaganda which were to be headed by party members thoroughly grounded in theory.[9]

Since then, Soviet party newspapers have been systematic-ally publishing articles on theoretical aspects of marxism-lenin-ism, and reporting lectures by acknowledged party theoreticians and propagandists. They also introduce 'consultation' colums in which, in reply to readers' letters, party propagandists discuss and elucidate ideological aspects of contemporary party policy.

The Soviet communists distinguish between the role of the party and non-party press in the dissemination of ideological propaganda. The propagation of ideology is a party matter; nobody but the party is allowed or qualified to interpret the dogma. The purity of marxism-leninism and the avoidance of any deviation or revisionist tendencies are the foremost essentials for the preservation of the party. Such an important task can only be fulfilled by the party press and by trusted party propagandists.

The non-party press, whether of general or specialised appeal, of central or lower level, has nevertheless to contribute to party propaganda by disseminating and explaining the decisions and decrees of the party and government on political and economic problems of the day.

This distinction between the tasks of the party and non-party press was also important in the new socialist countries of east Europe where there was a strongly established chain of 'bourgeois' newspapers. These newspapers had to be taken over by the communists and to be adapted to serve in the slow re-education of their readership, a readership disinclined to accept the crude propaganda dished out in the party, youth and trades union press.

The 'bourgeois' press, now under communist control and direction, tried to camouflage its propadandist effort and concentrated on exploiting the patriotic sentiments of the bourgeoisie by stressing those epochs and personalities in their nation's history which lent themselves to communist interpretation. Such, for instance, were the Hussite movement or the Munich episode in Czech history, the liberal uprising and the role of Kossuth in Hungary in 1848.

Propaganda in the Technical Press

The propagandist role of the press is not, however, confined to the propagation of marxism-leninism. The party attaches great importance to economic and technical propaganda by spreading knowledge of production processes in industry, agriculture etc. In fact, this type of propaganda takes the same amount of space in the columns of the central, republican, *kray* and *oblast* newspapers as political propaganda. In the local press and the specialised press at all levels, such as, e.g., *Selskaya zhizn* (Rural Life), or the newspapers of various economic ministries, it is the predominant factor.

Production propaganda includes articles on new production methods in the engineering, metallurgic and building industry; discussion of the means and advantages of the cultivation of new crops like maize, new strains of wheat, etc.

According to marxism, economic and production techniques are the determining factor in the evolution of any society, and the communist press shows great insistance on economic propaganda in general, the propagation of new methods approved by the highest party organs and special campaigns for their introduction. For example, all Soviet central newspapers and local press in the appropriate regions have been systematically pushing propagandist articles since 1955 for the introduction of maize, Khrushchev's favourite crop. Though the campaign started in 1955, even in 1962 the pages of *Pravda*, the central all-union paper, carried an almost daily article, news item, or picture connected with maize cultivation. Similarly all newspapers will carry, month after month, instructive articles on some new shockworker movement, and its spread from factory to factory.

Propaganda colours all major articles and features on cultural and historical themes, anniversaries of prominent personalities from all spheres of life, such as Pushkin in the USSR, Schiller in East Germany, Kossuth and Petöfi in Hungary, Hus and Komenský (Comenius) in Czechoslovakia, etc. In fact, important anniversaries are always seized upon by communist propaganda as a welcome occasion for prolonged propagandist and agitational campaigns in which the historical personalities are depicted as ideological allies and predecessors of communism.

AGITATIONAL FUNCTIONS OF THE PRESS

Propaganda and agitation have the same basic function in the communist press: to educate the masses so that without coercion or social pressures, they will follow the party and fulfil their assigned tasks in the communist program. They differ in their approach to their common task.

This difference is very clearly marked in the press where agitation utilises every news item and every opportunity to influence the sentiment and mood of the masses, to encourage patriotic enthusiasm to the point of willingness to make sacrifices, or to inflame hatred of the western 'imperialists' and inner 'parasites', 'enemies of the party' and 'dogmatists' in the communist world movement. Even more than propaganda, agitation pervades each page, every column of the press because of its effectiveness as an instrument for calling the masses to immediate action, for mobilising them for economic campaigns, production movements, and 'socialist emulation'.

While the press also uses leading articles and genuine features in its agitational work, it favours shorter, simpler means of journalistic expression. Information and news lend themselves to this purpose but even more suitable are headlines, slogans, photographs and political cartoons.

*Information and news** are not treated by the communist press as a means of giving the reader an accurate, objective, and comprehensive picture of events,[10] but to support the political aims of the party. Social values are entirely different from those of the democratic press, and the communist newspapers select different news items for publication, and even such selective items are treated in such a way that they will agitate.

Information and news from the communist countries—apart from official announcements, statements and speeches—are regarded as worthy of publication only when they represent some politically or economically important event, such as a challenge by individual workers or 'collectives' to socialist emulation, new records in production, or the surpassing of existing norms. In practice, very few items from communist countries are regarded as newsworthy enough to find their way into the newspapers. From foreign countries, only such information as fits into the official picture of the western world and supports the propaganda line is allowed publication.

Slogans and headlines are the most favoured agitational means for they can briefly, and pungently, express the agitational idea. Bold type and prominent placing can catch the reader's eye and make him read them. Colour can also add to their prominence. On special occasions both slogans and drawings are printed in red ink.

Any issue of a communist newspaper will illustrate the wide use of agitational headlines or slogans. A survey of two issues of *Pravda*, published on 9 and 10 October, 1962, on working days with no important home or foreign events, shows their application in daily practice.

The leader on 9 October had a non-agitational headline, 'The Criterion of our Progress', but the main story on the front page, a report on Premier Khrushchev's tour in Uzbekistan, carried the slogan:

* In the following paragraphs, information and news are briefly treated within the context of the agitational requirements. The communist conception of news as such is dealt with in full in Chapter 11.

THE TOILERS OF UZBEKISTAN WILL FULFIL
THEIR HIGH OBLIGATIONS

and on the second page, under a hate-evoking slogan

BRING PARASITES TO ACCOUNT!

the paper tried to show that existing shortages were the consequence of those who break the 'socialist legality'. Agitational intent is evident also in the slogan:

MAY SOVIET-GUINEAN FRIENDSHIP STRENGTHEN!

over a report of a reception at the Guinean embassy in Moscow, printed on the third page.

On 10 October, the headline above the leader improved on its agitational effect, claiming

A GRANDIOSE VICTORY ON THE ROAD
TO COMMUNISM

Exhortation and inspiration was the aim of other headlines on the front page:

NEW SUCCESSES ON THE GRAIN FRONT

THE GRAIN FLOWS FROM THE URALS

which accompanied news of progress in grain deliveries from *kolkhozes*.

The third page was entirely occupied by agitational articles on Soviet successes in the period 1917–62, and adorned with appropriate agitational drawings and slogans such as:

THE MIGHTY PROGRESS OF OCTOBER'S RULE

UNDER LENIN'S BANNER, FORWARD TO THE VICTORY
OF COMMUNISM

Agitational headlines appeared also over factual, short reports from abroad:

THE CO-OPERATION OF FRIENDS

(the visit of an official Indian delegation)

HALT THE AGGRESSION AGAINST YEMEN

(events in Yemen)

CUBA WILL REPEL THE ENEMY

(speech of a Cuban leader).

Slogans and headlines in the classical form of communist agitation become even more plentiful at the time of important international or home events. A study of *Pravda*'s issues during the Cuban crisis at the end of October 1962 is much to the point.

On Monday, 22 October, President Kennedy announced measures to ensure the safety of the United States by imposing a blockade on importations of nuclear missiles and other offensive weapons to Cuba from the Soviet Union and other communist countries. He declared also his determination to bomb or invade Cuba in order to secure the dismantling and removal of the existing Soviet missiles and sites aimed at the United States. Subsequently the Soviet government, deterred by America's firm stand, began by Thursday, 25 October, to retreat and by Saturday–Sunday, 27–8 October, officially accepted American conditions and announced the withdrawal of missiles and military personnel from Cuba.

On Tuesday, 23 October, Pravda published no report of President Kennedy's statement, since it was made after *Pravda*'s stop-press. (It took the Soviet news agency and radio nine hours to inform the public of the statement. This aspect of reporting is dealt with in the chapter on censorship.)

On Wednesday, 24 October, the paper printed slogans at the top of the front page:

BRIDLE THE HIGH-HANDED AMERICAN AGGRESSORS!
HANDS OFF CUBA!

The leading article was headlined:

FRUSTRATE THE CRIMINAL INTENTIONS OF THE
ENEMIES OF PEACE!

On the front page under a factual headline, 'The statement of the Soviet government', was published in full a lengthy Soviet official version of Kennedy's speech and the Soviet government's reaction to it. At the bottom of the page *Pravda* carried a photograph with agitational caption of a demonstration meeting in a Moscow factory.

Over pages 2 and 3 were spread the bold type slogans:

WE ARE WITH YOU, CUBAN BROTHERS!
STOP THIS DANGEROUS GAME WITH FIRE!

Another picture of a factory meeting appeared on the second page, together with the slogan:

THE IMPERIALIST WARMONGERS WILL MEET
CRUSHING RESISTANCE

MESSRS IMPERIALISTS, DO NOT THRUST YOUR
HEADS INTO FIRE!

THE IRE OF KOLKHOZ PEASANTRY

THE ANGRY VOICE OF MILLIONS, etc. etc.

(printed over reports of protest meetings organised all over the Soviet Union).

On Thursday, 25 *October*, two slogans were printed across the top of the entire front page; the first, showing complete lack of invention, repeating the headline of the leader of the previous day:

FRUSTRATE THE CRIMINAL INTENTIONS OF THE
ENEMIES OF PEACE!

and the second:

DEFEND AND STRENGTHEN PEACE ON EARTH!

In the same issue there were further repeated slogans:

IN THE INTEREST OF ALL NATIONS, IN THE NAME
OF GENERAL PEACE—REMOVE THE DANGER OF WAR!

ANGRY WORDS FROM THE SOVIET PEOPLE

THE PEOPLES OF THE WORLD ANGRILY DENOUNCE
AMERICAN ADVENTURERS

HANDS OFF CUBA

WE WILL DEFEND PEACE ON EARTH

Pictorial agitation was pathetically inefficient. On the front page, above the headline 'Angry Words from the Soviet People', *Pravda* printed a photograph of women from a factory meeting. A beautiful girl was prominently featured together with other women, attentively listening to the speaker. But neither she nor the other women showed the least sign of anger or emotion.

The second page carried a picture of two happily smiling 'cultivators of maize' with a heap of corn-cobs, apparently put

in to fill the agitational quota of items on maize stipulated by
some long-term editorial plan. An agitationally more topical
picture of demonstrators outside the American embassy in Moscow was reproduced quite small on the last page!

On Friday, 26 *October*, slogans significantly prepared for
the coming Soviet about-turn appeared:

DO EVERYTHING TO PREVENT WAR
REASON MUST TRIUMPH!

The angry agitational slogans were relegated to the fifth page,
and severely toned down:

THE FATE OF THE WORLD IS IN THE HANDS OF HUMANITY

THE ROAD TO WAR!

BRIDLE THE AGGRESSORS!

On Saturday, 27 *October*, big slogans and all mention of
'American imperialists and aggressors' entirely disappeared
from the front page, and only the foreign news headlines continued a mild agitation; it was not possible to cut off too abruptly
the campaign already started, and it was necessary to camouflage
the hasty retreat and defeat of Soviet policy.

Pictures and political cartoons have been increasingly used by
communist newspapers for agitation since 1953 and 1956. Before
1953 there were only one or two photographs in any issue of a
Soviet or other communist papers. They usually merely showed
party leaders, workers or farmers in the production processes, or
machines and buildings. In the following two waves of press
reform, this clumsy, rigid way of pictorial agitation was replaced
by a suppler and wider selection of pictures of greater human
interest.

With the greater variety in the communist press as a whole,
both within the Soviet Union and in the outer communist orbit,
the tendency to depart from the purely agitational character of
photographs and drawings gained impetus. Soviet newspapers
intended for less politically conscious people—the evening
papers in big cities (*Vechornaya Moskva*—The Evening Moscow), youth papers like *Komsomolskaya pravda*, or others like
Sovietskaya Rossia—began from 1956 to print from six to a
dozen pictures per issue (Soviet newspapers have only four or
six pages).

Certain forces within the party apparatus, firmly entrenched in past traditions and stalinist conceptions of life and the press, disapproved of this 'apolitical approach' manifested in the publication of pictures of pretty young (working, of course!) girls or picturesque photographs. They stressed that published pictures must always contribute in some unmistakable way towards the construction of communism, and educate the new communist man. Pictures, in their conception, should always have some 'content', some 'message'. In February 1958 *Pravda* published an article attacking the violation of agitational principles by the 'misuse of photographs by certain sections of the Soviet press'. The organ of the Central Committee denounced 'blind imitation' of the western press in publishing 'contentless' or sensational pictures, and, at the same time, deplored the use of illustrated advertisements 'in the style of the bourgeois press'.[11]

In general, Soviet newspapers lag far behind their counterparts in Poland, Czechoslovakia or East Germany in the use of pictures for attracting and influencing the reader. This is partly due to the lower level of technical skill among Soviet press-photographers and journalists, partly to the inferior technical level of the Soviet printing industry, but not least to greater rigidity and an unwillingness to apply the proved methods of western journalism.

Cartoons are used in the communist press almost entirely as a political weapon aimed at 'exposing' western 'imperialists and warmongers', and evoking hatred against them. Besides publishing drawings by the accepted communist cartoonists, newspapers frequently reprint political cartoons from the western press which are critical of the home or foreign policy of western governments.

The communist press never published cartoons critical of the party or government policy. Cartoons, or rather drawings, relating to home problems repeat the idealised images of workers, everyday 'reality', etc. Cartoons depicting party leaders were taboo and unknown until recently. It was a Bulgarian cartoonist who broke the ice when a newspaper there published in 1959, during Premier Khrushchev's visit to the United States, a cartoon showing him in an idealised image as an angel of peace. Since then this image of the Soviet Premier has been timidly imitated with the approval of communist authorities.

To sum up: agitation in the communist press is using all

D

journalistic forms of expression—leading articles, features, news, slogans, headlines, illustrations—to foster both the political and economic aims of the party. In the political sphere, the task of the press is agitationally to exploit any festive occasions, anniversaries, elections at all levels of the administrative structure, campaigns, movements and international events.

In the economic field, the press as collective agitator has an even greater task. The expansion of production is a fundamental precondition of communist success. Exhortation and persuasion by example and precept to improve labour discipline, to enlarge working norms, to introduce new methods, to join 'voluntary' Saturday or Sunday shifts or 'brigades', to economise in materials and electricity, to use machinery efficiently, to introduce new crops in agriculture, and not to neglect work on the *kolkhoz* fields in favour of work on private plots—these are but a few of the daily agitational tasks the press must perform.

ORGANISING FUNCTIONS OF THE PRESS

However important the propagandist and agitational activities of the communist press may be, they are not sufficient in themselves. The party demands more: it wants the press not only to educate the working masses, but also to help to organise them in the complex process of the creation of the communist state, to assure that they consistently and systematically perform their assigned duties in the desired way. This organising task provides, in fact, a kind of framework for production propaganda and agitation, a channel for a continuous flow of such material.

The function of the press as a collective or mass organiser in the new conditions of the communist system was defined in principle by Lenin in his draft article *The Next Tasks of Soviet Rule*. He described there the press as an instrument of the economic reorganisation and re-education of the masses. One of the most important tasks in this process was to teach the workers 'the new, socialist discipline of labour', which would be based on the 'organisation of emulation according to socialist principles'. The press, therefore, in Lenin's words, has the organisation of this emulation as one of its fundamental tasks. It must give publicity which will:

1 Acquaint all citizens of the state with the progress of economic development;
2 Compare the progress of socialism in one commune with another;
3 Provide the interchange of proven experiences (including the use of material and human resources).

The organising function of the press had been often wrongly interpreted (in the Soviet Union and consequently also in the western literature on this theme) as giving publicity to all party or governmental decrees, documents, instructions, circulars, and of enumerating the everyday production quotas or figures. From this misconception emanated the 'official gazette' appearance which—particularly in the years before 1956—characterised many of the communist newspapers in general, and more specifically those of the lower echelons of the press structure.

The organising role of the press in communist countries consists today of:

Supporting and organising, in co-operation with the party and trade union organs, all forms of 'new', 'socialist' methods such as socialist emulation between workers, factories, and districts; 'brigades of socialist workers'; and campaigns initiated 'from above' by the party or 'from below' by the workers.

Facilitating the exchange of experiences and comparison of productivity between individual workers, factories and *kolkhozes*.

Giving publicity to economic news of production progress in factories, *kolkhozes*, districts, regions or other socialist countries. In this category fall news and features on how the working masses react to different party decisions concerning economy.

Supporting all party decisions and actions aiming at the political and cultural 'education' of the masses in the spirit of communism.

The first two functions are represented in newspapers by lengthy technical discussions sometimes continuing for weeks, months, or even years, as in the case of maize cultivation in the Soviet Union. Technical discussions are inevitably supplemented by agitational material and pictures.

These articles are of little concern to the general reader and can interest only the few workers participating in the exchange of experiences or in socialist emulation. With the shortage of space in newspapers, the question arises: why does the party insist that such material should occupy so many columns, and so frequently? There are a number of reasons.

First, the party wants—even at the price of alienating the general reader (who has no other choice but to buy these communist newspapers)—to ensure that propaganda material reaches the widest possible circle of the workers concerned. Secondly, it wants to stress—by the amount of space and by continuity—the importance of new methods, emulation campaigns, etc. Thirdly, one has to remember that the press is but a part of the vast complex of the party's mass propaganda and agitation. Production is a continuous process, and so must be propaganda and agitation for the importance of production; and the organising activities of the press must therefore be constant and uninterrupted.

The organising function of the press is also seen in extra-editorial activities, in the organisation of production conferences, consultations, 'productivity verification' campaigns, emulation and 'innovators movements'. This type of work is closely connected with the so-called mass political work of the press and its editors, their link with the reader. The aim of such mass political work is to help the party to influence the thinking of the masses, in guiding and directing the entire state, production, culture. In practice there is, however, considerable confusion among journalists as to where lies the border line between the organising role and mass political work.*

CRITICAL AND CONTROLLING FUNCTION OF THE PRESS

As already mentioned above, Lenin attached great importance to criticism and self-criticism and considered the press to be the best suited medium for their application in the public sphere. The press could expose large groups or even whole segments of the population, such as factories, *kolkhozes*, industries, districts, regions, writers, artists, etc., to *criticism*

* Organising functions also overlap to some degree with critical functions and are discussed in the section 'Mass Character' in the following chapter. How the organising functions are fulfilled in practice is shown in detail by examples in chapter 13, 'How the Communist Newspapers Work'.

from the top, from the party or government organs, for not fulfilling their economic or political tasks. Criticism applied in the press had the great advantage of serving as a warning or exhortation to other similar groups. At the same time, however, the press was best suited for the transmission of *criticism from below*, from individuals, 'working collectives', or party and trade union organisations with complaints of shortcomings, mistakes or excessive bureaucracy in public life.

By opening its pages to such criticism, the press assumes, in the communist view, the function of a guardian of public interests against bureaucrats, parasites (but not against the party itself), and performs the function of a *public controller*. In this way the communist press fulfils, to a certain degree, similar needs to those met by its counterpart in a free society. There are, however, fundamental differences in the latitude and scope of its criticising and controlling functions. Criticism must never touch the foundations of the regime, marxist-leninist theory and party dictatorship, or its outward symbols and institutions. It must follow the party line and must only criticise with the party's approval.

Criticism and self-criticism are a constant feature of the newspapers. Practically every issue, from the central organ, *Pravda*, to the lowest city or factory paper, contains some type of criticism. It may be in the form of a survey of the work of a factory or *kolkhoz*; districts or regions may be criticised for failing to deliver on time their set quotas of grain, meat or milk; coal districts or the whole coal industry are exhorted to fill the gap between their lagging production and what has been planned; the Central Committee or the government may criticise ministries for neglecting to introduce new production methods into factories under their control, or party and government organisations may be put on the carpet for lagging behind in their political work.

As distinct from this official criticism from above, criticism from below takes the form of readers' letters, contributions from worker and peasant correspondents or from whole groups of such correspondents investigating the work of a factory, *kolkhoz* or a regional branch of industry.

Today, most of the critical matter not emanating from official quarters is the result of more or less organised, planned efforts, and only a small fraction of published material in the forms of readers' letters can be regarded as spontaneous. The

CHARACTERISTICS OF THE COMMUNIST PRESS

A PRESS which has to fulfil the functions and tasks assigned to it by marxist-leninist theory must base its work and methods on different principles from those of a free press.

The theory is that the communist press must be militant, truthful, principled, partisan, ideological, dedicated to the cause of the working class. The wide range of these principles, or characteristic features as they are usually called by communist journalistic theoreticians, can be reduced to three basic features. The press should have:

>Ideological character
>Partisan character
>Mass character.

Other features, such as its class or militant character, principled or truthful character, are inherent in the first two features above and can be treated within their context.

Such features and propagandist, agitational, organisational and critical functions determine the contents and methods of the press, its approach to such important subjects as freedom and independence, truthfulness, objectivity, tolerance and respect for other political or religious views, world outlook and ideology. They also determine its outward form and appearance, and set limits to possible changes and adaptation of the press to the tastes of readers or in the direction of the image of a responsible press as conceived by democratic society.

If the propagandist, agitational, organising and criticising tasks prescribed for the press influence its contents, these characteristic features shape even more profoundly the working methods and approach of communist journalism to the task of reporting and explaining news and events of everyday life.

The first two features—the ideological and partisan character—are only two facets of marxist-leninist theory in its strict application to the work of the press. They overlap and set practically identical demands upon journalists' work, as can be seen from the following communist explanations of the terms.

THE IDEOLOGICAL AND PARTISAN CHARACTER

The ideological character (*ideinost* in Russian) is generally revealed by 'thorough substantiation, defence and application of the social ideas of marxist-leninist theory'.[1] When applied to and in the press, it means expression of class interests by journalistic means.

According to the theory, the *partisan character* (*partiinost*) is the ideological tendency shown by the class approach to reality in defence of the interests of the working class. It demands that the press should evaluate every event and social phenomenon in the light of party policy, from the *class* viewpoint.[2]

This official interpretation of the terms shows that both the ideological and partisan characters are practically synonymous with the *class character*, since they all equally demand a class approach to events. They are directly derived from dialectical materialism, the philosophical foundation of marxism-leninism. 'Materialism', wrote Lenin, 'includes partisanship and requires evaluation of all events from the forthright and open standpoint of a specific social group.'[3]

To communists, the materialist basis of marxism-leninism distinguishes it as the only 'scientific', 'truthful' teaching. All other philosophical conceptions are therefore hostile and detrimental to the communist cause. A press basing its work on such ideological, partisan foundations must, in the communist view, be the *only truthful* press. 'Partisanship is the highest expression of historical truth, the result of a truly scientific and objectively faithful analysis of social phenomena.'[4]

Against this supposed 'objectivity' of the partisan marxist-leninist philosophy, Lenin contrasted 'bourgeois objectivism' based upon the 'fraudulent idea of non-partisanship'. According to him, 'the substance of the so-called non-partisanship in the question of the world outlook is the covering up of class contradictions'.[5]

The ideological and partisan characters must, therefore, the party insists, be the guiding principle in the work of communist journalists; they must permeate the whole content of the press and create an inner tendency easily recognisable and clearly understood by the reader.

Thus, the communist journalist must always ask himself why he is selecting a particular news item or theme for his article, feature, essay or satirical sketch, and how the material should be presented so that the reader knows from the very beginning what position the matter is written from, and what purpose or what class it serves. To deviate from these principles is to commit the crimes of objectivism and escapism.

Objectivism is the presentation of facts or events without their social or class evaluation. *Escapism* is the presentation of matter not relevant to social reality or political demands, and which therefore distracts the reader's attention from these imperatives. Journalists and the party authorities responsible for the press are alike haunted by the twin spectres of objectivism and escapism. The journalist can easily succumb to them, for he has many opportunities inadvertently to deviate.

Examples of *objectivism* are news and articles disclosing high levels of technique in the United States or western Europe, the scale of consumer goods production, and features on life, the arts, theatre, etc. which fail to show the class character of such phenomena. It must always be stressed that only the rich, the bourgeoisie and the exploiters can afford to buy the goods, and visit theatres, or own houses and flats. Western art and culture in general must be shown to be decadent. Items such as a correspondent's description of the scenic beauties in a voyage through Switzerland, feature articles on American skyscrapers or the vast number of vehicles on the highways, are condemned as *escapist*.

Objectivism and escapism are comparatively rare in the Soviet press. This is not only due to the rigid ideological training of journalists, but also to their ignorance of conditions in the west. The party tightly grasps the reins of the press in the Soviet Union, and journalists show less courage than elsewhere to express views even slightly differing from the official line. Even so, Soviet journalists are being constantly warned against deviation from the strict standard.

One rare case of a prominent Soviet journalist and writer being accused of objectivism and escapism was that of Viktor Nekrasov. Nekrasov, an architect by training, is a well-known writer who originally won fame by his novel about the battle of Stalingrad. Since then he had travelled widely in Europe, and in 1962 in the United States. His travel reportages, published in the Soviet press, were very popular with readers because of his keen observation and forthright way of comparing (and indirectly criticising) many aspects of life in the Soviet Union with those in foreign countries.

The literary journal *Novy mir* published in its November and December issues of 1962 his impressions of a journey to western Europe and the United States under the title 'Both Sides of the Ocean'. Nekrasov did not conceal the fact that he was impressed by the modern painting and architecture of Italy, France and the United States. In his account of the journey he ridiculed the practice of placing official watchdogs in groups of Soviet tourists abroad, and regretted the Soviet public's lack of opportunity to see the numerous experimental films being made by western film directors.

He indirectly criticised the censorship which prohibits Soviet readers from becoming acquainted with prominent western 'bourgeois' writers and poets, by describing his embarrassment at having to admit he had neither read Albert Camus nor even heard of Kafka. His favourite method was to report a western—in this case an Italian—communist who told him he could not understand why Albert Camus's works were not published in the Soviet Union. Camus, Faulkner, even Françoise Sagan, the Italian communist argued, were typical of their time, representing segments, views and moods of the contemporary world. 'They can be disliked, criticised—rejected if you wish; but they cannot be ignored.'

Nekrasov also gave a favourable account of the Guggenheim Museum of Non-Objective Art and an unfavourable comparison (for Soviet architecture) of modern housing estates and architectural styles by Le Corbusier in Europe and American architects in Chicago with the Moscow housing estate of Cheremushki, the pride of Soviet planners. Very cautiously, he tried to convey the realities of life in the west by objective balanced reporting, depicting the black as well as the white sides of life, especially in the United States.

The government organ *Izvestia* (20 January 1963) sharply attacked Nekrasov's reportages in an editorial under the heading 'Tourist with a Swagger-Stick', because he was 'applying the "fifty-fifty" method in a most serious matter: the comparison of the "two worlds, their two ideologies".' Such an attitude, said *Izvestia*, could only lead to 'declaring and confirming peaceful coexistence in the sphere of ideology'.

Criticising his account of life in the United States, *Izvestia* reproached Nekrasov for not saying for whom the apartment houses in Chicago and elsewhere were built, and indicated the right ideological and partisan approach: 'It is quite incredible how he fails to see the sharp social contrasts and class contra-dictions in American life, the war psychosis, fanned by the imperialist circles. . . . The crux of the matter is not [Nekrasov's] factual errors, but the thoughtless and untrue generalisations and parallels which lead to bourgeois objectivism and sterile descriptive methods which distort reality.'

The pitfalls of 'objectivism' are, however, much greater in the east European countries. There the communist parties have not succeeded in completely moulding the minds of jour-nalists. Experience and influence from the past remain vivid, and in favourable conditions an inner urge to write objectively and to entertain the reader prevails.

This became particularly evident in all east European countries in 1955–7. Even in Czechoslovakia objectivism and escapism were manifest in 1956. At the Congress of Czecho-slovak journalists in June 1957 the press was criticised for show-ing signs of these shortcomings, for applying the 'boulevard manners of the bourgeois press, the aim of which is not to serve the interests of the workers, and to exert an educational influence upon the reader, but to distract his attention' from the class war.[6]

Deviating journalists and newspapers were reprimanded in the journal of the Union of the Czechoslovak Journalists, on the instructions of the Agitprop department of the Central Committee.

In our press, [said the journal] objectivism and escapism are beginning to appear in the form of servile admiration of the 'miracles' of western technique, in reprinting nonsensical matter from the western press as, for example, 'How many pearls are there in Queen Elizabeth's necklace?' From such contentless materials no one can clearly tell whom and what class they serve, from what point of view they were written, and why, since the reader does not profit in any way by reading them, they were ever published.[7]

The article saw a 'horrifying example of how the imperative of class character is being violated' in writing about cars and motorism in general. 'Some newspapers and periodicals', it said, 'are losing all sense of proportion in their admiration for the creations of the western car factories; they report nothing so promptly as western motor shows; they are literally crawling on their knees before the capitalist west.'[8]

What in fact happened at that time was that the Czecho-slovak journalists dared indirectly to criticise the low technical standards of Czech cars which were several years behind the standard of western models, and contrasted the technical advance in the west with the backwardness in Czechoslovakia. The party castigated them for 'losing their class consciousness and the feeling of pride and dignity in what our own people can do'.[9]

THE MASS CHARACTER OF THE PRESS

The communist party is not satisfied if the masses merely buy and read papers; it wants them, as a whole or at least the most conscious, active section, to participate in the work of the press, to help it to reflect and shape 'social reality' in a proper way. Such participation of the masses, rather than mass cir-culation as such (though this also is desired, of course), gives the communist press its mass character.

Fulfilment of this task sets new demands upon the working methods of the press. The press is expected to maintain 'close ties' with the masses through various forms of *mass political work*, using readers' letters and worker and peasant correspon-dents, 'authors' *aktiv*' and especially 'non-staff departments'. These non-staff departments are the latest development in communist editorial practice, and represent a higher, more effective form of directing and utilising correspondents and activists to forward party policy.

The mass character of its political work is fostered by regular local and regional production conferences, 'all-national discussions' on political and economic issues connected with every aspect of the party program. The mass character or mass political work of communist newspapers is determined, in fact, by their filling the function of 'collective organiser', that is organiser of the masses for the fulfilment of the short-term and long-term tasks of building communism.

Until several years ago, the mass character of the Soviet press was poorly reflected in the circulations of newspapers. Figures for the press as a whole were very low, even for the most important central newspapers like *Pravda* and *Izvestia*. Since 1956, however, the situation has radically changed: the total and individual circulation figures have risen considerably and the party is conducting a vigorous campaign, using subtle and not-so-subtle methods of social pressure through agitators etc., to further the spread of the press among the broadest masses in the Soviet Union.

FREEDOM OF THE PRESS AND MARXISM-LENINISM

The characteristic features of the communist press, together with the functions enumerated in the previous chapter, prohibit it from playing the part of a free, responsible press in a democratic society. It cannot respond to public opinion, or attune itself to the interests and opinions of its readers. It suffers from complete lack of freedom and a total dependence on the party. It is inhibited by a biassed approach to objective reporting, a directed slant to all its comment, and by a preconceived evaluation of news.

At the root of the whole question lie the philosophically different concepts of freedom, objectivity and truth, stemming from the ideological foundations of the communist movement. Some of these concepts have already been discussed. Others, such as the approach to news, will be dealt with in following chapters. Here it is necessary to consider the attitude of communists to freedom of the press, and their interpretation of the concept of freedom itself.

Dialectical materialism, the philosophical basis of marxism-leninism, recognises neither free will nor freedom as absolute values. It only conceives of freedom as interdependent with necessity. Freedom and necessity are interpreted by dialectical materialism as a mutual relation between the actions of people and the objective laws of nature and society—as the recognition and application of objective laws of action, i.e. necessity, in the interests of society. Recognition of the absolute inevitability of the laws of nature and society transforms necessity itself into a freedom.[10]

With such philosphical concepts and with a teaching that subordinates the press, with other social institutions, to the dictate of the party or more precisely to a handful of leaders (if not an individual), there cannot be freedom for the press in the democratic sense. In a democratic society, the press must preserve its independence from the government or ruling group, and formulate its own responsibility towards reader and society. It must perform freely conceived functions such as objective reporting (news), and independent appraisal (comment), and entertainment of its readers, constantly resisting all attempts at interference or pressure from the state or other power groups. While independence from state and power groups is a precondition of press freedom, it is only the first. The second is a sense of responsibility towards public opinion and the reader: a sense which preserves the press from abusing its freedom or breaking the trust which it is or should be enjoying.

In communist society there is not even the smallest section of the press which could independently perform these tasks. According to Lenin it is impossible to live in a society and to be free from it. The communist press, therefore, cannot be free from communist society; it must be dependent on its leading force: the working class. The communist party is the outward, political expression of the will of that class, and therefore the press must depend on the party. But in the application of the dialectical method, recognition of the necessity of such dependence turns it into real freedom, freedom from capitalist profiteering, careerism, individualism—gives it freedom to serve the working class and its *avant-garde*, the communist party.

According to this concept, there *is* freedom of the press in communist society, derived from the 'recognition and application of objective laws of action, that is necessity, in the interest of society'.[11] Press and journalists are not, however, free to interpret those interests on their own, and therefore there is freedom only within the functions and methods strictly defined by the party and ideology.

It is sometimes argued (in the west) that the basic difference between the western and the communist concepts of press freedom is that in the west the stress is on freedom of expression, while in communist society it is on the free access to means of publication.

This view has its origin in accepting at face value the communist argument that even where capitalist society formally permits freedom of expression, the system makes it impossible in practice for the workers, individuals or independent groups, who lack the substantial capital necessary to launch a newspaper. Hence the argument that freedom of the press in capitalist society (as all other freedoms) is only for the rich few, who misuse it for their own interests. Lenin stated in 1921: 'Freedom of the press means freedom for the rich to buy the press, freedom to utilise their wealth for the fabrication and forging of so-called public opinion.'[12] Elsewhere in the same pamphlet he said: 'In the capitalist world, freedom of the press means the freedom to buy the newspapers and those who edit them, as well as the freedom to buy, corrupt and shape public opinion in their own interests.'[13]

Communists do not limit their concept of press freedom, however, to free access to means of publication. They maintain that true freedom is dependent both on the legal guarantees of freedom of speech and of freedom of the press in the constitution, and on the creation of suitable material conditions for the exertion of those freedoms: access to financial means, printing presses, newsprint etc.; and that only the communist state secures both.[14]

The constitution of the Soviet Union, since 1936, grants all these rights in paragraph 125. It stipulates: 'In conformity with the interests of the working people and in order to strengthen the socialist system, the citizens of the USSR are guaranteed by law: a) freedom of speech, b) freedom of the press.' The paragraph further says that the rights of free expression are ensured by 'placing at the disposal of the working people and their organisations' printing presses, newsprint stocks, communication facilities and other material requisites for the exercise of these rights'.[15]

However, the framing of this paragraph and of further laws, as well as the underlying ideology and practice, show that such freedoms are only formal and strictly limited by the communist concept. The 'interests of the working people' and the way to 'strengthen the socialist system' are interpreted entirely by the party, because it claims to be the vanguard or expression of the will of the working class who are the decisive force in the state. The press must aim solely at the strengthening of the system, which means it must support communist policy; it is not allowed to criticise its foundations, principles, organs or high representatives.

Paragraph 58 of the Soviet penal code, in fact, makes any anti-Soviet, anti-socialist agitation, and the publication and dissemination of such matter, punishable by imprisonment from six months to twenty-five years. Any view seriously conflicting with the accepted ideological dogmas, foundations of the regime, or general party line on economic and political matters, is regarded as anti-socialist or anti-Soviet.

The Soviet law of 1932 (on associations) and party decisions on the structure of newspapers and periodicals (quoted in the following chapter) further limit these 'constitutional freedoms' by excluding individual citizens or groups, who are not sponsored and recognised by the party, from access to any printing and publishing facilities. Only the party and government organs, and acknowledged communist-controlled public organisations, are granted the right to publish and given the necessary material facilities by the state. Any transgression of the law on association and publication is severely punished. Thus, the Soviet trade union organ *Trud* reported on 26 December 1962 that an unspecified number of Jehovah's Witnesses had been sentenced to prison terms for running three underground printing shops in Russia, and for printing and distributing several thousand copies of the sect's organ, *The Watchtower*.

To grant real freedom of speech, expression or of the press would be incompatible with the communist system since it would inevitably lead to questioning and criticising its ideological foundations and basic institutions, its general policy and the party leadership. Once started, such a process would result in the final liquidation of the system, as was threatened in 1956 in Hungary (and partially in Poland). Lenin was aware of this danger when, in 1921, he stated that freedom of the press in the democratic sense could not be allowed in communist Russia because 'it would mean facilitating the task of the adversary, helping the enemy. We do not wish to find ourselves committing suicide, and for this reason we shall not introduce freedom of the press.'[16]

5

DIFFERENTIATION IN THE STRUCTURE
OF THE PRESS TO REACH ALL LEVELS

A POLITICAL SYSTEM which pays such great attention to
defining the functions, contents and methods of the press as its
strongest tool for communication with the masses, can be
expected to be thorough in ensuring that the press reaches every
section of the population and speaks in an appropriate language.

A study of the structure, growth and adaptation of the press
in the Soviet Union and east European countries confirms the
assumption. The east European satellites provide instructive
examples of how local communist parties adapt the existing
(sometimes very highly developed) press system to their own
needs. The Soviet example illustrates the systematic, purposeful
build-up of all press media to suit the political, social and
economic needs of the new society.

When the bolsheviks took control in November 1917, the
press in Russia was at a very low level. Because of the widespread illiteracy in tsarist Russia, there were in 1913 only
859 newspapers. These had a total one-issue circulation of a
mere 2.7 million copies, which, among a population of more
than a hundred million people, works out at about one copy
per forty inhabitants.[1] Newspapers, with the exception of the
bolshevik and social democratic press, hardly affected the broad
masses. They were directed exclusively at the intelligentsia,
bureaucracy or bourgeoisie.

The propagandist and agitational work of the party among
the masses made it necessary to establish a new network of
newspapers and to increase their circulation. In the early days
of the Revolution, the bolsheviks commandeered the printing
plants and editorial offices of the existing newspapers in Peters-
burg and Moscow to produce their own papers. *Pravda* as the
central organ of the party, *Izvestia* as the organ of the government, and later *Bednota* and *Ekonomicheskaya zhizn*, were the
leading newspapers of the early period.

At the Eighth Party Congress a resolution 'On the party
and the Soviet press' was passed. It set out the program of
further development of the press and its tasks, and stressed that
'the press is a mighty instrument of propaganda, agitation and

E

organisation, an indispensable means of influencing the broadest masses', and that 'a strong, sound party and governmental apparatus is unthinkable without a well-founded press'.[2] The Congress also paid great attention to the military press for the Red Army units engaged in fighting counter-revolutionary forces.

Subsequent party congresses continued to deal with press problems, and after the Eleventh Congress (1922) the Central Committee made several decisions radically to improve local newspapers and periodicals, and to strengthen them ideologically by appointing party representatives to the staff. The importance the party attached to the increase in circulation as a means of reaching the masses is shown by the fact that, despite the very difficult economic situation and acute shortage of newsprint (at times the newspapers had to be printed on coarse brown wrapping paper or on sheets of paper-board), the circulation of newspapers grew by fifty per cent between the Eleventh and Twelfth Congresses, that is between 1922 and 1923.

The need for increased circulation and effective structure was underlined by Stalin when he stated that 'the press must grow not by the day but by the hour, since it is the sharpest and most powerful weapon of our party'.[3] The Twelfth Congress pointed out that the press is not only an important tool of propaganda and agitation, but 'at the same time plays the role of a communications channel between the party and the working class'. The Congress also instructed the Central Committee 'to take the greatest interest in this branch of party work'.[4]

The Twelfth Congress was an important milestone in the development of the Soviet press because it laid down the principles for its differentiation in structure and contents. It decreed as an urgent party task the creation of a complete network of central, regional, *gubernia* and *uyezd** newspapers and the lesser local press.

'It is necessary', said the decree, 'to establish a specific type of newspaper for every basic stratum of readership. The party, having the whole system of newspapers at its disposal, must assign to each its precise sphere of activity so that every newspaper operates for a defined stratum of the reading masses.'[5] In great detail, the Congress instructed the party to broaden and improve the network of newspapers and periodicals for the peasantry, national minorities, and in factories and large plants.

* *gubernia, uyezd*—former administrative territorial units.

The principles of differentiation laid down by this Congress are the basis of the present structure of the Soviet press and, with modifications to meet local conditions, also hold good for the press of other communist countries.

GROUPINGS AND LEVELS OF THE PRESS

Before considering this structural differentiation, it is necessary to recall that no individuals or groups have the right to publish newspapers and periodicals in a communist society. The right is available only to the party, to the government and its various departments, and to public organisations effectively controlled by the party. Accordingly there are only three groupings:

> The party press
> The government press
> The public organisations' press

A second, most important, differentiation is based on the territorial-production division of party organisations and administrative division of the state. In this differentiation the Soviet press is divided as follows:

> The central or all-union press
> The republican press
> The *kray* or *oblast* press
> The *rayon* and city press
> The local, factory and *kolkhoz* press

There is a further differentiation according to the vertical stratification of the readership to which the press is directed and its particular subject-matter, namely:

> The general press and
> The specialised press

General newspapers and periodicals are directed to all citizens of the respective administrative territorial unit, while the specialised press serves the needs (as conceived by the party) of different groups of the people such as farmers, miners, engineers, teachers, writers, artists, scientists, women, young people and children.

One can also differentiate the press according to language or nationality. There are two main groupings in the Soviet Union: the Russian and non-Russian language press, the latter including newspapers and periodicals of such peoples as the Ukrainians who number 40 million, down to the smallest minorities consisting of only a few thousand members.

A similar pattern, with modifications, is to be seen in the press of other communist countries. In eastern Europe and in China, too, the press structure, due to specific political conditions, also includes separate groups of newspapers which had belonged to former non-communist parties before the seizure of power. These parties are formally allowed to exist to give the appearance that the communists are continuing the former democratic order. These are part of the so-called National or Patriotic Fronts. With no political power or functions, they are a mere façade for the communist dictatorship.

The non-communist 'bourgeois' press usually has the character of central newspapers, but it may sometimes be on the provincial level. In Poland there is a strong group of catholic newspapers, mostly belonging to a pro-communist pseudo-catholic organisation, Pax. The catholic church is allowed to have some publications of its own, but no daily paper, and they are subject to state censorship.

The toleration of such non-party papers, though fully controlled by the communist parties, is only a matter of temporary, tactical concession, and will be gradually abolished.

The territorial structure is a framework which applies to the entire press; into it are fitted all types of newspapers: the party, governmental, youth and trade union newspapers, the general and the specialised press.

The Soviet press, as planned on territorial-production principles, shows the same pyramidical structure as the party. Omitting wall-newspapers, which are not usually printed, the base of the pyramid is formed by the most numerous group—the factory and *kolkhoz* newspapers—*mnogotirazhki* as they are often called. At the top are the few central newspapers. But when one compares circulation figures, the top group shows the largest total and individual one-issue circulation. The number of newspapers in each group and their circulation figures are shown in the following table:

Type of newspaper	Number published	One-issue circulation of the group	Average circulation of a newspaper
Central, all-union	22	23·5 mil.	1,070,000
Republican	180	13·3 mil.	73,900
Kray and *oblast*	401	13·1 mil.	32,750
Rayon and city	3,846	12·2 mil.	3,200
Factory and *kolkhoz*	5,092	6·6 mil.	1,300
	9,541	68·7 mil.	

Based on the figures for 1961, published in *Sovietskaya pechat*, October 1961, pp. 10–23.

Specialised journals in the Soviet press serve groupings important both in their influence and numerical strength. Thus, in 1961, party publications for children and youth formed a large group of 154 *komsomol* and pioneer newspapers with a total circulation at one printing of 15.2 million copies.[6] *Komsomol* newspapers to the number of 130 were printed for youth above sixteen, and their circulation was 7.7 million copies, with *Komsomolskaya pravda* (3·35 million) at the top. For the *pioneers*, children between nine and sixteen years of age, there were twenty-four newspapers with a circulation of 7.5 million, headed by *Pionierskaya pravda* (published twice weekly) with about 4,050,000 copies at one printing. The total number of children's and youth newspapers and magazines was proportionately spread over the republics, *krays* and *rayons*, and covered all important nationalities.

Important groupings also follow the demarcations of production, for example industry, transport and agriculture. Each of these specialised groups has newspapers from the lowest to the highest level. On the lowest level of factory and *kolkhoz* papers, there were 2,352 industrial and 2,740 agricultural newspapers in 1961.

It is important to remember that the specialised press may be published either by the party (for example the all-union agricultural newspaper *Selskaya zhizn* with 900,000 copies); or by the government (newspapers of various ministries for industrial sectors); or by the public organisations in co-operation with government departments. Examples are *Uchitelskaya gazeta* (Teachers' Gazette) or *Sovietskaya kultura* (Soviet Culture) published by the Ministries of Education and Culture together with the unions of teachers and professional workers in the sphere of culture; or by public organisations alone, such as *Trud* (Labour) published by the trade unions, or *Literaturnaya gazeta* (Literary Gazette) published by the Union of Soviet Writers.

In all these cross-sectional groupings the most important role is, of course, played by the newspapers published by the party organs at all levels. Their line, their criticism, their recommendations are law for the entire sphere of their influence, for they voice the will of the party. Similar in authority and importance to the central *Pravda* (which printed 6 million copies daily in 1961) in the all-union sphere are the other party newspapers right down to city or *rayon*, or even factory level.

The tendency in the last decade to stress the over-riding position of party newspapers was indicated in the preferential (directed, not spontaneous) increase in their readership. Their circulations were kept artificially high above those of other newspapers. This was not always the case. In previous years, and especially in the 'twenties, *Pravda*, for example, had a lower circulation than some other central newspapers. Even in 1953 *Pravda* and *Izvestia* printed almost the same number of copies, whereas in 1961 *Pravda's* circulation was approximately fifty per cent higher than that of *Izvestia*.*

FUNCTIONS ACCORDING TO THE LEVEL

At the top of the Soviet press pyramid in 1961 there were twenty-two central, all-union newspapers. The most prominent, and best known abroad, are *Pravda, Izvestia, Komsomolskaya pravda, Trud, Literaturnaya gazeta, Krasnaya zvesda, Sovietsky flot*. The others are newspapers of a specialised, industrial, agricultural or professional character.

The central newspapers derive their leading authoritative and official character from being the organs of the three main groupings through which the power, direction and executive functions of the state are exercised: the communist party, government and public organisations. As such they serve as

* A more detailed account of methods of circulation promotion is contained in chapter 13, 'How the Communist Newspapers Work'.

channels of communication to, and channels of influence upon, the entire Soviet population, and are obligatory reading for functionaries and bodies within each group. *Pravda* as the central organ of the party, and *Izvestia* as the official newspaper of the government, have an exceptional position and stand above all other papers.

In the central newspapers the general line in party, ideological, governmental and other matters of an all-union character, is laid down, together with changes in that line. The lower echelons of the press take their cue for attitudes to important and pressing problems from the central papers. These provide the Agitprop department of the Central Committee with its primary and most suitable channels for transmitting directives to lower organs which could not be reached so promptly and efficiently through the party machine.

The key position of this central group is indicated by its having the highest circulation of any newspaper group, namely 23.5 million copies, and an average one-issue circulation per newspaper of 1.07 million. These figures of 1961 were surpassed in 1962 when the total circulation of the central newspapers was over 26 million.[7] The circulation of the best known Soviet papers in 1961 was as follows:[8]

Pravda	6·00 mil.	*Trud*	1·54 mil.
Izvestia	4·10 mil.	*Selskaya zhizn*	0·90 mil.
Pionierskaya pravda	4·05 mil.	*Sovietsky sport*	0·85 mil.
Komsomolskaya pravda	3·35 mil.	*Literaturnaya gazeta*	0·62 mil.

The republican, *kray* or *oblast* newspapers fulfil to a degree the same functional tasks as the central press, so far as the party line and its changes in home policy and foreign affairs are concerned, since they can effectively transmit party and government information and instructions to much wider strata of the population by their local and linguistic adjustment. Apart from this, however, they must deal with political and economic problems from the point of view of their territorial unit, and in doing so they are expected to be more specific, to go deeply into problems rather than to generalise.

The newspapers of this group are practically unknown abroad, not only because they do not print any relevant all-union news which is not also published in the central papers, but also because there are restrictions on exports of papers at the *oblast* level press.* Only names of newspapers like *Sovietskaya Rossia* (Soviet Russia), with a circulation of 2 million in the Russian Federal Republic, *Radyanska Ukraina* (Soviet Ukrain) or *Leningradskaya pravda* are worth mentioning.

The circulation of *kray* or *oblast* newspapers has been constantly increasing. In 1950 their average was 23,900 copies per issue and at the beginning of 1961 had risen to 32,750. Examples of the largest papers in this group are: *Molot* (Rostov), 200,000; *Volzhskaya kommuna* (Kuybyshev), 160,000; *Stavropolskaya pravda* (Stavropol), 109,000; *Altayskaya pravda*, 105,000. The extent of the general growth of these newspapers is shown by the Tulsk *oblast* paper *Kommunar*, the circulation of which rose from 5,000 in 1922 to 110,000 in 1961.[9]

At the lowest level relating to state administrative divisions are the *rayon* and city papers. Since they are closer to everyday life and local economic and social problems, they are charged with more specific tasks of propaganda and agitation than newspapers at the higher levels. They are used extensively for direct organising and critical functions, almost entirely adapted to local needs. But their work is considerably handicapped by shortage of qualified journalists and by poor printing facilities. Their circulations are small and they reach too few readers. To overcome these shortcomings, and to raise the journalistic and technical level, the Soviet authorities decided to establish newspapers of a new kind.

In 1962 so-called inter-*rayon* newspapers (*mezhrayonnye gazety*) were launched in a number of republics. They were set up to implement a decision of the Central Committee of March 1962 and are now slowly replacing the inefficient small *rayon* newspapers. In the Russian Soviet Federal Socialist Republic there were, in 1962, about 400 of these, and about 190 in the Ukraine. Their circulation is much higher, the average being about 20,000 copies compared with the 3,200 average in the *rayon* and city group.[10]

At the lowest level, that of the territorial-production division, are the factory and *kolkhoz* newspapers. Their sphere of influence, their readership and their tasks are suggested by their name. They are published in the larger industrial plants, factories, collieries, offices, *sovkhozes* and *kolkhozes*. Their

* Owing to the agitational and critical functions of the local papers, their export might publicise shortcomings in production and output, or bureaucratic failings which are only for domestic consumption.

circulations vary according to the size of the production unit, and may range from 500 to 20,000. They may be published monthly, weekly or daily.

The ultimate printed link with the workers, the factory and *kolkhoz* newspapers must be most specific of all in translating important party and government decisions into terms relative to the particular industry and production unit. They have to be the most specific in agitation for the fulfilment of the targets assigned to plants, departments and individual workers. Together with local party and trade union organs they must be efficient in organising socialist emulation, exchange of experiences and introduction of new working methods and norms.

The picture of the combined communist press, propaganda and agitation system would not, however, be complete without mentioning that special phenomenon, the *wall newspapers*. These consist of hand-written or painted slogans, typewritten material and photographs or press cuttings pasted up and displayed on notice-boards or walls. Each has its own 'editorial commission' nominated or elected by the party primary or sectional organisations, trade unions or youth committees. Their basic and perhaps only function nowadays is to be agitator, critic and organiser in the microcosmos of smaller enterprises and offices, departments and workshops of larger plants, institutions, ministries, etc.

Wall newspapers, due to their vast number and immediate impact, are regarded by the party as an important link in the agitation system. In the past, they tended to be regarded as of only minor importance and merely as ordinary notice-boards. The 'editorial commissions' used to limit their function to showing, with emotional slogans and pictures clipped from newspapers and magazines, the happy life in socialist countries in contrast to the exploitation and misery of capitalist countries, or to exhorting workers—with slogans cut out from newspapers or specially issued posters—to fulfil and exceed targets and norms. Only a very small fraction of these wall newspapers fulfilled the demands of the party. Their effectiveness was limited by the prescribed agitational contents and by the fact that they gave no scope to free expression of workers' views.

Wall newspapers were a significant development in the Soviet Union in the 'twenties when, in a way, they were newspapers brought right down to the working masses, and when they were the result of a spontaneous movement 'from below', freely criticising the misdeeds of factory management, government and party executives. Later, their influence declined as they became engulfed in the party apparatus and the bureaucratic agitation system. The appearance of factory newspapers, or house organs, whose predecessors they had been, hastened their decline.

Since 1956, however, the communist party in the Soviet Union has been trying to revitalise wall newspapers in an all-out drive to bring new life into mass propaganda and agitation. In smaller plants they are now even replacing factory newspapers with very small circulations. Similar developments are taking place in Czechoslovakia. There the number of factory newspapers was drastically reduced in the years 1955–60. From a total of 1,380 factory papers in 1955, only 433 remained at the end of 1960; their functions were taken over by wall newspapers.[11] The 'editorial commissions' of the revitalised wall newspapers are provided with help from professional editorial and technical (design and print) staff.

PERIODICALS

Soviet periodicals show, even more clearly than newspapers, striking evidence of their official planning and integration in a system thoroughly organised to serve both political and technical propaganda by an appropriate blend of both.

The network of periodicals inherited by the bolsheviks from tsarist days was quite unsuited to their needs and to their concepts of the function of this section of the press. Almost immediately they began with the liquidation of existing periodicals hostile to their cause or unwilling to support it unquestioningly, and virtually finished the process by 1919. At the same time, they began to publish their own political, literary and artistic periodicals. These, however, were short-lived and were, in turn, replaced after 1922 by new ones in the thorough reorganisation of publishing.

Instrumental in this reorganisation was the decision of the Eleventh Congress, 'On the press and propaganda', adopted in 1922. It defined the type, character and tasks of the new party and other periodicals. The existing state publishing house for political literature, Gospolitizdat, was reorganised and a new one, Partizdat, was formed which took over the production of the entire network of party and other political publications. The years 1922–5 saw the appearance of many new (and mostly still existing) literary, artistic, scientific and political periodicals and general magazines including: *Oktyabr* (1924), *Zvezda* (Star, 1924), *Novy mir* (New World, 1925), *Ogonyok* (Small Light, 1923), *Krokodil* (1922), *Rabotnica* (Woman Worker, 1923), *Krestyanka* (Woman Peasant, 1922), and *Bolshevik* (1924) which was renamed *Kommunist* in 1952.

In the following years, 1925–31, the founding of new periodicals continued. There appeared numerous technical, industrial, medical, educational, theatrical, musical and other journals. In connection with the great industrialisation drive announced in the First Five-Year Plan, technical periodicals multiplied spectacularly. In the territory of the Russian Federal Republic, 1927 saw the publication of forty-six periodicals dealing with industrial and technical problems, and in 1932 there were already 140 periodicals for the heavy industry alone in the whole Soviet Union.[12] Collectivisation of agriculture was also reflected in many new agricultural periodicals.

This mushroom growth, however, had serious drawbacks. By 1931 the quality of most published periodicals was low; they did not work systematically or with any clear purpose. In many fields parallel publications doubled each other's work, while at the same time all lacked qualified editorial personnel, and publication was irregular. Typography, layout and illustrations were of poor quality, and above all the party found such periodicals lacking in the most important quality: militant political consciousness.

To improve the political and general level of periodicals, in 1931 the Central Committee issued the decree 'On the work of publishing'. The decree included regulations aimed at raising quality and at strict differentiation, eliminating duplication, especially among government publications (technical magazines published for industry by various ministries). The decree defined the sphere of activities of the various publishing bodies, *viz*. Ogiz, the Unified Government Publishing House; Partizdat, the Party Publishing House; Gostekhizdat, the Government Technical Publishing House; and scientific institutions and ministries.

While some periodicals were closed down, many new ones, especially in non-Russian languages, were launched. In the period 1932–4, mainly due to the appearance of publications in non-Russian territories, technical periodicals increased from 337 to 387, literary and artistic periodicals rose from 108 to 136, and medical periodicals from 87 to 142. The growth of non-Russian periodicals continued. By 1937 their number reached 393, whereas in 1913 there were only 109 such publications in non-Russian territories.[13]

Another comparison illustrates communist efforts to reach the broadest non-Russian masses and draw them into the constructive process. In 1913 peridoicals in tsarist Russia were published in twenty-nine languages. After twenty years of communist rule there were, in 1937, already periodicals in fifty languages. For many nationalities, the progress was remarkable. In tsarist times they had not even had their own written language or primitive literature. Now they could boast not only of newspapers but also of literary, technical and political periodicals. In those years, for the first time in their history, periodicals were published for such national groups as Buryats, Bashkirs, Kazakhs, Chuvashes and others.[14]

Apart from organisational problems, the party paid great attention to political contents. The Central Committee, and Stalin and Zhdanov personally, sharply attacked the editorial line of certain prominent publications, and gave a strict warning to other possible deviators and independent thinkers. Significant in this respect was the decision of the Central Committee in 1946, 'On the periodicals *Zvezda* and *Leningrad*', dealing with ideological matters. Other decisions included one on the improvement of the political content of the magazines *Krokodil*, *Ogonyok* and *Molody kolkhoznik*. They stressed that periodicals are 'powerful instruments of the Soviet government in the education of the Soviet people, and especially youth, and must therefore be guided by what constitutes the vital basis of the Soviet system—its political principles'.[15]

Ideological strictures and directives especially referring to literary and artistic periodicals were contained in a decision of the Central Committee of 1949, 'On the periodical *Znamya*'. It sharply reprimanded the editorial board for publishing literary material 'divorced from life', and emphasised the duty of every communist periodical to print work which depicts 'life in its revolutionary development' and 'reveals the high moral qualities of the Soviet people—the builders of communism'.[16] Requirements of this so-called *socialist realism*, to show the entire life of communist states in the idealised form, left their mark not only on literary and artistic works, but on all forms of Soviet journalism: reportage, human interest stories, features, leaders and essays.

The broad outline of the network of periodicals for the Soviet Union was completed by 1937–8. The organisational structure of the publishing houses, their task, and also the differentiation in the contents of periodicals, made it possible to cater, according to communist notions, for the varied needs and tastes of the whole population.

The growth of Soviet periodicals since 1938, which is still continuing apace, is planned and executed within the broad outline referred to above. Today, every branch of Soviet economy, science, culture and public life has its own periodicals differentiated by territory, language and other aspects, as is shown by the following thematical division of periodicals published in 1950:[17]

	Subject	Number of titles
1	Party, politics, economics	265
2	Science, mathematics	222
3	Industry, technology	250
4	Agriculture	128
5	Medicine, public health	103
6	Education	139
7	Literature, arts	156
8	Press, bibliography	103
9	Miscellaneous	42

The list shows the preponderance of scientific, technical and industrial periodicals which, taken together, are numerically almost twice as strong as those on party, political and economic subjects. This structural characteristic has not only been maintained, but even strengthened in the last ten years. While in 1950 the two groups (covering the Soviet Union as a whole, that is including periodicals published in individual republics) were represented by 472 titles, the catalogue for 1963 published by Mezhdunarodnaya kniga (an organisation for the export of Soviet publications) listed altogether almost 700 corresponding periodicals which are exported. The actual number of technical industrial and scientific periodical publications must be consequently higher, since many of them are barred from export by the censoring organ, Glavlit.

According to *Sovietskaya pechat*,[18] in 1961 there were 923 periodicals with a yearly one-issue circulation of 577 million copies. If one adds also periodical publications such as the *Notebook for Agitators*, various periodic reviews, annuals, technical reference publications and bulletins, then the total number of titles rises to 3,761 and their circulation to 778 million copies.

At the beginning of 1962 there were already 950 periodicals and, with other similar types of publications, the total number of titles was 4,121 and their circulation increased by 94 million.[19]

Of popular magazines, however, there are only a few and the reader today has almost no choice. The circulation of these few magazines is relatively far behind comparable magazines in western countries. Practically the only magazine of general appeal in Russian is *Ogonyok*. Two magazines for women, *Rabotnica* (Woman Worker) and *Krestyanka* (Peasant Woman), are, as their titles suggest, aimed at readers of two different social classes and are published only monthly.

The circulation of the most popular magazines in 1961 was (in millions): *Rabotnica*, 2·5; *Krestyanka*, 2·2; *Ogonyok*, 1·85; *Krokodil* (satirical magazine), 1·5.

The party theoretical periodicals—*Kommunist*, *Partiynaya zhizn* and *Agitator*—had in 1961 circulations of about 500,000 copies each.[20]

It is obvious from what has been said on the structural differentiation of the Soviet press that it is a thoroughly planned institution. Apart from the party, only government and public organisations controlled by the party have the legal right to publish. These three groups perform their publishing activities on the bases of strict planning according to political needs. The outward expression of this attitude is reflected in the inclusion of the press in economic development plans. Not only is the structure and number of newspapers within each grouping planned, but their circulation as a whole and individually, technical equipment, the construction of printing plants, and even the number of journalists and their education are strictly regulated.

Such planning is made possible only through public (i.e. state) ownership of all printing and publishing facilities, and by total control of the entire cultural and spiritual sphere of life. It is made possible also because finance, profit or loss do not count in a society where political requirements over-ride all other considerations.

To a great extent, the system proves efficient in rational utilisation of the limited resources for political purposes, and in efficiently concentrating on the most important and necessary areas where development under communist direction is required. But its efficiency is manifested chiefly in the technical and scientific fields where there is little ideological influence, propaganda or agitation (though even the most serious publications are not free of them). In other fields its efficiency is dependent on the successful application of the other aspect of differentiation: differentiation in contents. Here, however, the chances of success are severely limited by propagandist and agitational requirements.

There are some signs that the structure of the press as conceived in the 'twenties and 'thirties, like many other Soviet institutions, no longer meets the requirements of the more diversified Soviet society of today. Some opinion considers there should be newspapers and magazines differentiated according to the varying educational and cultural levels of the population. In the east European countries with higher social development and higher journalistic traditions, the structure of the press, despite many inept interferences since 1947–8, is much better suited to the population's varied needs. Soviet journalists and authorities are aware of these shortcomings and are now considering the possibility of some modifications in the structure of the press.

6
DIFFERENTIATION IN THE CONTENT OF THE SOVIET PRESS

THE TERRITORIAL and other cross-sectional structure of the Soviet press was supposed to provide a variety of newspapers through which, in Stalin's words, the party could speak to the masses in the necessary language. The structure was there, but variety was conspicuously absent from the newspapers. The ideological rigidity and absolute party control of the press by the party's bureaucratic apparatus, even down to the minutest detail, combined with the terror of Stalin's rule— under which the least deviation from the line meant professional and often physical liquidation—imposed a stamp of uniformity on the Soviet press as a whole.

The communist party was instrumental in creating this uniformity not only by imposing functions and contents on the newspapers but also by intervening in the technical details of editing, layout etc. The instructions issued by the Central Committee in 1921 for the local press stipulated its basic task to be the mobilisation of the workers for the construction of the new social order. Beyond these political tasks, the instructions listed in detail the individual themes for news and articles, such as industry, agriculture, transport etc., and decreed where and at what length they should be printed.[1] Similar instructions were issued by the Central Committee for the regional newspapers. It prescribed, in fact, the whole layout of the newspaper. The leader, from 80 to 120 lines of a concrete character, was to contain information and facts on some issue of local political and economic life; the second major article was to be a 'practical' or 'technical' discussion about problems of local construction; the remaining space was to be distributed as follows: life of the nation—120 to 150 lines; foreign affairs—80 to 100 lines; agriculture—100 to 150 lines and so on.[2]

A. Inkeles, in his book *Public Opinion in Soviet Russia*, compared this prescribed pattern with matter published in *Pravda* and *Izvestia* in 1947 and 1948 and found that the pattern was clear and consistent up to that date.[3]

The uniformity of the Soviet press, especially of the

regional press of the 'thirties and 'forties, was reinforced also by slavish imitation of *Pravda*'s typographical layout and by reprinting its editorials and main articles on party and ideological matters, on economics and foreign policy. Fear of committing political errors, or of being found insufficiently enthusiastic in praising the party and Stalin, or of offending the local party leaders, created the deep-rooted habit of using well-known phrases and quotations, and repeating, with only slight changes of words, whole passages from party decisions and leaders' speeches.

Journalistic initiative, independence in searching for news or themes for reporting and criticism, originality in journalistic expression—these were utterly unknown to the Soviet journalism of those years. The modest differentiation of contents, of treatment of different subjects by different journalistic methods required by the structure of the press, was almost totally obscured behind the stereotyped propagandist and agitational approach, and by the low professional standards of journalists.

The same pattern and methods were applied to the press of the east European countries after 1947–8, as the communists gradually gained power. Within a short time the press of Czechoslovakia, Poland, Hungary, Rumania, Bulgaria and East Germany, regardless of differing conditions in these countries, was transformed in contents and layout into a faithful replica of the Soviet press, though the latter's standards were much lower.

The degrading and damaging effects of such rigid enforcement of Soviet methods were openly admitted and deplored in 1956–7 by communist journalists in many countries. They protested that, in this submission of the press to the theoretical requirements of the party, the considerable differences in the level and tasks of the press were neglected or disregarded. These differences which were being ignored arose out of the specific conditions in individual communist countries— differences in economic development and national traditions, and in the level of political control of the country's life.

Further differences lay in the degree of distribution of the press among the population, as shown by the number of newspapers and periodicals per head or per worker in the industrial branches. Closely related to the distribution factor were press traditions influenced by readership habits and demands in the past.

F

Thus, for example, in Czechoslovakia the people were used to a wide choice of newspapers and to free expression of varying political views. Journalistic standards and the circulation of the newspapers had been high, whereas in the Soviet Union at the time of the beginning of communist rule, the general public were not accustomed to reading papers or to free expression of different views. Its notion of newspapers and periodicals was formed by the image of the stalinist press.

The traditions of the press of any country are the result of historical development, and are to be seen, not only in its scope and tone, but also in its structure and its typographical and technical level. These in turn are dependent on the level of the country's industrialisation, on the technological level of the printing and paper industry in particular, and on communications in general. Other factors which contribute to press traditions are style, layout and journalistic forms used in the newspapers, methods of editorial practice, division of duties, and availability of journalists trained in different conditions and coming mainly from the middle class.

All these considerations were over-ridden in the political drive to bring the press nearer to the 'matchless Soviet model', to the detriment of its efficiency and its functions.

A leading Czechoslovak communist journalist, analysing such faults of the years 1948–52, wrote:

It is necessary to say that, in the past, specific features of the Soviet press were sometimes mechanically transferred into our press without taking into consideration the different conditions, our national traditions, *genre* forms which had deep roots (such as Neruda's feuilleton column etc.), and the popularity of the press. . . . It often happened that some partial Soviet experience was proclaimed to be a principle which it was obligatory to follow. In the years 1948–52 we also often mechanically applied usages in the editorial and organisational work of the press, graphic layouts, forms and style peculiar to the Soviet press.

We took them over together with the shortcomings which were inherent in the Soviet press in the time of the personality cult. . . . All those mistakes found expression in our press in the simplification of the problems of socialist construction, in a schematic attitude to life, to questions of construction and to the reader. We used to write as if life consisted only of percentages, production norms, technical and organisational problems of production; as if there were nothing else in man's life but work; as if health, housing, culture, recreation, the whole complex of questions of living standards, of man's spiritual life and of human relations between people ceased to be an important part of life.[4]

This frank admission illustrates how the press in the entire communist orbit was reduced to a uniform image of drabness and dullness. Yet, despite these descriptions, the western observer, accustomed to the vivid presentation and wide variety in the appearance and contents of his national and provincial press, can hardly imagine the state of the Soviet and satellite press of that time. A clearer idea may be provided by the following:

Before me lie several issues of provincial and territorial newspapers published on the same day. Above all, one is arrested by the striking similarity of the papers. Like twins, they can hardly be distinguished from one another. If it were not for the names of the papers and the names of districts, factories and collective farms which are mentioned in them, any one of the papers could be substituted for another, and neither the reader nor the staff itself would notice.

These words are from a critical survey of the Soviet press by a high official of the Central Committee's propaganda and agitation department in Moscow, published in the authoritative party periodical *Kommunist* in April 1955.[5]

It should be noted, moreover, that these remarks relate to the press in the post-Stalin period, more than a year after the highest party representatives started a vigorous campaign to change the deadening uniformity and stereotypy.

CHANGES AFTER 1953

The 'thirties and 'forties, years under Stalin's rule and of the blindest application of marxist-leninist theory to every aspect of social life, show very little differentiation and variety in the Soviet and other communist press as far as methods and contents are concerned. Real differentiation started in 1955 and 1956 with a wave of 'liberalisation'—a mixture of deliberate policy from the top, expression of ideological uncertainties and loosened party controls (in some countries) resulting from the contest of the old and new tendencies.

The impulse came at the end of 1953 from the First Secretary of the Communist Party of the Soviet Union, N. S. Khrushchev, who, at a conference convened by the Central Committee, urged editors to use new methods of presentation in order to make the press more efficient and more attractive to the reader. In words often quoted, he said: 'The firmly rooted stereotypes and time-worn methods whereby everything is written according to a single pattern must be vigorously driven from the newspaper pages. . . . Material must be more varied, and more thought must be given to content and form of presentation.'[6]

While the press in some satellite countries was ready and eager to take up the offered opportunity, and—as was the case in Hungary and Poland—even exceeded the limited liberties, Soviet journalists were very slow in adapting newspapers to the new party requirements. The passage already quoted from *Kommunist* (April 1955) is proof of it. The party authorities had, indeed, to push the press into changes. In 1956 and 1957, on the Day of the Press (5 May), *Pravda* still castigated Soviet newspapers for being 'insipid, lifeless, deadly dull and difficult to read', without realising that it was, even at that very time of writing, the prototype of all the enumerated sins.

It took the courage and example of the editors-in-chief of *Komsomolskaya pravda* and *Sovietskaya Rossia*, who had the personal backing of Khruschev himself, to show a fresh spirit and give an impetus to new journalistic ventures in 1956-8. Adzhubei, the editor-in-chief of *Komsomolskaya pravda*, and Khrushchev's son-in-law, was transferred in 1959 to *Izvestia*, and with the aid of a party decree on the reorganisation of the paper effected similar changes to those made in his previous paper. The readership of *Izvestia*, which was previously falling away, returned. Attracted by the more vivid presentation, shorter articles, and other innovations, the circulation rose. In 1961 the paper's circulation was 4.1 million copies, almost three times that of 1957. Readers reacted favourably to another lively newspaper, *Sovietskaya Rossia*, which prints short items, more interesting features (compared with the stalinist diet) and photographs. Within three years, it achieved a circulation of 2 million.

Since then Soviet newspapers in general have become more lively and varied both in presentation and contents. Regional newspapers now rarely reprint editorials or articles from *Pravda*, and instead publish their own articles and features. Though the general line on the preponderance of economic and political agitation and propaganda over all other aspects of the press's functions (such as information and entertainment) persists, editors are given a free hand in journalistic methods and presentation; and, to some degree, a spirit of competition, both for readers and higher standards, is now apparent in the press in the Union and in other communist countries.

Perhaps the most important feature in the differentiation of contents lies in the fact that editors are no longer rigidly bound by outdated regulations as to how many lines or how much space must be given to specified material. Instead, the party has demanded that contents and layout should be varied, and that each newspaper should cater for the taste of its readers (while, of course, keeping within the still unchanged functions of the press—defined as a collective propagandist, agitator and organiser).

The order to 'cater for the taste of readers' required reallocation of space reserved in some newspapers for certain types of matter. Ideological and economic propaganda had to be compressed, though not eliminated, to make place for other material of interest to the specific strata of population at whom the papers were aimed. Out of the former faceless, uniform mass of dullness emerged several newspapers or groups of newspapers distinguished by specialised contents, livelier and even bold layout, and greater use of photographs and drawings.

The most outstanding examples of this new journalism are the youth papers, with the central *Komsomolskaya pravda* at the head, followed by the *Pionerskaya pravda* and other papers in the republics and *krays* or *oblasts*. Articles on ideological problems are not so frequent and, when published, are brief and better adapted to the level and scope of interest of young readers. Political propaganda is less obtrusive, compared with its previous clumsy ways, and is worked into the generally popular travel reportages, short stories, humorous features, and above all sports news and features which are the most appreciated and the items most sought after by the readers. Headlines in the youth papers are to the point and often striking in wording and typography. The most outstanding feature of the youth press is the generous use of illustrations.

Another group notable for their changed face and contents are the evening newspapers. They are published in big cities like Moscow, Leningrad and Kiev, and concentrate on local news and features, film, theatre, sports, etc. They avoid all heavy propaganda and print even the most important speeches and documents in a highly compressed, almost telegrammatic form.

Literary newspapers also take their place in the new 'progressive press' with livelier journalistic spirit and differentiated contents. There were ('62) three literary and cultural newspapers in the Soviet Union: *Literaturnaya gazeta*, *Sovietskaya kultura* and *Literatura i zhizn*, all published three times weekly, competing for readers not only by interesting contents but also by differentiated attitudes to the problems of literature, culture and the arts.

The total effect of these changes on the Soviet press in general is, however, slight. They are only significant when compared with the extremely low standards of the pre-1953 period. Not only to the western observer, but also to critical Soviet observers, the Soviet press still presents an uninspiring picture. Speaking to journalists at a reception in the Kremlin on 14 November 1959, Khrushchev had this to say: 'There is still very much dullness in our newspapers. You take a paper, go through it quickly and put it away—and you don't even remember what was in it.'[7]

CHANGED CONTENTS AND APPEARANCE OF PARTY ORGANS

The trends in the Soviet Union affected, of course, other communist countries. Hungary and Poland stood out from countries where more rigid systems were entrenched, but even in the latter the leaders were to follow the Soviet lead. With growing independence from the Soviet Union, specific national features came to the fore, and the satellite countries' earlier slavish imitations of *Pravda* were replaced by party organs showing more individuality.

Today the organs of the individual communist parties differ in outward appearance. There is varied distribution of matter over the pages, the inclusion of sections and columns more clearly reflecting the interests of readers, the cultural level and traditions of the country and national press characteristics. A brief survey of the issues of the Soviet *Pravda*, Polish *Trybuna ludu*, Czechoslovak *Rudé právo* and Hungarian *Népszabadság* on a typical day—9 October 1962—clearly reveals the differences (and their affinity, too).

On that day *Pravda* had four pages, *Trybuna ludu* and *Rudé právo* six, and *Népszabadság* twelve pages of smaller format equalling six pages of the other papers.

Front page

Pravda has in the first two left-hand columns a typical leader exhorting better organisation of work and higher productivity, under the indifferent headline 'The criterion of our progress'. Under the leader is the full text of Khrushchev's congratulatory telegram to the Premier of Uganda, complete with full address, date etc. At the top of the page over the remaining four columns are placed a photograph and long caption agitating for the introduction of new working methods in engineering. Underneath with a headline 'The toilers of Uzbekistan will fulfil their high obligations!' is a thousand-word report (by four correspondents) of an official party meeting in Tashkent, called on the occasion of Khrushchev's visit to Uzbekistan, with the speeches of officials.

On the lower part of the front page, spreading over three columns, is another exhortation: 'Complete the work in the fields more quickly!' Apart from these items, the front page contains only one short report of a meeting in Orenburg convened to express 'patriotic pride and joy' over congratulations sent to the region by the Central Committee after the completion of state grain deliveries, and three short items on successes in the fulfilment of the Seven-Year Plan targets in factories.

Trybuna ludu prints on the front page, beneath the headline 'Cuba is ready to negotiate with the US', a three-column telephone message from its own correspondent at the United Nations on President Dorticos' speech in the General Assembly; below it a two-column report from the Yemen, a short report on Polish films in Finland, and another factual report on Laos. After a one-column report on Algeria's membership of the UN the paper spreads over the top of three columns a lively and factual 'own information' account of the expansion of Polish production of pulp and paper. Three other larger items on the front page are: a report on economic talks between Poland and East Germany; on a 'rich cultural program for the celebrations of the 45th anniversary of the October Revolution'; and on an exhibition of Van Gogh's pictures in Warsaw.

The front page contains further shorter items of information, one of them noting in six lines the telegram of Premier Cyrankiewicz to Uganda's Premier, and another (sixteen lines) mentioning the similar telegram of Khrushchev. One photograph (production of specialised lamps) and a map of Uganda are also on the page.

Rudé právo prints in the same position as *Pravda* an exhorting leader, 'The force of communists' personal example', and next to it—under bold headlines, 'Search for savings: prevent losses in the interest of higher economy in the consumption of electric energy!'—agitational items from good enterprises and some bad examples. Another report, with statistics, exhorts farmers to speed up potato deliveries.

The front page also contains official matter: the new Canadian ambassador presenting his credentials to the President; the President's telegram to Uganda's Premier (fourteen lines); and a reception held at the East German embassy in Prague. The page is completed by a reportage on the use of glass waterpipes accompanied by a photograph, and another 'pictorial reportage'—three pictures with explanatory and agitational captions—on deliveries of sugar-beet and work in sugar factories.

Népszabadság has a leader filling two columns of the smaller format (five columns in all) on 'Careful Economising'. Other space is occupied by a report on Dorticos' speech in the UN and on fighting on the border between Yemen and Saudi Arabia, accompanied by a photograph of jubilant masses in Yemen's capital, both spread over three columns. Algeria's new membership in the UN is also reported.

Further contents

On further pages *Pravda* follows the established pattern. Page 2 is filled with lengthy articles on 'Profit as the basic criterion'; on the experience of maize cultivators from Ryazan accompanied by a photograph; and with two other items—

on the fight against 'parasites and shirkers', and on short-comings in housing construction.

Foreign affairs are dealt with on the third page: a longer account of Dorticos' speech, a long article on Uganda, and a very lengthy official report on the reception at the Guinean embassy in Moscow, with speeches. Beside some short items on production in the section 'From the socialist countries', the page contains a more or less objective, factual report on the American astronaut W. Schirra's press conference. Some more reports from foreign countries (British communists' appeal to free Britain from dependence on the United States, the situation in the Yemen, and an appeal of the communist Peace Council in France to the French people) appear on the last, fourth page. The bulk of this page is filled with short news from the USSR, a report on the world chess Olympics, and an article on the Soviet theatre.

A cheerful picture of smiling, pretty girl-folkdancers and short programs of the Moscow theatres, radio and television complete the last page.

Trybuna ludu continues in its usual way to give readers a wide selection of foreign news on the second and third page. In fact, this paper usually gives two and a half times more space to foreign news than *Pravda*, and by better handling, selection and cutting, gives the reader a much wider view of world events, though, of course, from the communist angle. The angling, however, is not very obvious, and many items are purely informative and factual in character. Reporting of home events, political and economic problems is also factual, vivid and interesting, and is almost entirely free from the clumsy Soviet agitational or official approach.

Thus, *Trybuna ludu* of all communist organs comes nearest to the western conception of a newspaper. It pays great attention to the varied problems of the country, has special sections for Warsaw and the regions, for women, children etc., informs the reader widely and deeply enough on cultural events at home and abroad. Its sport section is very good.

Rudé právo fills its second and third page with readers' letters and contributions to a nation-wide discussion on economic, political and cultural shortcomings and problems. The discussion had been conducted by the paper for several months as preparation for the party Congress.

The fourth page is therefore, in fact, a typical second page on normal days. It is run on a stereotyped pattern, modelled—with more vivid adaptation—on *Pravda*.* It contains a critical article against speculation in fruit and vegetables; an official announcement of new regulations concerning the sale of cars and a 100 per cent increase in their prices; a section 'Briefly from the homeland' with very short items; a column 'On the margin of the day' with a typical selection of items—one criticising, one praising; an article on the 250th anniversary of the Harrachov glassworks; and at the bottom, across the whole page (the place usually reserved for long articles), is an article by the Minister of the Health Service. Three photographs from factories and one pictorial landscape are printed, which is usual for that page.

The last two pages also show the typical pattern of the distribution of matter and layout. The first two columns on page 5 are filled with 'cultural material' and the remaining five columns with foreign news and articles. In the foreign news and commentaries, also in headlines, the paper shows, as always, more militancy and partisanship than any other communist organ. Characteristic of this attitude is the report on Schirra's press conference which selects only passages presenting the American space achievement and program in the most unfavourable light. This piece of reporting, based entirely on western agencies' materials, is in sharp contrast to the reporting of that event in the other papers surveyed.

The other items on the fifth page are: a report by the New York correspondent, headlined 'Another failure of the US in the anti-Cuban crusade'; an account of the American press's uneasiness about Ben Bella's forthcoming visit to Cuba; a speech of the General Secretary of the British Communist Party; and articles on Uganda (with map) and on the situation in Laos.

Foreign news is also carried, as usual, on five columns of the last page, with longer items on Dorticos' speech, the French referendum, fighting between the Yemen and Saudi Arabia, and Ulbricht's press conference. A wide selection of one-sentence

* In 1962 it was noticeable that *Rudé právo* was trying to get right away from the pattern of *Pravda*, and not only on the front page. During 1963 the pattern and layout of both pages 1 and 2 were changed so that they become quite distinct from *Pravda* and more vivid and interesting, and in January 1964 the paper underwent a radical typographical change. Materials and sections were also radically reallocated to give *Rudé právo* the air of a modern newspaper with a new outlook.

items, printed in the regular section '24 hours abroad', concludes the foreign news part. Three columns are filled with sports news and radio and television programs, and theatres and cinemas in Prague. There are two photographs on both the fifth and sixth pages—altogether fourteen in the issue, while *Pravda* had only four, or one per page.

Népszabadság prints on the second and third pages home news and two features, one on a Hungarian communist underground fighter executed twenty years ago, and another on women active in public life. Foreign news is continued on pages four and five with a somewhat different selection from that of *Pravda*. The report on Schirra's press conference is conspicuous by its objectivity and includes even some entertaining episodes.

On the sixth and seventh pages the paper prints a novel, serialised in parts, and a 'human touch story' about an 87-year-old woman doctor, 'Auntie doctor'. The remaining space is filled with home news. Page eight is fully occupied by cultural items, and page nine by a popular article on electronic computers. Page ten contains more home news, radio, television and theatre programs.

Characteristic of *Népszabadság* are advertisements,* usually included in the entertainment and information pages. In the issue surveyed there are four larger advertisements, by an enterprise producing neon lights, a departmental store, etc. The whole of page eleven is reserved for classified advertisements (on some days two full pages are reserved for this purpose). The last page is always devoted to sport.

* For further remarks on advertisements in the communist press, see chapter 13, 'How the Communist Newspapers Work'.

DIFFERENTIATION IN THE CONTENT OF THE EAST EUROPEAN PRESS

DIFFERENTIATION in the contents and appearance of newspapers, is even more obvious in some east European countries. In the pursuit of their political aims after 1953, the communist regimes had to take into account the existence of wide strata of opponents of communism—the petty bourgeoisie, intelligentsia and the adherents of the former non-communist, democratic parties—and also the fact that the population had, until recently, been accustomed to higher journalistic standards and a wide variety of newspapers, news and features.

The means to reach and influence these strata of readership were there: the newspapers of the former political parties. In most countries, the communists retained both the newspapers and the parties, and integrated them into the transitional political system of 'people's democracies'. The only problem was how to use the newspapers to the best advantage for their cause. The pre-1953 method of *Gleichschaltung* into the dull and ineffective carbon copy of the stalinist Soviet press had failed, but the period of revitalisation offered new opportunities.

In the process, the proportions of ideological, political, economic and cultural matter, entertainment and sports were adjusted to correspond better with the functions the papers had to fulfil. The preponderance of ideological, economic and production propaganda and agitation was reserved for the party press, especially the central organs; other newspapers were given the task and, to a certain degree, also a free hand, to adapt their contents to their readership, with more stress on entertainment and culture.

Thus a higher degree in differentiation was attained even in countries with rigid party controls, such as Czechoslovakia and East Germany. Poland and, to some extent, Hungary stood apart. Especially in Poland liberalisation of the press, the loosening of most party controls and an unheard-of liberty in licensing new papers and periodicals in the short period from October 1956 to summer 1957, was of great significance for the rest of the bloc.[1]

CHANGES IN THE POLISH PRESS

The wave of liberalisation and ferment after Stalin's death started in Poland as a spontaneous movement of journalists and writers 'from below'. The journalists exerted great pressure upon the party whose leadership was split into two factions: the stalinist wing and the 'liberal' wing with Gomulka as its representative. By their pressure and bold attitude they paved the way to important political changes later. The movement of change got out of the control of the party as early as the spring of 1955 and had a very profound influence on the attitude of journalists in general, including party members, and this was reflected in the contents of the existing press.

The new, bold and independent spirit appeared originally in a group of literary periodicals like *Nowa kultura* and *Przeglad kulturalny* (later also in *Życie literackie*), and soon also infected journalists on other papers, economic periodicals and newspapers. They were all voicing demands for democratic freedoms, and trying to adjust the contents of their publications to suit their readers rather than the party and state organs. The most audacious and prominent in this respect was the student weekly, *Po prostu*, which became a rallying point for all young radical intellectuals.

These changes alone provided a sufficient differentiation in contents within the existing structure. However, differentiation went further with the appearance of new publications (or reappearance of some newspapers previously suppressed during the 1947–53 period), which not only catered for different tastes of general readership, but also represented certain groupings among the population not connected with, and not welcomed by, the party. This, of course, involved a change in the structure of the press. Such, for example, were *Tygodnik powszechny*, the weekly from Cracow, formerly banned, representing the catholic church, and the cultural monthly *Wież* published by the Catholic Intelligentsia Club in Warsaw, and several student and cultural periodicals.

Among the variety of new publications which appeared both in the capital and in the provinces were, for example, two weeklies *Wyboje* and *Tygodnik zachodni*. They were started in Poznan late in 1956. The staff of *Wyboje* was composed of members of the former (communist) Polish Youth Union who resigned from it. Intellectuals, students and artists began to publish a cultural periodical *Kronika* in Lodz, *Nowe sygnaly* in Wroclaw, *Przemiany* in Katowice, *Poglady* and *Pod wiatr* in Lublan, *Zebra* and *Od nowa* in Warsaw. New satirical periodicals—*Kaktus* in Poznan, and *Karuzela* in Lodz (with a circulation of 350,000)—competed for readership with the existing popular *Szpilki.*

The Polish press of 1956–9 presented, despite the noticeable party pressures after the second half of 1957, a lively picture compared with that of other communist countries. In the new conception of journalism the press tried as far as possible to assume the function of a genuine two-way channel between the people and the party and government, as Lenin spoke of it, giving people and journalists the opportunity freely to express their views: that is to say, to give voice to public opinion and thus to be truthfully informative. The press in general, and even the party press, had to adapt itself to the new trends, and tried at the same time to reduce to proper dimensions the formerly 'over-politicalised' contents and methods.

With the increased number of publications, there was competition to cater for the varied tastes of readers. Articles for light reading on sport, the film industry, theatre and television were a regular feature of the press. Leading this field were illustrated weeklies filled with travelogues, fashion news, cartoons etc. There were even such specialised publications as *Jazz, Brydz* (Bridge), *Auto-Moto-Sport, Film na swiecie.*

Growing competition and financial difficulties (the party either limited or totally withheld financial subventions to any journals but its own), efforts to increase circulation and to replace formerly popular (but later prohibited) controversial political and ideological matter with attractive materials, led to the increasing use of illustration, often resulting in sensationalism, and the printing of pictures of scantily dressed and even nude women. The effect in some respects was an unwelcome trend towards yellow journalism in contents and methods, and even included the running of contests for readers with the offer of numerous prizes.

The party, however, was soon dissatisfied and alarmed by the liberalist, even radical, trends and by the situation in the press generally. From the autumn of 1957 it embarked more or less openly on a policy of reimposing its controls and systematically reducing the numbers of certain newspapers and periodicals, and limiting the circulation of others. It was claimed by party officials that in a socialist country there was no need for a wide range of publications which only duplicated each other's work and contents since there were no opposing classes or ideologies.

The communist party (United Workers' Party) increasingly used censorship with its irritating methods to suppress the politically inconvenient or otherwise unwanted newspapers and periodicals which appeared after 1956. The first victim of the new policy was the radical student weekly, *Po prostu*, which had continuous clashes with the Chief Press Control Office, the censoring organ. The post-vacation issue in September 1957 was completely censored and the publication was stopped.

Censors or party organs extinguished some new publications even before they could show their character. The most notorious case was that of a Warsaw periodical *Europa*, intended as a review of western literature and culture. The first issue was scheduled to appear on 1 November 1957, but the censoring organs rejected several drafts, and on their recommendation the party withdrew the licence even before the first number appeared on the news-stands. In October 1957 the popular *Przemiany* was liquidated because the censor objected to its 'revisionist' line. In December of the same year two periodicals, *Nowe sygnaly* and *Poglady*, met the same fate after approximately one year of publication.

Since then a tendency to reimpose the former party controls, supervision and direction of the press is more and more apparent. Artur Starewicz, head of the party's press section in the propaganda department, discussing the shortcomings of the Polish press and its gradual subordination to the party dictate, said in 1963 that 'there are certainly enough directives' issued by his department ordering the press how to write—especially about life in the west. He also expressed some satisfaction with the transformation of the press into a more efficient tool of propaganda:

In spite of deficiencies and various weaknesses, our press has made substantial progress in the last few years and is certainly more militant nowadays. In order to achieve this, we have had to wage quite a difficult fight against revisionism, especially in the years 1957 to 1959. We fought primarily against people who were obstinate in maintaining these views and did not want to abandon them. We discussed with people, but at the same time we carried certain personnel changes. The composition of the editorial boards of the press, the radio and TV underwent a fundamental renovation. Our ties with the journalists are stronger now than with other groups of the intelligentsia.[2]

The latest open interference by the party in journalistic affairs occurred in the summer of 1963 when two weeklies, *Nowa kultura* and *Przeglad kulturalny*, which were still pursuing 'revisionist' or independent editorial policies, were ordered to cease publication, allegedly because of shortage of paper. *Le Monde* (18 July 1963) reported that a heated discussion on the affair went on for some weeks and that the First Secretary of the party, W. Gomulka, convened a plenary meeting of the editorial staff of both weeklies. After much excitement and many protests, Gomulka, it was said, banged with his fist on the table and made it clear that the closure had been decided by the party and therefore could not be further discussed. Both weeklies were replaced by a new one called *Kultura*.

As a result of all these changes and pressures, the Polish press today is a far cry from its best years 1956–7. With limited freedom for discussion, news reporting (dealt with in the chapter on the communist conception of news) and criticism it has lost most of its former vigour and independence. This has had an adverse effect upon readers—naturally, they have lost much of their interest and faith in the press. Yet the Polish press still stands out from that of other Soviet bloc countries.

CHANGES IN THE HUNGARIAN PRESS

The movement for liberalisation of the entire social life in Hungary began with notable impact in 1954–5 under the government of Imre Nagy. Again, the writers and journalists stood in the vanguard of the development and in fact initiated the wave of freedom which culminated in the Revolution of October 1956.

From the summer of 1954 some newspapers, with *Irodalmi Ujság* (Literary Gazette) at the head, fought against the rigid stalinist controls, especially open censorship. Despite the suppressive methods of the rigid party regime of Rákosi (who deposed the liberalist Premier Nagy), pressure from journalists increased from the end of 1955 and into 1956. Prominent in the fight was the Petöfi Circle where journalists and writers met regularly to discuss the political and cultural problems of their country.

At a tumultuous meeting of the circle in June 1956, certain journalists demanded freedom of the press and one of them declared that 'nationalisation of the Hungarian press is responsible for its decline and incredibly low standards'.[3]

During the short period of the Revolution in the last week of October and first days of November 1956, Hungarian journalists, and it has to be noted that they were mostly former members of the communist party, tried to create a truly free democratic and responsible press as a defender of truth and civil rights of individuals.

Liberalisation of the press was brought to an abrupt end with the suppression of the Revolution by Soviet tanks and troops. The new regime clamped down on the press and jailed many journalists who played prominent parts in the pre-revolution period and during the uprising. Later in 1957, it allowed some so-called independent newspapers, among them two pseudo-Catholic publications, but prohibited the expression of all independent attitudes.

The return of political oppression and inept propaganda created widespread apathy in the political, cultural and economic life of the country. Not until 1958, when the nation's entire life was dangerously stagnating, did the Kádár regime begin to understand the lessons of 1956. For two years it manoeuvred cautiously between the pressures from the old stalinist forces and the demands for political and economic revitalisation, and around 1960 it started to foster 'peaceful coexistence' with the entire population under the new slogan, 'Who is not against us is with us'.

The slogan, signifying new, officially initiated and controlled 'liberalisation', meant in general that the regime was prepared to tolerate political indifference, but not active ideological or political opposition. In the new situation details of method in the construction of socialism could be criticised, but not the program itself, or communism, marxism-leninism, or the party.

In this campaign ideological, economic and political propaganda and agitation were reduced in the press generally in favour of lighter, entertaining and cultural matter. Changes were much more pronounced than in neighbouring Czechoslovakia and Rumania, though they did not go as far there as those in Poland. The trend has been maintained up to 1963 and at the

G

moment the Hungarian press differs considerably from what it was in the pre-1953 period. It is more vivid, and nearer to what it was before the communist era.

Even the party organ *Népszabadság* was made to play the new role and was changed, as no other party organ had been except *Trybuna ludu*, so as to make it attractive for the broad non-communist masses, while not neglecting its ideological duties. The brief sketch of its contents given in the previous chapter (p. 91) showed the adaptation to some extent, but the weekly pattern of special sections appearing in the newspaper during 1961 illustrates the case even better.[4]

Among the regular sections (the paper is not published on Mondays) were:

Tuesday: 'We have read': two columns of quotations from the foreign press, not more than half the page; 'Science and Technology': articles or features in popular style with illustrations on a whole page.

Wednesday: 'From our villages': approximately 60 lines of short features or items on life in the 'socialist village'; 'Advice to parents': on education, schools etc.; 'Advice to co-operatives': a whole page, also on Fridays, in rural editions only.

Thursday: 'Cinema': short reviews of new films; 'The reader wants to say': readers' replies and comment on readers' letters.

Friday: Editorial replies to readers' letters.

Saturday: 'News from party life': short summaries on the initiative and methods of party organisations; 'Readers' views': 2 to 3 letters on articles published in the paper; 'At home': a whole page for women with features and information on various subjects like flat-planning, kitchen furniture, advice on make-up, fashion, meal recipes; 'Economic notes': short items on smaller or bigger problems of the Hungarian economy; 'A week of international affairs': short comments.

Sunday (16 pages): 'Sunday letter': a contemplative article of about 75 lines by one of the three best known communist writers; 'Cultural life': a supplement of four pages; 'Crooked mirror': satirical section; 'From the courts': reportage, mainly on pillaging of 'socialist property' or violation of 'socialist good-neighbourliness'; 'Monologue': profiles of positive or negative types taken from everyday life; 'Merry Sunday': political, satirical and entertaining cartoons, anecdotes, with a story written by the most popular Hungarian humorist; crosswords etc; 'For our children': section of entertainment for children.

The last page of the paper is always reserved for sport which is very popular in Hungary. It also contains features, but even 'here, on the sport page, we conduct political educational work', as the editor has said.[5]

This review of the sections shows that the paper tries in many cases to imitate popular sections of newspapers of the pre-communist period.

CHANGES IN THE CZECHOSLOVAK PRESS

The Czechoslovak Communist Party adopted, with some modifications, the new Soviet trends in press and propaganda as early as 1954–5. Cautious, officially induced changes were also reflected in modified methods of press direction and supervision. The propaganda and agitation department of the Central Committee of the party began to replace former bureaucratic, detailed circulars and decrees with directives by 'personal guidance', direct contact with editors in matters concerning the new line for the changed contents, and reallocation of tasks for the entire press.

In this reallocation *Rudé právo*, the central organ of the party, was given the function of ideological, doctrinal mouthpiece, filled (more or less as before) with appropriate propagandist and agitational matter. It was, however, enlivened by the generous use of photographs, many in each issue of pictorial or entertaining interest. Further improvements included the introduction of satire, humour, reportages, and regular travelogues.

The organ also served the party, with other theoretical periodicals, as a watchdog over the rest of the press, criticising and sharply rebuking those papers which, in the tumultuous years of 1956–7, strayed too far from the tolerated 'liberal' line. *Rudé právo* has always been the most rigid and dogmatic of the satellite central organs. Its line on foreign policy in relation to the west is even more militant and uncompromising than *Pravda's*.

In ideological and economic matters *Rudé právo* was supported by the regional press of the party, and by the trade union paper *Práce* (Labour) which was given, however, a more popular character and printed less theoretical matter. The stress in *Práce* was on good reporting from industrial plants, building sites etc., linking explanations of economic and political problems with the workers' everyday life and using very simple language and journalistic methods of presentation. But *Práce*, in general, failed to achieve much interest and never attained popularity.

The central youth papers, *Mladá fronta* (The Youth Front) in Prague and *Smena* (Shift) in Bratislava, with the central newspapers of the 'bourgeois' parties, *Lidová demokracie* (People's Democracy), *Svobodné slovo* (The Free Word) and the Slovak *L'ud* (The People), were ordered to adapt their contents the better to meet the tastes of their readers, while remaining tailored to the wishes of the communist authorities.

The youth newspapers faithfully followed the example of their Soviet counterparts in copying their kind of content and journalistic methods, with bolder headlines, wider use of photographs and drawings, and arresting layout.

Lidová demokracie, organ of the so-called People's (christian) Party, had to beam its adjusted contents to the catholic section of the Czech population in cities and villages, and influence their loyalty to the regime by claiming that the basic demands of christian socialism had been fulfilled by the communists. *Svobodné slovo* had to influence the petty bourgeoisie, artisans, white-collared and skilled workers who previously formed the bulk of the (national) Socialist Party (whose organ nominally it still is) and the right wing social democrats. Both newspapers were also given the common task of convincing their peasant readers of the advantages of collectivised agriculture. The considerably diminished propaganda, varied contents, and the return to many formerly popular features and columns, made these papers very popular. On Sundays they printed 250,000 copies each, but could have easily sold twice the number. The communist party would not, however, allow them to increase their circulations.

The Slovak *L'ud* had essentially the same propagandist tasks as *Lidová demokracie*, since Slovakia is an agricultural and catholic country. For the catholic population the communists also started a special newspaper *Katolické noviny* which, however, was run by the pro-communist pseudo-clergy and the communists themselves.

But these formal changes introduced by the party did not satisfy the journalists. They became infected by events in neighbouring Hungary and Poland. Ferment was most noticeable in the spring of 1956 among the Czech and Slovak writers. But before it could spread among journalists in general and develop into a broad movement, the party leadership took firm measures against liberalising tendencies. The pressure by journalists for even small reforms, mainly in news reporting, continued in 1957 and resulted in relatively better presentation of life, as is shown in the chapter on the communist conception of news. Due to the pressure and demands of readers, in 1957–8 the Czechoslovak press became even brighter and more entertaining and contained less propaganda. There were also general tendencies towards more objective reporting of events at home and abroad.

From 1959 onwards, communist authorities in Czechoslovakia applied the old practices of strict party supervision of culture and the press, and of suppressing 'liberalist' tendencies, although preserving many outward aspects of the differentiation introduced to relate contents to different strata of population. The authorities reverted to the old methods of 'ideologising' the contents of all newspapers. Even in the 'bourgeois' newspapers, propagandist matter appeared more frequently; news and features were once again heavily slanted and imbued with a militant, partisan spirit. The rather subtler methods introduced for a time were replaced by heavy and clumsy propaganda and agitation.

Thus, *Lidová demokracie* printed on Easter Day in 1962, instead of a catholic meditation on Christ's Resurrection, a political leader by J. Plojhar, an excommunicated priest and Minister of Health Service, entitled 'Eternal Legacy'. It said among other things:

> The name of Vladimir Ilyich Lenin will stay forever connected with the new era in the history of mankind, begun by the Great October Revolution, and the ensuing unfolding of the forces of socialism. The resurrection of a true humanity, the opening of new horizons for all peoples, the renewal of the moral greatness of mankind is forever connected with his name. The great socialist thinker and statesman V. I. Lenin is forever enrolled in the golden book of human history; his work will remain for us a source of instruction, inspiration and strength.[6]

One can well imagine the reaction of catholic readers, to whom the paper should appeal, when they saw Christ replaced by Lenin in the most offensive and clumsy way. The same propagandist line was applied in news reporting and evaluation of prominent personalities in culture, theatre and music.

The same newspaper, reporting the eightieth birthday of Igor Stravinsky, presented him as a 'Soviet composer' with no connection at all with the United States or the west. The reader was led to believe that Stravinsky had lived all his life in the Soviet Union and was an ardent, though sometimes slightly deviating, supporter of the communist regime.

This item, which can serve as a model of the method of distortion used, said:

> The prominent representative of contemporary modern music, Soviet composer Igor Stravinsky is celebrating his 80th birthday today. He studied music under Rimsky-Korsakov and, with his unusual talent and endeavour, soon took his place among the most outstanding composers of the twentieth century. He has also lectured at universities and published several theoretical works, but his importance lies in the creative field. His most important works were composed during the period of his co-operation with the Diaghilev Ballet. Part of his work is influenced also by jazz (Ragtime). In some of his works he experimented too much, and this evoked critical disapproval among the musical public.[7]

The gradual tightening of the screw in the entire cultural field could stifle their voices but it could not still the critical mood of journalists and writers wanting to probe and openly discuss the causes of serious economic troubles and stagnation in the cultural and political life of their country. The smouldering revolt of the intellectuals was brought to the surface in the spring of 1963. The protracted economic crisis, culminating in a disastrous winter, and chronic shortages of certain foodstuffs brought widespread discontent. Further, there was general dissatisfaction at the reluctance of the leadership to admit its responsibility for the continuation of 'stalinist' methods and failing fully to rehabilitate victims of previous persecution.

First to lead the still muted attack were some communist economists who complained in the press that previous economic plans had overestimated the country's potential, setting unrealistic targets and subordinating economics to politics. After March 1963 there was a growing chorus of voices in the press criticising the 'cult of personality', 'non-leninist methods' and innumerable past and present misdeeds. Prominent among the rebellious papers were the cultural weeklies *Kultúrny život* (Slovak), *Literární noviny* and *Kulturní tvorba* (Czech), and the Slovak youth paper *Smena*. Even *Pravda*, the organ of the Slovak Communist Party, on many occasions lent its pages to thinly veiled attacks on the central party leadership in Prague for its past and present policies.

In the forefront of the struggle stood the Slovak communist journalists. In the years 1951–4 many prominent Slovak communists had been sentenced to death or long-term prison sentences for alleged crimes of 'bourgeois nationalism'. The central leadership in Prague was refusing to rehabilitate them legally and politically. In addition the Slovaks had certain grievances against the centralistic tendencies of the Prague leadership.

Political ferment was brought to a new head at congresses of writers and journalists held in April and May. The most outspoken attacks were made at the Congress of Slovak Journalists. The Premier and member of the presidium of the Czechoslovak Communist Party, Viliam Široký, was openly accused of sharing personal responsibility for trials of 1951–4, and Miro Hysko, one of the most prominent Slovak journalists, accused the party leadership that it was, in fact, maintaining the discredited 'cult of personality' (that is stalinist methods) from 1949 until 1963, and that the 'promising developing process of revival which began in our country after the Twentieth Congress of the CPSU has been impeded by intervention by the authorities since the end of 1956 onwards'.[8]

The general tone of criticism voiced at the congresses and subsequently in numerous articles in certain newspapers whose editors refused to submit to the directives and supervision of the discredited party leadership, was also aimed at the total subordination of the press to the ideological and political demands of the party. Rebellious journalists criticised (as the party organ *Rudé právo* admitted) the party for having 'over-ideologised' the newspapers and the whole journalistic output, totally subordinating it to party decisions, and thus allegedly depriving journalists of an active, 'independent' function. They complained that 'journalists became victims of service to the party, of their faithfulness to an ideology which allegedly they only blindly followed'.[9]

Pressure from journalists and writers, supported by the younger generation of communist officials at lower levels of the party machine reinforced by the general dissatisfaction of the people, had some notable successes. In April and September 1963 Premier Viliam Široký, Karol Bacilek, First Secretary of the Slovak Communist Party, and many other party functionaries and ministers responsible for the political trials and for the existing cultural oppression and economic crisis, were dismissed.

The new revolt of journalists was reflected in much better and freer discussion of economic, political and cultural problems of the country in daily and weekly newspapers. Reporting of events from abroad became rather more objective, but the changes could not go very far because journalists were mostly dependent for news on the official agency service which was very little affected by the ferment.

In autumn 1963 the party leadership began a slow and cautious, but deliberate, counter-attack on the dissident journalists. They were accused of spreading 'chaos, frustration and defeatism' among the population and of undermining the position of the party. A similar process was set in motion within the party machine as that in Poland after the autumn of 1957, aiming at the gradual elimination of 'liberalising' tendencies and unreliable journalists.* The First Secretary of the party, Antonín Novotný, struck the keynote of the campaign by declaring:

> . . . We shall never admit any compromise, we shall always relentlessly defend the positions of our party. . . . We shall not change one iota of the principles and policies of our party. We cannot therefore agree to the . . . spreading

* But in January 1964 the editors of *Literární noviny* and *Kultúrny život* were still continuing their fight against party control. The acting editor-in-chief of the former went so far as to declare, after his paper had been criticised at a plenary meeting of the Central Committee: 'The lazy, passive obedience and undiscriminating repetition [of party decisions and criticism] are no longer a perfect sign of political consciousness. Newspapers do not merely accept and comment on the party program: they also participate in the formation of the program, or at least they should do so. . . . The party's Central Committee acts in the name of the party, expresses the will of the party; but this does not mean that it, instead of writers, will write novels, or edit and write newspapers instead of journalist-communists.' (*Literární noviny*, 18 January 1964.)

of petty bourgeois views. . . . Our party will support any factual, constructive critical voice, but will resolutely refute every attempt at criticism which would aim at weakening the leading function of our party in the state and which would impair the unity of socialist society.[10]

CHANGES IN THE EAST GERMAN PRESS

The uprising of workers in Berlin and other East German cities in June 1953 was, for many journalists, a clear sign that the old methods of propaganda and agitation in the press were no longer effective. Prominent communist editors demanded radical changes, especially in news reporting (see chapter 11) and in the space given to propaganda and agitation in the newspapers.

Although the party leadership successfully suppressed the threatening revolt of journalists at the outset, to some degree it learned its lesson and made concessions in news reporting. It also made changes in the differentiation, tasks and contents of newspapers similar to those allowed in neighbouring Czechoslovakia, since both countries had similar social, economic and political conditions with two 'bourgeois' parties and their own newspapers.

The reallocation of tasks, propaganda and agitation and the resulting greater differentiation in the contents of East German newspapers is confirmed by a detailed study of the main newspapers undertaken by the Munich *Infratest Institut* at the request of the Federal Ministry for all-German affairs.[11]

For its research the Institute selected one paper of each type or group from the 39 dailies (with 277 local editions)—namely:

One central and district paper of the ruling communist party, the Socialist Unity Party (SED), *i.e. Neues Deutschland* (New Germany) and *Volksstimme* (People's Voice).

One district paper of the Christian Democratic Union (CDU), *i.e. Die Union.*

One of the Liberal Democratic Party (LDP), *i.e. Sächsisches Tageblatt* (The Saxon Daily).

Two dailies of the public organisations, *i.e.* the trade union *Tribüne* and the youth paper *Junge Welt* (The Young World).

The economic weekly *Die Wirtschaft* (The Economy) published by the party.

The contents of the issues of these newspapers, published in January 1957, were analysed (with further samples taken during June-December 1957) and grouped under subject-matter such as politics, ideology, economics, culture and entertainment, sport and advertising. The researchers found that the practice of 'ideologising' economics and 'economicising' ideology, and the mixing of both elements with politics, made the distinction between subject-matter difficult. Nevertheless, analysis proved fruitful.

The results of their research are shown in the following table (the figures give percentages of the total contents):

Subject Matter	NEUES DEUTSCHL.	VOLKS- STIMME	DIE UNION	SAECHS. TAGEBL.	JUNGE WELT	TRIBUNE
Political	29	20	23	18	17	24
Ideological	16	10	5	3	19	14
Economic	18	14	4	6	8	24
Topical	3	3	2	2	3	1
Other events	2	9	5	5	1	1
Culture and entertainment	18	16	30	31	34	19
Sport	8	9	7	10	11	8
Readers' letters	1	0	0	1	4	3
Advertising	4	17	23	22	3	4
Other items	1	2	1	2	0	2
	100	100	100	100	100	100

It is obvious from the table that the central organ of the party plays the role of chief indoctrinator. The readers of the 'bourgeois' newspapers are given a relatively small dose of ideology and economics though the proportion of political material is still high enough; but in this section are included also 'necessary' party political documents, speeches, etc. so that purely political articles are rather rare. In the 'culture and entertainment' section, which predominates in this group, the researchers found it was not exploited ideologically as much as one might expect. (But the inquiry was carried out in the period of the communist regime's political retreat—the period of 'liberalisation'. Since then 'ideologisation' and the tightening of party controls has considerably increased, and with it the proportion of ideological propaganda, not only here, but in all communist newspapers in the Soviet bloc.)

In economics the emphasis was on news from the industries. The treatment was close to real life and well presented graphically. The section 'culture and entertainment' showed a different approach to cultural life from that of western newspapers. Stress is laid in the 'cultural and historical heritage'.

In distinguishing the groupings of the newspapers examined, the researchers observed that the structure of contents in the SED press was fully in line with the task of developing the party members' political consciousness, and that other possible functions of the press—those of entertainment and information —gave way to this political educational function. Also significant was the relation of political, ideological and economic matter in the central *Neues Deutschland* and the provincial *Volksstimme*. The smaller ratio in the latter reflects the lower level of party members and general readers at whom it is aimed.

The trade unions have to attract and win over the non-organised, politically unconscious and uninterested workers for communist construction, say the researchers. Their newspaper, *Tribüne*, therefore comes most closely to *Neues Deutschland* in its proportion of the first three subjects. It differs, however, in methods; the presentation is much simpler, uses more illustrations, and material is drawn from everyday life in factories, construction sites and transport. The youth paper gives almost half its space to light reading and sport which are of interest to young people.

In the 'bourgeois' newspapers the researchers found that all matter attempted to cultivate loyalty to the 'workers' and farmers' state', and that the communist party attempted to use christian-socialist or liberal-nationalistic ideology to bring readers nearer to the communist cause.

For someone intimately acquainted with both the press and life of another similar country under communist rule, like Czechoslovakia, it is fascinating to read the findings of the inquiry and the analysis of newspaper contents. They tally exactly with the picture and structure of the Czechoslovak press of 1957, in the groupings of the newspapers, their contents, and their approach. The East German *Neues Deutschland*, with its ideological rigidity and dogmatism and even layout is, but for local and national distinctions, a faithful counterpart of *Rudé právo*; the trade union *Tribüne* is mirrored in *Práce*, and *Junge Welt* in *Mladá fronta*. Also both 'bourgeois' newspapers have their replicas in the christian-democratic *Lidová demokracie* and the (national) socialist *Svobodné slovo*—liberal in tone before 1948.

The 'bourgeois' press, though controlled by the communists and adapted to fulfil the specialised task of channelling communist propaganda and agitation to specific segments of the population, will be tolerated only so long as the communists consider it necessary for their purposes. As soon as the theoreticians and party leaders decide that the construction of socialism has been accomplished and that classes have disappeared, there will be no place for such newspapers.

The differentiation in contents to suit the tastes of different sections of the 'classless society' will remain, however, and with improvement in journalistic standards, better printing facilities and supplies of newsprint, which are still at a very low level, it will continue to grow. Hunger for differentiated newspapers, magazines, journals etc., is apparent in all communist countries.

One must, however, bear in mind that such differentiation does not mean any differentiation in political and ideological line or attitudes. The functions of all newspapers and periodicals remain the same as in Lenin's days: they must serve in their particular way the realisation of the political aims of the communist party. The most careful scrutiny of decisions of the Soviet or any other communist party and of the contents of the communist press as a whole reveals not the slightest deviation from these functions. There is freedom for technical and professional improvements, but no freedom for ideological or political matters.

The differentiation in contents and journalistic forms, as an aspect of the 'liberalisation' process initiated in the period 1953–6, and halted after 1958, is consequently confined to the better use of the existing structure, and does not in any way represent a partial approach to the functions of the independent and responsible press of the democracies.

CHANGES IN THE YUGOSLAV PRESS

The situation is, however, different when the policy of the ruling communist party undergoes significant changes. Then the press, which has to serve the party, can benefit for a period, if not permanently, in many ways, as is seen in the example of Yugoslavia. At present, this country still stands aside from the Soviet bloc with an independent policy in foreign and home affairs, and an individual interpretation of marxism-leninism.

The break with the communist bloc in 1948 brought a wave of 'derussification' and later a wave of liberalisation of the press. In both cases the changes were initiated by the communist party which has, however, maintained the marxist-leninist principles of the press's functions. It had kept a firm hand on the press, allowing—with a short lapse in 1952–3 (due to ideological differences at the top of the party)—greater freedom where and when it considered this suited its policy.[12]

But since the policy was in many respects different from that of other communist countries, the press and readers benefited. Changes for the better were first noticeable in the sphere of reporting international affairs; news, articles, comment were more objective. In the cultural field also the break with the Soviet bloc proved beneficial. But changes in reporting and commenting on events in Yugoslavia were slow and less significant, though the scope of liberty to criticise the administration and even certain high ranking personalities (but not the leaders and the regime) was much wider than in neighbouring communist countries.

Relative freedom of expression was gradually limited after reaching a short-lived climax in 1952–3. In November 1952, Milovan Djilas, who as member of the Politburo was then responsible for propaganda, encouraged writers and journalists to greater use of freedom in information and criticism, later setting an example by his own articles criticising even the principle of the dictatorship of the party and the conduct of the new ruling social class. Writing in *Borba*, the party's central organ, he demanded democratic freedoms: 'The first duty of a socialist democracy, and indeed of any democracy, is to permit the free expression of ideas and to guarantee that no one will be persecuted for his ideas.'[13]

For these attitudes Djilas was expelled from the Central Committee, and stricter controls were imposed on the press in general.

In 1958, at the Eighth Congress of the Yugoslav League of Communists, President Tito stressed that journalists must write in conformity with the country's interests (which are represented and interpreted as in other communist countries solely by the party), and that the press could not be considered, in the revolutionary period of transition, as an independent and autonomous factor in society.

The Yugoslav press is thus but a tool of the party, and has only such freedom of expression or objectivity as party interests allow. Nevertheless, it is still freer than its counterparts in the Soviet bloc, informs its readers better, caters more for their tastes, and shows a more responsible regard for public opinion.

The Yugloslav press shows great variation between the central and provincial newspapers, the latter having—due mainly to the multinational structure of the state—much higher standards than in other communist countries. Considerable variety is to be found among the weeklies, cultural periodicals and magazines. The difference between the party and non-party press is much less pronounced since the party press does not enjoy such marked preferential treatment as in the Soviet bloc. In many cases the non-party press stands above that of the party both in editorial quality, general prestige and even in circulation. Thus the most prominent daily newspaper is not the party organ *Borba* but the 'independent' *Politika* which has high journalistic standards, though maintaining a communist viewpoint, and a large number of pages. Its prominent place and popularity are shown by the fact that while the circulation of *Borba* dropped from 500,000 to 250,000 in the period 1950–5, that of *Politika* shot up above the half-million mark.

The liberal attitude towards licensing cultural periodicals and magazines and the policy of withdrawing state or party subsidies and putting the finances of the press on to a commercial basis (discussed in chapter 13) led to a situation similar to that which the Polish press faced in 1957–9 and resulted in financial difficulties and the forced closing down of many publications.

A problem of the Yugoslav press is the stricter application of ideology in journalists' everyday work which is being brought to the fore by the rapprochement between Yugoslavia and the Soviet bloc in both the state and party spheres. The problem became sharper after 1962–3 when L. N. Brezhnev, Chairman of the Supreme Soviet, visited Yugoslavia in September 1962; President Tito went to Moscow in December; and in August 1963 Premier Khrushchev paid a visit to Yugoslavia. Some observers saw a tightening of Yugoslav control over writers and journalists as a result of this rapprochement.

Speaking at the November session of the Central Committee after Brezhnev's visit, Tito said that in future the activities of writers would be more closely watched by party authorities. 'We shall not permit anyone to write nonsense and to caricature or render monstrous our social life,' he said. 'We thought nobody would get hurt if everybody could be permitted to say and write what he wanted. But we have gone too far.'

After his return from Moscow, President Tito said that Yugoslavia, though not changing her independent policy as the result of reconciliation, would be guided by the interests of the communist movement. He has been more critical of western ideas which have penetrated into his party, has attacked the intellectuals and their 'liberalism' and praised the workers who, he said, were called upon to direct and control the policy of the party.

In February 1963 President Tito discussed the problems of the press with members of the board of the Federation of Yugoslav journalists, again stressing the necessity of 'ideologisation' of the press. He said that in his view 'the most important problems of our press that we have to solve are its material and ideological aspects, and its organisation'.

According to an account published in the *Review of International Affairs*[14] President Tito said in the discussion about material and organisational problems:

I fully understand your position and the difficulties you are facing. I have never believed that the weaknesses of our journalism are merely subjective. There is also something objective in them. Take commercialism, for instance. One must exist somehow, and that is understandable, but commercialism allows all kinds of things to creep in. . . . How can a way out of this be found? First of all, I think, it should be asked whether it is necessary and serves any purpose to issue such a great number of small magazines published weekly, fortnightly, etc. As in our economy, splitting has proved to be damaging here, too. That is why we must encourage the integration of the press, and it will be also necessary for us to offer our press some material facilities. I do not say that this will solve everything, but we shall have to help the leading journals in one way or another.

Turning to the ideological aspect, Tito said:

What purpose should our press—our daily and other
newspapers—serve? It should serve to form our socialist
man and to develop our socialist relations; and it must be
directed to this end. Of course we have no idea of having
a directed press in which every article should be scrutinised
by those at the top. But if our press is to answer its purpose,
the ideological side should be on a higher level. The
journalists should have more ideological training and the
Federation of Journalists should organise the necessary
schools for them to attend. . . .

Throughout the discussion Tito was, however, stressing
that the party and government would not try to dictate to the
press how to solve its material and ideological problems, but
would leave it to the journalists themselves to act upon the
advice of the party, which again should not be interpreted as a
directive. The general tone of Tito's remarks on the press
and the general practice throughout 1963 have shown that the
Yugoslav party does not intend to change its policy towards the
press in any radical way, and that it intends to continue to
leave the press that greater freedom in reporting and comment
which distinguishes it so markedly from the press of other
communist countries.

8

DIRECTION AND SUPERVISION OF THE PRESS

THE PREVIOUS CHAPTERS have shown how carefully and thoroughly the communist party in the Soviet Union had laid the foundations for its total grip over the press. The party decided that the press must not fall into the hands of its enemies, and made sure that 'freedom of expression and of the press' were granted only to organs of the party and government and of public organisations effectively controlled by the party.

The party had also laid down, firmly and uncompromisingly, the principle that the entire press must base its work on marxist-leninist ideology. It decided the methods, contents and organisational structure of the press; incorporated it into the framework of its political propaganda and agitation; and controlled the selection and appointment of editors.

One might think that, by doing all this, the party could consider that its direction of the press was complete. But, as already stated, the communist press 'bases its activity on the general line of the communist party, helps to effect its decisions, is guided by its instructions and advice'. The party must, therefore, 'make sure that it does fulfil its tasks, and does not deviate . . .'[1] This, of course, involves a continuous direction and supervision of the press in the most detailed way, and the issuing of long-term and short-term, even daily, instructions. From the practical, executive point of view, it requires an adequate, effective system for direction and control.

In communist society such a directing and controlling system has a double task: to ensure that the press prints what must be published, and to keep out everything which would clash with the official propaganda line. The two tasks are so closely interlocked and of such equal importance to communist propaganda that the problem of supervision of the press cannot be narrowed down to one of censorship alone, as is the case in dictatorships or countries of a different social order. Censorship as a governmental, bureaucratic institution does exist in the communist states, but it stands at the bottom in the hierarchy of the means of control and supervision.

The communist system offers the party many ways of ensuring that the press serves its purpose. They may be classified as follows:

H

1   Absolute dependence of the press on the communist party for licensing facilities and financial matters, i.e. allocation of printing presses, newsprint, printing and editorial premises, and funds;

2   Staffing the newspapers only with selected and politically trained, reliable journalists generally, and leading editors in particular;

3   An efficient system of direction by the party and government organs in ideological, political or organisational matters;

4   An effective system of supervising and controlling the fulfilment of directives;

5   Censorship.

The issuing of broad directives and instructions concerning ideological, political or organisational matters has been touched upon in previous chapters. But the range of party interest and interference in the affairs of the press is much wider and deeper. Almost every section of political and economic life of the USSR and correspondingly also all aspects of the work of the press are covered by decisions and instructions issued by the congresses and central committees of the CPSU and republican parties.

The thoroughness, scope and volume of these are shown by an examination of the collected decisions of the Communist Party of the Soviet Union on the press. These collections are reissued at more or less regular intervals and their volume is constantly growing. The last edition was published in 1961. It is instructive to look through some of the individual chapters and sections.

Previous editions followed the territorial and functional levels in their sections, gave an outline of the problems with which the journalists had to cope, and dealt with organisational and technical aspects of publishing and editing. The present edition has a somewhat different method.

SOVIET PARTY DECISIONS ON THE PRESS

The 1961 edition[2] reprints decisions taken by party congresses and conferences, the most important decrees, instructions and letters of the Central Committee relating to the press, and other documents connected with the work of newspapers, periodicals, publishing houses, etc. Since the previous edition of the collection (1954) many significant changes have taken place. New newspapers and periodicals have appeared, circulations in general have considerably increased, and content and layout have improved. The Twentieth and Twenty-first Party Congresses (1956 and 1959) called for more active mass political work. Important decisions and resolutions on the work of the press issued by the Communist Party of the Soviet Union in the years 1956–61 would alone fill 220 pages of the 1940 edition.

The 1961 edition, which has almost 800 pages, had therefore to drop a series of outdated documents with only indirect relation to the press, but inserted many new equivalents. The collection is divided into nine sections with the following headings:

I   The press as the most important weapon in the fight for the revolutionary transformation of society;
II   The press as the sharpest weapon of the ideological work of the party;
III Economic construction and the tasks of the press;
IV   Party and government activities in the pages of the press;
V   The work of the party among the masses, and the worker and peasant correspondents' movement;
VI   The character of the newspapers;
VII General questions relating to the press;
VIII Publishing houses, their role and tasks;
IX   The grand program of communist construction and the tasks of the press.

Section I contains documents since the foundation by Lenin of *Iskra* (the first bolshevik newspaper) up to the October Revolution. Among others, there is the 'Statement of the editorial board of *Iskra*', resolutions of the Second and Third Congresses of the Russian Social Democratic Revolutionary Party on party literature and its central organ.

In Section II are resolutions and decisions on the press made by the Seventh, Eleventh, Twelfth and Thirteenth Party Congresses; the 1924 decree of the Central Committee, 'The principal tasks of the party in the sphere of the press'; that of 1925, 'The policy of the party in the sphere of belles lettres' etc. The determination of the fight against ideological deviations is shown in the decree 'On the periodical *Under the Banner of Marxism*'.

The section contains relevant decisions from the periods during and after the second world war, such as that 'On the improvement of quality and the increase in volume of republican regional and district newspapers'; 'On the newspapers *Molot* [Rostov-on-Don], *Volzhskaya kommuna* and *Kurskaya pravda*'. Of great importance for communist literary and artistic periodicals was the decision of 1946 on the periodicals *Zvezda* and *Leningrad*.

Among the latest party decisions, taken at or after the Twentieth Congress (1956) and included in this section, are: 'The work of *Izvestia*'; 'On serious shortcomings in the contents of *Ogonyok*'; 'On the periodical *Sovietskaya pechat*'; 'Improvement of the work of the periodical *Smena*'.

In these decisions the Central Committee elaborated the working program of the Soviet press, gave detailed instructions on how the problems of everyday life should be approached, on ways of increasing topicality. The main theme of the press, the Central Committee emphasised, should be the construction of the communist state in all phases and aspects.

Decisions on *Kommunist* and *Voprosy filosofie* dealt with theoretical problems of communist ideology and with the work of theoretical periodicals.

Of special interest in Section III are decisions: 'On the situation of the periodical press in connection with the fight for the regime of economy' (1926); 'On oral and press agitation for the rationalisation of production and for attracting the working masses into the campaign for the rationalisation of production'. The tasks of the press in postwar construction are dealt with in the decisions: 'Measures to improve the management of the periodical *Molodoy kolkhoznik*', and 'On the *Ekonomicheskaya gazeta*'.

Sections IV, V, VI include various documents relating to the 'explanatory work' of the press in connection with party and government activities, and also to the 'mass political work' of the press.

Here are reprinted all important decisions from 1925, 1926 and 1927 on the *rabselkor** (worker and peasant correspondents) movement, and also the latest party decree for its reactivisation after the Twentieth Congress, 'On improving the

* See chapter 13.

guidance of the mass movement of the worker and peasant correspondents'. Among articles dealing with readers' letters, it is worth mentioning the decree of the Central Committee 'On shortcomings in the work of the editorial board of the newspaper *Sovietskaya Sibir* with readers' letters'.

Documents in Section VII contain instructions for the improvement of management and for introducing modern methods in newspaper production, and organising their distribution.

Section VIII gathers together material on the activities of Soviet publishing houses, on production and on the distribution of literature. Their grouping reflects the phases of the party's progressive seizure of absolute control in the publishing field from January 1918 onwards. There is the principal decree, 'On publishing work', issued in 1931, and the latest document from 1959, 'Establishment of the Chief Administration for Publishing, Printing and Bookselling'—a department attached to the Ministry of Culture of the Soviet Union. This document decrees not only the organisational forms but also the political tasks of Soviet publishing houses.

Section IX contains party documents which, although they have no direct relation to the press, do define its general tasks in the contemporary period now that 'the foundations of communism are laid'. Here are: the resolution of the Twentieth Congress on the detailed report of N. S. Khrushchev; the resolution of the Twenty-first Congress 'On control figures of the development of the national economy of the USSR in 1959–65'; and speeches by N. S. Khrushchev: 'For close ties of literature and arts with the life of the people'; 'Serving the people—the noble task of the Soviet writers'; and 'The Soviet press must be the strongest and the most militant instrument'.

Also included are the decrees of the Central Committee on mass political work among the workers of the (former) Stalin region and on the tasks of party propaganda in present-day conditions.

★

However important these party decisions may be, they provide only a general line for the work of the press. The Communist Party of the Soviet Union soon felt the need for closer contact with and direction of the press. The application of the party line in day-to-day work and compliance with the often complex and tortuous party policy in home and foreign affairs made it necessary to establish a system of daily guidance for the press.

Such a system evolved slowly in the Soviet Union—and later in the new, east European socialist countries. In his recollections, a former Soviet journalist, A. Kotlyar,[3] gives an interesting and instructive glimpse into the gradual bureau-cratisation of the press and the evolution of a system for guidance and supervision. According to his account, the Soviet press originally enjoyed much greater freedom within the prescribed bounds of ideological and political tasks than one would suppose from the practice of today. Control of the press in the 'twenties was only loosely exercised; editors had some measure of liberty in printing news or discussing the country's problems.

By the end of the 'twenties, however, the situation had changed, and the press began to receive directives concerning the type of information that could be published. In 1929, for example, the Ukrainian newspaper *Kommunist*, on whose staff Kotlyar was working, was instructed more and more frequently —via the official news agency—how to handle economic and other news.[4] Thus, it was prohibited from making any mention of Soviet grain exports since the country was experiencing serious food shortages. These instructions were sometimes given in the body of the text of an official release and were transmitted by the news agency. They were unsigned so that it was impossible to know whence they originated. It was, how-ever, obvious that they were issued not by the party but by the government, probably by the commissariat of foreign trade. 'These were the first portents', wrote Kotlyar, 'of bureau-cratic control of the press. Later this control spread, though not necessarily through written instructions.'[5]

The basic features of this brief description of the evolution of the apparatus for directing press activities are discernible today. The present structure and practice of day-to-day direction and supervision is, however, better known as it exists in the satellite countries than from inside the Soviet Union. Since these countries took over practically all the principles of press functions and guidance from the Soviet Union, it can be fairly and logically assumed that circumstances in the satellites are very similar to those which apply in the Soviet Union, at least as far as party-government duality, predominance of party direction in political and ideological matters and its control, are concerned. Specific differences arise where special bodies exist for the direction of the 'bourgeois' newspapers.

DIRECTION OF THE PRESS

A good example is provided by the system of press direction in Czechoslovakia. It is based fully on the division of functions between party and government bodies. The party, through its propaganda and agitation department in the secretariat of the Central Committee, directs and supervises the entire central and provincial party, youth and trade union press, news agencies, radio and television. To fulfil these functions, the structure of the department is adapted as follows: the press section is subdivided into subsections for the party press, the other central press, provincial press, news agency, radio and television. It also has a subsection for the 'bourgeois' press, but does not directly intervene in its affairs, in order to preserve a semblance of 'independence'.

The head of the propaganda and agitation department organises regular press conferences or briefings for editors-in-chief of the news agency, radio, television, youth and trade union newspapers at which he gives directives concerning the propagandist and agitational line, articles, features, and reports on agricultural, industrial, transport and other economic and political problems. The department also calls 'briefing-sessions' before or after special occasions such as meetings of the Central Committee, the issue of important party decisions, or whenever serious political and economic incidents and difficulties arise (as frequently occurred during the destalinisation process in Czechoslovakia). At these press conferences heads of departments in the secretariat and even top party leaders occasionally speak.

Besides issuing instructions, the head of the Agitprop department or his assistant may also use this opportunity to criticise individual sectors of the mass communication media for shortcomings or negligence in the fulfilment of previous orders.

The existence of the 'bourgeois' newspapers poses a problem, since they are—formally—beyond the reach of the communist party and since their editors are not communists. Political directives for these papers from the propaganda department are channelled through the press department of the Prime Minister's Office (to which they are subordinated) or through the National Front, a front organisation uniting all 'political' parties.

The directives given by the Agitprop department of the Central Committee are political and ideological. They outline tasks, such as support for autumn agricultural work, introduction of new working methods, or socialist emulation in industry; they stress the main points and requirements, but do not go into technical details. The same is the case in matters of foreign policy. The party spokesman sums up the line and the main points which the press is to follow, explains the international situation, say the Cuban crisis, but he omits complicated details.

Guidance in practical and technical aspects, and especially day-to-day instruction, is left to the appropriate government departments. Thus the Ministry of Foreign Affairs convenes a regular weekly 'instruction conference' at which the foreign editors of all central communication media are informed on international developments; the attitude of the Czechoslovak government to main problems in the United Nations Organisation or at forthcoming international conferences and meetings; the state of relations with individual countries; the desirability of publishing only favourable reports about countries with which the government is conducting negotiations or trying to improve relations; the need to attack other foreign governments, their policies or their representatives.

In the same way regular briefings are organised for editors and reporters by the ministries of Agriculture, Industry, Transport, Culture, etc. Here journalists are supplied with the technical instructions and details necessary for carrying out the political tasks required of the editors-in-chief by party spokesmen.

Similar briefings and press conferences are, of course, organised by government bodies in western democracies. But the difference between these and briefings in the communist states is that the communist press must obey the instructions, must support government policy, and cannot take an independent or critical attitude, inquire into the correctness of government policy or suggest alternative solutions for short-comings and difficulties.

The party press enjoys a special privileged position in the system. The editor-in-chief of the central newspaper *Rudé právo* does not, or is not obliged, to attend the briefings given by Agitprop since he receives his instructions direct from the presidium (politburo) or party secretaries. The editors of *Rudé právo* usually attend the instruction meetings at the ministries, but they have access to special, most confidential briefs from the highest officials which are denied even to editors of such important bodies in communist communication media as the news agency. This applies especially to the ministries of Foreign Affairs and of the Interior.

As for the provincial press, the problem is simplified by its being published by the party and therefore directed and supervised by the appropriate party organs as far as local matters are concerned. As for central problems, the provincial press merely reprints the news, commentaries or articles supplied by the news agency or by the editors of the central newspapers working as special contributors, particularly on foreign affairs.

The existence of national dualism—Czechoslovakia is a state of two nations, Czechs and Slovaks—and the predominance of Czechs relegate the Slovak press, party and non-party, to the role of the provincial press. This situation is analogous to that in the Soviet Union, where only the Russian newspapers published in Moscow are treated as the central press, and the press of the other half of the population is regarded as peripheral, provincial.

The leadership of the Czechoslovak Communist Party is aware of this discrepancy and tries to remedy it by publishing the central *Rudé právo* also in a Slovak edition. Since 1960 *Rudé právo* has been published simultaneously in Prague (Czech edition) and in Bratislava (Slovak edition). The obvious intention is slowly to replace the existing organ of the Slovak Communist Party, *Pravda*, and thus achieve greater centralisation and, with the central organ printed in their own language, give the Slovaks a feeling of full participation in central party and state affairs.

The importance and influence of government departments in news reporting is significant. Practically no news concerning the least aspect of policy or of even the slightest connection with official bodies or ministries, may be published without their approval. Similar regulations also apply to the publication of news and articles about national industries.

Editors and reporters must 'verify' their news or ask appropriate ministries for approval even in cases of small, unimportant news items. Thus, for example, all news concerning Czechoslovak foreign relations must be approved by the press department of the Ministry of Foreign Affairs even if it is a short item such as that a Czechoslovak ambassador in some foreign country has handed in his credentials.

In the same way all news concerning foreign trade must be 'verified'. When, for example, the Minister of Foreign Trade concludes a trade agreement, the news agency must have the approval of the ministries of Foreign Trade and of Foreign Affairs prior to the publication of the news filed by its correspondent. Any breach of this unwritten law—even if the item may seem trivial—is angrily rebuked by the ministry or department concerned.

In 1958 the London bureau of the Czechoslovak news agency despatched a very short item about the arrival of the Czechoslovak cargo ship *Lidice* in the port of London, following upon a previous request by the head office (on the instructions of the Foreign Ministry) to give full publicity to all events concerning Czechoslovak political or trade activities abroad. Later, the foreign editor informed the bureau that the Ministry of Foreign Trade had complained about the publication of this innocent information. The fault was not with the London bureau, but with the foreign department of the agency in Prague which had not seen any harm in publishing the item, and therefore did not consult the Ministry. The Ministry, however, wanted to keep the ship's London call as secret as possible (though its arrival in London was reported in the local commercial press), since it was unloading there a cargo of rice bought in communist China on the understanding that it was for Czechoslovak home consumption only, and would not be sold in western countries to the detriment of Chinese exports. The large bureau of the Chinese news agency Hsinhua in Prague had picked up the item on the *Lidice* and—again on instructions from its Ministry—forwarded it to Peking.

This tight system of subordination makes the communist press, in fact, no more than a part of the vast party and governmental bureaucratic machine. Bureaucratisation has affected the working methods of the press and especially its news reporting to such a degree that 'news' is little else than a series of official press releases.

In Czechoslovakia the communist party had tried as early as 1945 to create a proper organisation for the direction of the non-communist press. A Ministry of Information was created which, after the communist *putsch* of 1948, was able to fulfil this function. The Ministry had power, in co-ordination with the National Front, to issue or withdraw licences for the publication of newspapers, to allocate supplies of newsprint etc. It also had control over the Journalists' Union. After 1948 this Ministry issued instructions to the 'bourgeois' and non-party press (that is the youth, trade union, cultural and agri-cultural papers) on how to publish certain news and on what news was to be suppressed. The Ministry was maintained until January 1953 when its functions relating to government direction and supervision of the non-party press were handed over to the press department of the Office of the Prime Minister.

Instrumental in the transmission of instructions of the former Ministry of Information and of the press section of the party Agitprop department was the Czechoslovak News Agency. On the instructions of these two bodies the news agency issued 'memos to editors', called 'blues' or 'pinkies' (they were mimeo-graphed on blue or pink paper; at that time there was no tele-printer circuit between the agency and the newspapers, and the news bulletin was supplied to editors mimeographed on white paper, page by page).

'Blues' ('pinkies' were reserved for the most important warnings) contained very detailed directives for handling certain items, official speeches or documents. A 'memo' could, for example, stipulate that the speech of the president and chairman of the communist party should, in such and such newspapers, be published in full over the entire front page under supplied headlines and accompanied by an attached photograph, while other newspapers should spread it only over the first three columns of the front page with different headlines, with no photograph and reduce it to so many lines by dropping certain paragraphs. (This was in cases where it dealt with party organisation matters; otherwise speeches and party or govern-ment documents had to be published in full by the entire press.)

After Stalin's death, with the wind of change blowing through the communist world, the formerly frequent 'memos' began to be used more sparingly and more judiciously, but they are still used by the party and government as a convenience.

The news agency has proved to be a particularly useful medium for the direction of the press and the regimentation of its contents in other ways. After 1948 the agency was put under strict communist supervision, all non-communists in leading positions were removed immediately, and non-communist journalists gradually eliminated, so that by 1950 it was ready most efficiently to serve the needs of propaganda. It was then turning out material adapted to the required line, and with its monopoly in reporting home and foreign news the contents of the Czechoslovak press were soon *gleichschalted* (regimented), as far as news was concerned, to the party's satisfaction. Under constant fear of committing 'political error' in reporting or assessing home and foreign events, editors eagerly used agency material because it was 'reliable' and had been vetted by all levels of the communist press control.

Thus press direction in Czechoslovakia is conducted by a system consisting of the following levels:

1   The propaganda and agitation department of the Central Committee,
2   The press department of the Office of the Prime Minister,
3   The news agency.

In this system, the party organ takes the dominant position giving instructions both to lower levels and to the press departments of all ministries, and directing the work of other organs concerned with the work of the press, such as the Union of Journalists or the censoring organ. The news agency, however, has no executive power, and cannot give instructions or directives of its own to the press; it serves only as a convenient channel for quick transmission of urgent, day-to-day instructions of a purely technical nature, and also, of course, for the central distribution of news and comment, censored and adapted to the official line.

It is interesting to compare this Czechoslovak system of direction with that of another communist state with similar conditions. Richert, the East German scholar, in his work on propaganda and agitation methods in East Germany[6] analysed the system and came to the conclusion that the East German press was directed by three organs:

1   The propaganda and agitation department of the Central Committee of the ruling communist party, SED, and

the agitation commission attached to the committee, co-operating closely with the department,

2 The official news agency, ADN, which has practically the monopoly of news reporting,

3 The state organ, the former Office of Information whose duties were taken over by the Press Office of the Prime Minister.[7]

The core of this tripartite direction system is the propaganda and agitation department of the party. The Central Committee, as Richert points out, had, from the earliest days after 1945, organised regular press conferences at which the party line for all topical questions was laid down. These conferences or briefings were for the central party press and for party members on the staff of other newspapers and the radio in Berlin. The directives given at these briefings were also transmitted to the lower party organs in regions and districts which, in their turn, instructed newspapers and radio stations in their area. The instructions were reflected also in regular issues of the SED Press Service which adapted its work according to the 'main points of the line', and supplied editors with ready-made propagandist and agitational articles and information on inner-party matters.

Such press conferences enabled the party also to direct the work of the Office of Information and of the ADN news agency whose leading representatives attended them. The news agency was, in Richert's words, important because 'its material could be used by newspapers without hesitation since it was already sifted and arranged from the standpoint of the existing political power'.[8]

Later, when the regular Soviet censorship, which in fact worked as a directive and not only as a prohibitive instrument, was replaced by irregular post-censorship and control, and the risk of possible deviations from the official line increased, the role of ADN grew. All important posts in the agency were occupied by communists through whom the party (and at the earlier stages also the Soviet occupational authorities) exercised influence.

The Office of Information, known under the abbreviation AfI (*Amt für Information*), was founded in 1949, but had predecessors in the press offices attached to the regional (Länder) governments and district councils. The AfI had, of course, much wider tasks than issuing information on the country's economic or cultural affairs. The SED had here an organ with executive, government authority well suited to enforce the practical realisation of party directives. Richert characterised this office as a 'counterpart of the propaganda ministry of the national socialists'.[9] Its functions included the power to issue or withdraw licences for the publication of newspapers, and the allocation of newsprint.

The powers and duties of the AfI were transferred in December 1952 to the 'Press Office of the Prime Minister'. This office organised regular briefings in Berlin and in the provinces through subordinated sections in regions and districts which were attended by all editors-in-chief (except those of the party press). The main departments of the office, 'Peace and (economic) Planning Propaganda' and 'Foreign Information', supplied editors with material partly in the form of pamphlets, partly in the form of an 'Article and Feature Service', depicting the 'successes' of economic and social construction in East Germany and other communist countries, in contrast to 'low living standards', 'misery', and 'warmongering' activities in West Germany and in the west in general.

With one small adjustment—placing the news agency in third place where it may also belong in East Germany—comparison of the systems of press direction in Czechoslovakia and East Germany shows striking similarities. The development in the system, whereby government press control has been transferred from the Ministry of Information to the Office of the Prime Minister, is significant in understanding communist methods and ways of thinking.

SUPERVISION OF THE PRESS

Though the party staffs the press only with reliable and trained editors and journalists, and issues both broad and daily instructions, nevertheless, it considers it highly important to have at hand an appropriate system and apparatus for ensuring that its line is followed and that at all levels directives are properly carried out. The means to this supervisory control function are at hand in the elaborate territorial and cross-sectional structure of the party, governmental and public organisations press. All that is necessary is to create a unified system of methods, and to endow the particular echelons of the structural apparatus with such tasks and powers.

The Agitprop department of the Central Committee's secretariat, as already shown, is the chief organ for all directing and supervisory activities concerning the press. In the Soviet Union, the department is divided into sections for the central press, the press of the republics, regions and districts, and for the local press. Each section supervises the newspapers at its corresponding level. Sections dealing with other than the central press co-operate closely with the corresponding press sections of the Agitprop departments of party secretariats in the republics.

With the decentralisation tendencies of 1956–7 and attempts to free the party apparatus from over-bureaucratisation, inherited from the Stalin period, the supervising role of the particular sections in Moscow was considerably curtailed and the emphasis is now more on local supervision. The propaganda department of the Central Committee, particularly the press section, exercises its functions more in a co-ordinative way. Reading or following regularly even the 180 papers in the central sector of the press in the republics would require a very large staff (especially when one considers this press is, to a large extent, non-Russian), not to mention the lower levels. Even in the large union republics, the press sections of Agitprop departments rely on the lower echelons for supervisory work.

The system for supervision is basically identical at all levels of the party press apparatus. Newspapers falling within the sphere of a given press section are carefully read and scrutinised. Mistakes, and tendencies to deviate from the general party line or to neglect certain aspects of propaganda and agitation etc., are brought to the notice of the editor-in-chief and publisher of the newspaper, that is to say the appropriate party, government organ or public organisation, with a reprimand and order to take corrective action.

If the ideological and political, or the general journalistic level of work continues to be defective, the press section takes steps to criticise sharply the offending newspaper, editor or editorial board in public. The form of criticism may vary from case to case. If the work of newspapers in a region, district or city is generally on a low level, the Central Committee may single one out and by its example show the main defects and suggest ways of improvement. This may take the form of a decree or of a critical review in central organs such as *Pravda*, *Kommunist*, *Partiynaya zhizn*, etc. Otherwise the criticism is published in papers of the corresponding territorial level.

The co-ordination of supervisory activities between the echelons of the party apparatus is based on regular reports on the press of their sphere submitted by the lower organs to the higher, by regular consultations and conferences between lower and higher organs and by visits of the workers of the central, Moscow, press section of the propaganda department to press sections in the republics and regions.

It is often assumed in the west that, apart from this critical supervising role of the party organs, the newspapers themselves conduct such activities by regular 'reviews' and criticism of the lower echelon press, according to the sectors of the party, government and public organisations press, and on the basis of territorial structure. In this scheme, the Soviet trade union newspaper *Trud*, for example, would criticise similar newspapers at republic level, which in their turn would do the same in relation to the regional trade union papers and so forth.

In practice, however, a higher newspaper would very rarely criticise its lower counterpart on its own initiative; the initiative comes almost entirely from the party organs who merely utilise the existing channels most suitable for their purpose. Even today, when freedom to exercise the rights (and duties) of criticism is much greater and less subject to limitations by the party organs than was the case up to 1956–7, all criticism in the pages of the press must be done only in consultation and co-ordination with the party.

The east European communist parties took over the Soviet system of supervision and control of the political contents of their press practically with no modifications whatsoever, and thus the system applies to all communist countries in general. Some details of the supervision by the party organs in practice are, nevertheless, useful to complete the picture.

The press section in the Agitprop departments exercises its function by approving the 'working' and 'perspective' plans of newspapers, radio, television and news agency, and by supervising the newspapers' compliance with instructions to conduct systematic campaigns on economic and political questions, and their treatment of the 'reaction' of the working masses to important party decisions (that is to say, how they report the enthusiastic and approving voices even to such measures as monetary reform or increases in food prices).

As for campaigns, in the pre-1956 period the press sections used 'quantitative methods' of control. The relations between the economic campaigns (say socialist emulation, spring field-work) and political campaigns (such as that against the 'titoist clique' or 'unmasking of western warmongers') were fixed by number of articles or percentage of lineage of the total contents and editors adapted their editorial plans to these quantitative requirements.

Instructions to this effect were given to editors orally at the briefings, but party functionaries criticised the laggard fulfilment of these 'political tasks' by enumerating the lines or articles published on the themes. This general practice was admitted by a Czechoslovak communist journalist when, in 1957, he criticised bureaucratic methods. 'Many journalists and functionaries', he wrote, 'often previously judged the participation of the press in the fulfilment of important tasks in a formal way, according to the number of lines and articles pertaining to this or that task. . . .'[10]

East German party organs and the *Presseamt* (Press Office) used the same 'lineage' method. They elaborated, with perhaps even greater vigour and German thoroughness, such quantitative analyses of the contents of the party and non-party press. Like the Czechoslovak communist organs, they issued instructions to editors to this effect, as is evident from a description of briefings by an editor who fled to West Germany: ' . . . Therefore, the issues over a week or a month', so ran the instructions, 'should be standardised more or less in this sense: about the Oder-Neisse line or the Soviet Union only so-and-so many lines were published in this newspaper whereas the average in the republic amounts to a multiple of this number of lines on the same subjects.'[11]

The supervisory—and enforcing—powers of the party organs were so discredited by such bureaucratic methods that journalists began, in the years of 'liberalisation', to disregard the still valid, though modified, instructions on planning and publishing prescribed numbers of articles and contents percentages for different campaigns.

They also deliberately defied instructions to support party decisions by pretending in the 'reaction campaigns', which were always organised by the party and were never spontaneous, that

I

they were approved by the workers. This only temporary decline in press control was by no means limited to the press of Hungary and Poland, where liberalising and defiant tendencies were most pronounced, but was apparent in countries with rigid party control such as Czechoslovakia and East Germany.

The tendency to ignore bureaucratic instructions of the stalinist era was deplored in 1957 by the Czechoslovak journalists' organ which said:

> There have appeared lately among some comrades ideas as though the Soviet experiences, especially those concerning the organising duties and mass political activities, did not work in our country and as if it were necessary to drop them. This was, for example, said about the reaction campaigns to various decisions, important events, etc. They said that it was stereotyped, uninteresting phrase-mongering which did not give the reader anything new. So many editorial boards stopped publishing reaction campaigns. Today, it happens very often that some great event is passed over by many newspapers and periodicals in dead silence, without any reaction, with the result that it disappears like ephemera. . . . [12]

In fact, not only the 'reaction campaigns' disappeared almost totally from the Czechoslovak and other communist newspapers in 1956–7; socialist emulation, shockworker drives and other similar 'mass' movements, enforced upon the workers by the party and previously depicted by the press as spontaneous movements 'from below', were banned by editors who gladly submitted to readers' wishes and took advantage of the decline in the party organs' powers in the ideological turmoil and strife between the old and new factions of the top party hierarchies.

9
CENSORSHIP

WORKING hand in hand with mass and organised propaganda and agitation activities in communist countries, are the measures to prevent the dissemination and publication of any ideas, news or other matter running counter to the official line and approved picture of life at home and abroad. It would be useless to conduct propaganda on a mass scale if at the same time it was allowed to be undermined by discordant news and views. The success of propaganda is determined as much by what is suppressed as by what is published.

It would therefore be wrong to underestimate the function of communist censorship. Such an underestimate could easily result from too narrow a concept of the meaning of press censorship, or from relying too much upon official communist pronouncements (which of course play down the importance and extent of censorship) without personal knowledge and experience of the everyday communist practice of suppressing everything embarrassing to the regime.

The censorship of the press in communist countries is more than the operation of an organ appointed by the government to eliminate from newspapers, radio and television any matter which editors, critical of the government or regime, may try deliberately to publish with a view to discrediting and defeating the regime. This may apply to countries outside the communist orbit where, short of suppressing the opposition press, such methods are the only ones available to the government.

The situation in a communist state is quite different. There the rulers, the party, hold all power in their hands and all the means to ensure that their instructions are followed efficiently. Moreover, there is no open opposition to the regime, no independent or hostile press. On the contrary, editors-in-chief, through their membership in the executive committees at the appropriate level, directly participate in the execution of power. Journalists are regarded as party functionaries of considerable importance and rank.* The press, therefore, in normal conditions is intent on co-operating actively to ensure that nothing gets published which is damaging to the party's policies and

* For a fuller account of the position of the journalist under communism, see chapter 14.

aims. It is only in exceptional times of ideological and power conflicts within the party itself that this equilibrium is broken and that views, and news too, inconvenient to the group holding power, or to the party as a whole, find their way on to the pages of newspapers. Such was the case in 1953 in East Germany, in 1955–6 in Hungary and Poland, and in 1963 in Czechoslovakia.

Communist censorship is a wide activity in which various echelons of the editorial and party hierarchy participate, and normally co-operate. An institution designed specially to fulfil some censorship duties exists in all communist states and is modelled closely on the Soviet *Glavlit*, the official censoring organ. In the hierarchy of organs involved in the censoring of the Soviet press, Glavlit comes, however, at the very bottom and its contribution and importance are not very significant, as will be shown later.

INDIRECT CENSORING

The process of censoring everything against which the party organs could object, starts with the journalist himself as he writes his article, feature or news item. This *self-censorship* of his is motivated either by his political consciousness, or by concern to evade the risk of political errors that would brand him as politically unreliable or ideologically immature, which could mean the end of his journalistic career. It is difficult to define all that is covered by the term of 'objectionable matter' which has to be kept out. Journalists and editors have to learn how to proceed from training, experience and political instinct.

Generally the following are regarded as taboo: any news or views which could be interpreted in the least way as critical of or contrary to marxist-leninist theory, the foundations of the communist order, party and state; anything critical of other communist states and parties (unless otherwise ordered, as was the case with Yugoslavia, and is now decreed against Albania and China); foreign or home policy; anything which contradicts the officially proclaimed division of the world between the happy, peaceful present and future of the socialist camp, and the misery, decadence and warmongering in 'capitalist' countries.

If in this self-censoring process the journalist has doubts, he consults his editor or editor-in-chief who in any case undertakes the second stage of censorship from an even stricter point of view. Should they be unable to decide the matter themselves, they refer for guidance to the head of the press section of Agitprop; if the matter is of grave importance, the head of the Agitprop department, a secretary of the Central Committee, a member of the presidium (politburo) or even the First Secretary—the head of the party—may be asked to decide. In matters concerning government departments and ministries, the editor contacts the appropriate press officer, head of department or deputy minister.

In some cases the process of voluntary self-censorship is reversed, such as when the top party leaders issue through party and government channels strict instructions that certain matters of foreign relations, ideological and power struggles inside the party or between communist parties (such as the differences between the Chinese and Soviet parties in the 1959–62 period), or specific home or foreign news cannot be handled without prior approval from the leaders themselves.

Since most important news, official speeches, documents, etc., regarding events at home and abroad are published by the news agency, and important political, ideological articles and similar items are published only in the central party press, censorship is considerably facilitated. Speeches of party leaders, documents, reports from party congresses and conferences, and of meetings of the Central Committee are supplied to the news agency already fully vetted and ready for publication.

Vetting and adapting speeches of party leaders is a common thing and even heads of the parties have their speeches 'censored', usually with their agreement, of course, and the revised text may be published only with their approval. Khrushchev is notorious for making frequent remarks or slips in his speeches which when published could harm official propaganda or disclose aspects of policy which should be kept secret for the time being. Thus in May 1953 in a speech in Prague Khrushchev boasted that the Soviet Union already possessed the hydrogen bomb and could devastate 'capitalist America'. Strict orders were given not to mention this in agency dispatches. (The official announcement of the first explosion of a Soviet hydrogen bomb was made in August 1953.)

In 1962 and 1963, during a serious political crisis in which party chief Antonín Novotný had to face the liberal wing's accusation of 'stalinism', his speeches were on several occasions censored and purged of remarks which were not approved either by all the members of the presidium or the Central Committee. Thus in February 1962, in a speech broadcast by radio, Novotný accused his rival Rudolf Barák amongst others of plotting to overthrow the party leadership and seize power by force. This passage was omitted from the text of the speech published in the official party organ. In the middle of June 1963 Novotný asserted in another public speech that his views on the need to fight Slovak 'bourgeois nationalists' and liberals among journalists and writers were 'the views of the party presidium and the whole Central Committee'. Again this was omitted from the published text in *Rudé Právo*.

In normal conditions party leaders voluntarily submit to the vetting and censoring of their speeches. But in cases like the speeches of Novotný and when there are differences among the party leadership, the censoring by a small, select group (described below) is done even against the will of the particular party leader who, of course, has no longer the absolute control of the apparatus.*

A similar situation arises when there is an open struggle at the top and nobody has yet assumed full control over the machine. Then conflicting speeches and views are sometimes published as in the case of Hungary in 1954 and later when Rákosi and Nagy, the former heading the party apparatus, the latter the government, and both with their adherents in the party leadership and in the government, fought each other and issued decisions and decrees which the other side tried to nullify by counter-decisions. But once the scales tip decidedly to one side, the full weight of censorship is imposed on the adversaries who are thus deprived of any opportunity to make their political platform public. This was clearly demonstrated in the Soviet Union in 1957 when Malenkov, Molotov and others were defeated by Khrushchev.

The speeches of presidium (politburo) members are nor-

---

* The intricacies of the system for determining when to censor and when to release speeches, even of the highest leaders, whether for limited or general consumption, were well illustrated in another case involving Antonín Novotný. On 14 December 1963 Novotný accompanied L. N. Brezhnev, President of the USSR, on a visit to the Mladá Boleslav car factory near Prague. The speeches were being broadcast, but as Novotný began his listeners heard him say: 'I must ask if this is going out generally or if it is an internal broadcast, for this has happened to me before. . . .' After about three minutes, the broadcast ceased abruptly, and an announcer explained: 'Because the speech by comrade Antonín Novotný is meant only for the workers of the Mladá Boleslav car factory, we have concluded the relay.' Radio Prague then substituted music, which continued until a news report twenty-five minutes later.

mally edited by a small group from the secretariat, consisting of
the secretaries in charge of the propaganda and other departments concerned, but usually all important speeches have to be
approved in advance by the presidium (so that the group's task
is made easier) and any serious deviations from the approved
text are censored.

In the case of party congresses or conferences, a special
editorial commission is set up, consisting usually of representatives from the propaganda and agitation department, the party's
central newspaper, and the news agency. This commission edits
all speeches made by the leaders, documents and 'discussion
contributions' (as the speeches of other congress delegates are
called) by carefully eliminating passages expressing dissatisfaction with or criticism of the leadership. It thus maintains an
illusion of complete harmony and unanimous approval of the
policy of the leadership. No texts other than those edited by the
commission may be published, and individual newspapers are in
most cases 'advised', according to their territorial level and readership structure, what and how much they are to publish from the
lengthy and voluminous party material.

Despite the fact that journalists are well trained and
regularly briefed, censoring in the form of advice or instruction
solicited by journalists from party and government organs is a
frequent, almost daily occurrence, especially in a communist
news agency. In most important cases, and sometimes also in
matters quite trivial by western standards, the journalists try to
shift responsibility on to the editors, these again on to the editors-
in-chief, who, in their turn, deem it safer to be covered by the
decision of the higher party organ.

Thus in 1953, when the economic situation in Czechoslovakia was precarious and dissatisfaction ran high among the
people, the foreign news department of the Czechoslovak News
Agency published a very short statement that the Bulgarian
government had reduced prices of some seasonal foodstuffs by
10 per cent. People paid no attention to the report, but the
Politburo immediately reacted, reprimanded the agency's
director for publishing news which could 'incite the people to
demand similar price reductions'.

When a month later the East German party and government reduced the prices of shoe-cream, shoe-laces, marmalade
and similar unimportant goods, the editor of the foreign department asked advice from the general director of the agency who

did not want to decide the matter himself, and telephoned the head of the propaganda department. The latter declined to make a decision about publication, and the foreign editor had to take the news item to two top party officials: the President of the Republic and Chairman of the party, and the Prime Minister. They were attending a theatre performance with a foreign delegation, and the editor had to disturb them in the presidential box. After long consultations the President and the Prime Minister decided in this 'important matter of state' that it would not be 'in the interest of the people' to announce the price reduction of shoe-cream and laces in East Germany.

Censorship, of course, is usually concerned with more serious cases which could, indeed, do harm to communist propaganda. At the end of August 1962, U Thant, acting Secretary-General of the United Nations, visited Moscow to discuss with Khrushchev and other Soviet officials the problem of the Congo. Moscow radio and the official news agency TASS asked U Thant for an interview before his departure. His statement, critical of Soviet policy in the Congo and of Soviet methods in not objectively informing its people, was not broadcast in the home service and was reported only in bowdlerised versions in the foreign services of Moscow radio.

The statement, as the London *Times* reported,[1] was either censored or ignored by the news agency and by the Soviet press. *Pravda* was the only paper to mention the statement but omitted U Thant's complaint that the Soviet people were not being told both sides of the Congo story. TASS, both in Russian and English, failed to publish U Thant's more critical remarks and tried to assume an air of objectivity by releasing, only in a shortened version, his remark that fear and suspicion were still in evidence both in the west and east.

The passage in U Thant's statement which the Soviet authorities—no doubt after consulting Khrushchev himself—censored, said:

> Fear and suspicion, which for so long have characterised international relations, are still in evidence here as in the west. Let me be candid. When Soviet foreign policy concerned itself with what was happening in the rest of the world—for instance, in the Congo—it did so out of fear and suspicion; fear of losing potential friends and suspicion of what it regarded as imperialist designs.

He then added—and this was the part most objected to by the Soviet authorities:

> I beg to be excused for saying that the Russian people do not fully understand the true character of the Congo problem. This lack of understanding is probably due to absence of presentation of the other side of the coin, and I am sure that if only they could have the means of knowing all the facets of the problem, they would certainly revise their opinion of the nature of the United Nations involvement in the Congo and decide to shoulder their share of the heavy responsibilities now being undertaken by the world organisation in seeking a peaceful solution of the Congo problem.[2]

The suppression of the last passage, even at the price of a minor scandal, was understandable since it touched the very core of the propaganda system in the Soviet Union. Coming from such a high official of the United Nations and a representative of an uncommitted nation whom some people even regarded as favourably inclined to the Soviet Union, it would have done irreparable damage to party propaganda in the eyes of the Soviet people.

Communist propaganda is very often confronted with the dilemma that certain matters, which may be very useful in its activities abroad, may be harmful at home. In such cases the matter is simply censored for publication at home, and widely broadcast to foreign countries by radio and news agency. An instance was the TASS report on the opening of the Ecumenical Council of the Roman Catholic Church in Rome in October 1962. In its foreign languages service TASS made a favourable reference to Pope John in an effort to bolster the communist propaganda line for peace and nuclear disarmament and against the 'warmongers' in the west.

It was common knowledge, TASS said, that Pope John had repeatedly come out in favour of peace, against the atomic arms race, and for the settlement of controversial international questions by negotiation. But, TASS added, 'the point is that catholic statesmen who were the highest leaders of the United States, France and Germany, had by no means always followed the pope's advice'.

The TASS report had not, however, been broadcast by the home news service and was not printed in the newspapers since it would have clashed with the campaign against religion and churches in the Soviet Union.*

Another example of such censoring and of the double voice of communist propaganda was the case of the publication of the Hungarian *White Book on the Crimes of the Counter-Revolutionaries*. It was published at the end of 1956 by the Hungarian Communist Party under Soviet and Czechoslovak pressure. It was intended at the time for use in other communist countries and in the west where much propaganda was made out of it. But the Hungarian people, who so clearly rejected communism in October of the same year, were not told at that time about the book.

In the first half of 1956, the Czechoslovak authorities arranged a rather important press conference in Prague for foreign correspondents at which Artur London, one of several persons accused in the Slánský trial, revealed the manner in which false confessions had been extracted from him in 1952. But the Czechoslovak press did not even mention this conference. At the same time the correspondent of the French agency AFP in Prague managed to find out, in the course of an interview with the Director of Religious Affairs, that Mgr J. Beran, the archbishop of Prague, was no longer in prison but under house arrest, and that two Slovak bishops had been released 'some time ago'. This news, which was immediately reported to the whole world, was not taken up by the official news agency and was not published in a single Czechoslovak newspaper even though it originated from the country's own Office of Religious Affairs.[4]

A further example of official suppression and subsequent manipulation of news on important home events was the case of labour camps for political prisoners in the Soviet Union. Under Stalin's rule their existence was hotly denied and allegations about them were branded as 'imperialist lies' aimed at the denigration of communism. The strikes and other incidents which occurred in the spring of 1953 in the camp of Vorkuta, and later in other places, were completely ignored by the Soviet press. Since the amnesty of 17 September 1955 the press has never mentioned the number of political prisoners set free, although there were hundreds of thousands of them. Even in

---

* Later, after almost a year of vacillation, Soviet propaganda began to publish, even for home consumption, some of the pope's statements, and also reports on the proceedings of the Ecumenical Council.

the later years of destalinisation their existence was hardly mentioned and it was forbidden to write about them.

However, in 1962 the November issue of the literary monthly *Novy mir* (New World) published a short novel by Alexander Solzhenitsyn entitled *One Day in the Life of Ivan Denisovich*, describing the horrors of life in a Siberian concentration camp in 1951.* The story of its publication is typical of the continuation of old methods of suppressing or censoring important information, even in literary form, in the Russia of Khrushchev, who professes to have made the USSR completely different from Stalin's Russia.

Western correspondents and diplomatists in Moscow learned that the manuscript of Solzhenitsyn's novel had been refused publication and that it had been circulating among the members of the Central Committee for several months, producing sharp and at times angry debate over the advantages or disadvantages of publishing this story of life under Stalin. Officials and many party leaders wanted to suppress the novel, but Khrushchev's intervention secured its publication. Khrushchev, wishing for political reasons to strengthen his position among the people against his rivals, chose to authorise publication at the height of a new destalinisation campaign, which he launched in autumn 1962.[5]

Obviously writers and journalists in Russia are no more free today to publish what they regard as relevant and important for the public than they were before 1953; only the political considerations of those holding power or gaining the upper hand in the inner struggle are the real arbiters of what the public in communist countries is allowed to read.

The pre-publication censorship of press contents by any of the supervising organs is so widespread in communist countries that examples could be quoted *ad infinitum*. In this respect it is important to note the procedure in cases where news or incidents cannot be suppressed altogether. In such cases the authorities apply delaying or distorting tactics to give the official propaganda apparatus time to prepare itself and the public for the matter that has eventually to be released.

The Cuban crisis of October 1962 was a clear example of these tactics. The news of President Kennedy's statement, made on 22 October, announcing the blockade of Cuba in an

* Published under this title in the translation of Max Hayward and Ronald Hingley in 1963 by Frederick A. Praeger, New York and London.

effort to prevent further build-up of Soviet rocket bases and rockets on the island, and his administration's determination to enforce the dismantling and removal of the existing bases and missiles manned by Soviet troops, was not reported to the Soviet public until the afternoon of the following day (Moscow time). Even then there was only a brief and distorted announcement from TASS. It was left to a government statement, issued in the late evening hours, almost twenty-four hours after Kennedy's broadcast, to 'explain' in full the 'aggressive act' and 'piracy' of the United States. But not even this statement mentioned the Soviet missiles and bases in Cuba.

The labours of communist propaganda were noticeable, however, in the writing of the commentators. The editorial article of *Pravda* on 24 October, presenting the American quarantine as the action of 'cowardly beasts of prey', did not inform its readers about the American allegation that a new factor—the Soviet missiles in Cuba—had been brought into the situation, nor was it mentioned by Moscow radio's home service. The most direct reference to the American charges about the existence of aggressive rockets in Cuba was contained in a Moscow radio home service broadcast which accused the US Department of Defense of using 'faked photographs'.[6]

The existence of these Soviet aggressive weapons and their sites was withheld from the Soviet people until some days later when Khrushchev, in a political somersault, admitted under the firm American stand that there were, indeed, such Soviet weapons and troops on the island, and agreed to withdraw them.

GLAVLIT—THE SPECIAL CENSORING ORGAN

Practically all censoring in the communist press is done, as was shown in previous pages, in a two-way process either as primary self-censorship and the more or less willing co-operation of journalists with higher echelons of the press and party hierarchy, or by strict orders and detailed instructions from the top through lower and lower steps of the ladder. Yet the Soviet communist party was not satisfied with all these controls, and comparatively soon established a special organ charged with the execution of formal censorship of all material prepared for publication in the press or books, or reaching the general public through other media.

This government censorship organ, known under its

abbreviation *Glavlit* (Glavnoye upravlenie po delam literatury i izdatelstvo—the Chief Administration for Literary and Publishing Affairs) had been in existence since the late 'twenties, but its authority was officially legalised by a decree of the Council of People's Commissars in 1931. Formally it is attached to the Ministry of Education, but in practice its officials are members of the state security services, the political police.

The duties of this organ were to control practically all material intended for publication either in the press (such as news, articles, manuscripts, photographs), or in other printed form (books, pamphlets), and similar material for radio broadcasting. Its aim was to prevent publication of any matter containing anything deleterious to the political, ideological, military or economic security of the state. Today the censors of Glavlit also sit in the editorial offices of television.

The scope and authority of such an organ, established in the first years of Stalin's thorough bureaucratisation of the whole of Soviet life, was bound to be severely limited in the clash with a more efficient and flexible system of party and government controls and direction.

The first restrictions were revealed when the Unified State Publishing House, Ogiz, was empowered to censor all books through its own editors who were formally appointed representatives of Glavlit. In addition, the party press and the party publishing houses, together with the government newspaper *Izvestia* and publications of the Academy of Sciences, were freed from the political and ideological control of the censoring organ. By being eliminated from political control over a very considerable part of published material, Glavlit was relegated to the lowest rank of all the organs supervising and censoring the press. Its importance and authority were, therefore, never great and its function was only of a secondary nature.

The role and functions of Glavlit as the official censoring organ have been described in detail in several western works on communist propaganda or press, such as *Public Opinion in Soviet Russia* by Alex Inkeles, and by a former Soviet journalist, A. Gayev.[7] The International Press Institute in its very useful survey of *Press in Authoritarian Countries* also sums up the operations and functions of this organ.

All surveys of Glavlit come to the same conclusion: that political and ideological guidance and supervision are so overwhelming that this additional instrument of state censorship can only have subsidiary functions. Details of the way Glavlit functioned in the pre-war period are contained in the so-called Smolensk archives which came into the hands of German troops in 1941 when they occupied the city. Documents covering all the reports from local offices of Glavlit in the Smolensk *oblast* for the years 1931–9 were taken over by the American army and are now housed at Alexandria, Virginia. They show that officials of Glavlit never enjoyed great authority among the editors. Censors often complained in their reports that editors were almost always disobeying, and even ridiculing, their decisions. The censors followed a secret bulletin containing confidential rules and an index, called *perechen*, which enumerated all items to be censored. The *perechen* was constantly revised and supplemented.

Glavlit's censorship during the Stalin period was highly fastidious. There were at least two censors on the editorial staff of each newspaper. They thoroughly examined the proofs at make-up stage, especially making sure that units of the Soviet Army were never referred to by number or their garrison towns by name, eliminating all information of enterprises concerning national defence and secret inventions. Censorship went so far as to eliminate data on production capacity and the size of the labour forces of factories. Censors also scrutinised every illustration to make sure there were no distortions in the faces of the party leaders, or signs which could be interpreted as swastikas or similar 'counter-revolutionary' symbols, and in fact anything which could be held to ridicule the communist system or endanger state security. They also examined every text in order to detect any allusions judged inopportune from a political point of view.[8]

The limited importance of Glavlit suffered even more in the years of 'liberalisation' and nowadays it is responsible only for keeping material connected with state security out of the press. In this sphere its organs operate throughout the entire Soviet press, including *Pravda* and other party newspapers.

With the general relaxation of stalinist control of the press came a softening in the conception of what constitutes a state secret. Former ridiculous rules were relaxed and the press is now publishing data on production capacity, number of employees in factories and other facts, disclosure of which before 1953 would have been regarded as treason.

The Glavlit organs perform their duty in two ways: by

pre-publication censorship of manuscripts and by post-publi-
cation checking of the printed text against the approved original.
As confirmation of their censoring, Glavlit organs affix to each
issue of censored publications a number which, in the case of
newspapers, can be seen at the bottom of the last page.

Glavlit also supervises the restriction of export of Soviet
publications from the standpoint of state security. These considerations and perhaps plain bureaucratism tend to prohibit
the export of all newspapers and periodicals below the central
and republican level. Disclosure of technical secrets is the
main reason why numerous scientific and industrial publications
are not allowed to be exported, though meanwhile the Soviet
Union imports and thoroughly exploits a vast number of technical periodicals and books published in the west.

A much more important role played by Glavlit is the
censorship of all outgoing dispatches and telephone calls of
foreign correspondents based in or visiting the Soviet Union.
Here its powers used to be widely and frequently exercised, but
after Stalin's death Glavlit's interference slowly petered out,
and finally, on 23 March 1961, the Soviet government abolished
prior censorship on outgoing news dispatches. Nevertheless,
correspondents were warned that they would be held responsible
for the transmission of 'incorrect' reports.[9] In fact, by this
warning the Soviet authorities forced foreign correspondents
to exercise a similar self-censorship to that of their Soviet
colleagues. Otherwise they risked expulsion, which both the
correspondents and their employers (and this applies mainly to
western news agencies) try to avoid. Since the abolition of prior
censorship several foreign correspondents have been expelled
for sending 'incorrect' reports, or because their newspapers
published such reports.*

Glavlit is regarded by Soviet journalists and party leaders

* Thus, for instance, in August 1962 *Newsweek's* correspondent, Whitman
Passon, was expelled, and a year later Frank Burkholtzer, correspondent of
the National Broadcasting Company (of America), was asked to leave, and the
NBC office in Moscow closed, because of a TV program relayed in the USA
of which Soviet authorities disapproved. In February 1964, Reuter's correspondent in Moscow, Peter Johnson, was 'denied the status of a foreign
correspondent' and told to leave the USSR because, allegedly, his 'dispatches
containing gross slander were designed to poison the atmosphere in the relations of the USSR with other countries—including the African states'. The
Soviet authorities took exception to his reporting of demonstrations by
African students in Moscow in December 1963.

today as an expression or survival of stalinist bureaucratisation of life by substituting control through security organs, which should be exercised by politically conscious workers themselves. It may be abolished sooner or later since formal censorship is now regarded as a means of the dictatorship of the proletariat which has now, according to theory, been superseded by a higher stage of development of communist society within the Soviet Union.

CENSORSHIP IN THE EAST EUROPEAN COUNTRIES

The satellite countries, without exception, took over the Soviet system of legal censorship, but they took it over at varying stages. In Poland, for example, the communist party established a censoring organ, the Chief Press Control Office, by a law of 5 July 1946 while in neighbouring Czechoslovakia their organ, the Chief Administration of Press Supervision, only came into existence in 1953.

Since, however, the political situation in the east European socialist countries is different from that in the Soviet Union, censorship is regarded by the parties as a very useful stand-by in case political controls over the press slip out of the hands of the party apparatus, should it be discredited by political developments.

Poland

Events in Poland vividly illustrate the application of the broadly defined scope of the censoring organ. The law establishing the Chief Press Control Office stipulated[10] that:

The Chief Office has the task of supervising the distribution of all kinds of works executed, among other things, by means of the printing press, in order to prevent:

a) Attacks on the system of government of the Polish state.
b) Disclosure of state secrets.
c) Damage to international relations of the Polish state.
d) Violations of law and order.
e) Misleading public opinion by the publication of in-accurate information.[11]

In the stalinist period in Poland censorship was, as in the Soviet Union, applied rigidly, especially against the non-party

press; after the temporary consolidation of communist power
it became less necessary and less obvious. But since 1954-5 it
has been used again and again in attempts to suppress news and
articles from dissident journalists. These were times when the
communist party lost a considerable degree of control over the
press, and was, for tactical reasons, unwilling to enforce party
direction and control. Polish journalists, who were reluctant to
collaborate with party or state organs in self-imposed censorship,
had been feeling the efficient pressure of this office which was
generally supposed to be of little importance. Consequently on
many occasions they demanded abolition of press censorship.

On 20 September 1956, the executive committee of the
Polish Journalists' Association passed a resolution against 'the
unjust and unjustifiable interference of the Chief Press Control
Office' and demanded the creation of a committee of journalists
whose function would be to keep an eye on the activities of the
Control Office and to delimit the scope of its prerogative.[12] On
the same occasion the committee of the Association denounced
interference by certain party organs in editorial affairs, their lack
of comprehension with regard to the new role of the press, and
above all their frank hostility towards journalists.

The annual plenary assembly of the Journalists' Association,
meeting from 30 November to 2 December 1956, also adopted
resolutions in the same spirit. On 18 October, the vice-president
of the Peasant Party, Stefan Ignar, called for the abolition of
pre-publication censorship, and the Warsaw committee of the
communist youth organisation made the same demand, declaring
that the reform of news reporting was not making sufficient
progress.

These views even had sympathisers within the Chief Press
Control Office itself. The censors of Poznań voted a resolution
urging that they be disbanded! The Warsaw censors—as the
IPI Survey notes—did the same, but citing of their resolution
was censored from the newspapers to whom they had delivered
it for publication, on the orders of the higher censorship
authorities.

At the end of the year the struggle for suppression or substantial relaxation of press control remained undecided. In
December the director of the Polish radio's news service was
dismissed for having deliberately disobeyed orders from the
censorship. At the beginning of 1957, the editor-in-chief of
Po prostu, Eligiusz Lasota, who was elected as a communist

K

deputy in the elections of 20 January, called for the abolition of censorship. 'Censorship', he declared, 'is anti-democratic, and without democracy there can be no socialism.'[13]

Though the Chief Press Control Office was never abolished, its functions, during the most liberal phase of 'Gomulkism' until autumn 1957, were restricted to the following items:

1   Military information, in particular anything concerning troop movements and new armaments.
2   News concerning foreign affairs liable to provoke the Soviet Union.
3   Expression of opinion openly opposed to communism as a philosophy and a political system, as well as attacks against the government and its members. On the other hand, it was possible to say almost anything in the form of suggestions purporting to reform or improve communism.[14]

'Censorship', declared the editor-in-chief of *Po prostu* to the correspondent of *France-soir*, 'stops articles that are written explicitly against the government, but it cannot intervene in discussions which are ideological or which are considered as such.'[15]

The tactical retreat and concessions made by the communist party to the press were, however, short-lived, as the same editor of *Po prostu* had soon to learn. From the autumn of 1957 the party embarked cautiously, but firmly, on a new policy of taking the controls over the press into its own hands. Censorship was a handy means to this end. It was used again and again to suppress rebellious and unwanted publications (as was shown in the previous chapter on developments in the Polish press). Gradually tightening press control revived opposition to censorship, as indicated by press comments in 1961. Premier Cyrankiewicz tried to defend his government's press policy by asserting that, despite the censorship—which he described as very mild—the press in Poland was much freer than that in the west. He said:

The high social role of our press and the dignity of the profession of journalism in our country become that much more prominent when we compare them with the capitalist press which calls itself free. And this press, which calls itself free, remains, in the overwhelming majority in practically every capitalist country, under the absolute financial and personal influence of . . . a few all-powerful press concerns which control publications, printing plants and advertising. . . . It is true that the Polish press, the socialist press, does not enjoy such freedom. Its duty is to tell the truth, to present reality such as it is—to present the perspective of its transformation and to unmask the falseness of reactionary propaganda. We have no reason to conceal the truth from public opinion, because truth and reality speak for us, for our policies, for socialism. . . .[16]

In communist dialectics, the increased use of censorship is fully compatible with the presentation of 'reality such as it is' and helps to 'reveal the truth before public opinion'. The truth must be, of course, in accord with the marxist concept, that is 'the recognition of social reality, the laws of society's evolution and subordination of one's actions to this recognition'. The Polish press today is allowed by the state and party censorship to dispense the truth only in small doses and to exercise criticism only within narrowly defined limits.*

Czechoslovakia

In Czechoslovakia, where the communist party was much more successful in keeping the reins firmly in its hands, there were no troubles with the censorship and no open protests against it. It worked smoothly and unobtrusively after its late introduction in 1953. It kept to the Soviet model and its influence and sometimes even its existence was hardly noticeable to ordinary journalists.

The censorship agency was restricted from its beginning to preventing the disclosure of state secrets, and it was never involved in controversial cases of censoring political or ideological opinions in articles, since the party organs either had

* On 19 March 1964, prominent Polish writers, journalists and intellectuals delivered to the Office of the Prime Minister a letter of protest against increasingly strict censorship and restriction of intellectual freedom. The letter, which was signed by 34 personalities, remained secret until 27 March when the political police arrested and questioned Jozef Lipski, a journalist. They charged him with collecting signatures for the letter. The signatories then circulated the letter among foreign correspondents in Warsaw. The only 'reply' they had received by mid-April from the Prime Minister was an instruction to the press, radio and television forbidding the editors to publish any materials from the rebels.

full confidence in the appointed editors (some literary publications which clashed with the rigid party line on the arts were quietly suppressed by the party, without fuss even in the limited circle of poets, writers or artists), or had full control over the entire press. The Chief Administration of Press Supervision was established after a series of unpleasant—for the communist authorities—misprints, such as 'our *fiend* the Soviet Union' instead of 'friend', and after facts on industrial production, regarded as secret, had appeared in the press.

The censorship in east European communist countries will, apparently, be retained much longer than in the Soviet Union, since they lag behind in progress towards the goal: the establishment of the classless communist society. The residue of old ideologies still lingers among the remnants of the old classes and the influence of 'reactionary western ideas' may still find fertile soil. The censoring organ is a strategic reserve in case indoctrination and control of journalists should prove inadequate in turbulent times to come.*

This attitude was openly expressed in the official Czechoslovak journalistic publication in an article entitled 'The materialistic conception of press freedom'. The author declared that the censorship in Czechoslovakia is today an expression of the ideological power, an act of the state. In a transitory period censorship is a necessary protection against bourgeois ideas and their dissemination. 'Only very naïve people can believe', writes the author, 'that the communists who did not hesitate to ban the bourgeois newspapers would perhaps hesitate to ban all expressions of counter-revolutionary bourgeois ideology in the pages of the legal press or even in the socialist press. We communists

---

* Shortly after this chapter was written a situation arose in Czechoslovakia where the party leadership had to use censorship to suppress views and criticisms of dissident journalists and writers. In the first months of 1963, an entire printed edition of the Slovak literary weekly, *Kultúrny život*, was confiscated on party orders because a leading article indirectly criticised some communist leaders. On 21 March 1963, the weekly *Kulturní tvorba* was censored at the direct instruction of the party leader, Novotný, and the new issue appeared only several days later, without the 'defective' leading article demanding thorough destalinisation and minus several items against which the leadership raised objections as being 'liberalistic'. In subsequent months there were frequent clashes between editors and censors, sometimes ending with compromise, sometimes with the editors' refusing to submit to censorship. Inner struggles within the party enabled the editors in such cases to disregard the censoring organs who themselves were sometimes confused.

are not supporters of so-called free competition in the field of ideology!'

Exchange of views is possible only within the frame of adherence to marxism-leninism; the communists 'are saying openly that they do not tolerate dissemination of all views'. Censorship is necessary not only in the period of transition to communism, but it has basic 'revolutionary character because it helps to destroy the political organisation of class enemies'.[17]

THE IMAGE OF LIFE IN THE
COMMUNIST PRESS

WITH ITS PROPAGANDIST functions so clearly defined, its contents and approach to events so rigidly prescribed, can the communist press truthfully reflect communist life? What image does it present of the greater world in which the communist peoples are living? The answer to these questions, touched upon marginally in the chapters on the ideological foundations and characteristic features of the press, lies in the ideology and partisan or class character from which stems the concept of a world split into two camps.

According to this concept there is, on one side, the world of the communist countries where the people, under the wise leadership of the party, live a truly free, happy and prosperous life. Here everything is done most democratically by the party leadership, with the fullest knowledge and consent of the people, and affairs of state are conducted in the interests of the people and peace.

On the other side is a world where the life of the people is bleak and dreary; unemployment and the cost of living are constantly rising (wage increases are rarely reported); workers are exploited; governments and 'ruling circles' conduct a policy directed against the interests of the people, and are forever preparing for war against the socialist camp.

The duality applies, with adjustment according to the degree of development of the particular country, also to life within the communist states. The bright, positive side is represented by the communists and all 'progressive elements'— the working class. The dark side consists of all those who resist communist policy and are branded by such terms as reactionaries, parasites, hooligans, as class enemies, enemies of the state or the people, and so on.

Though this split-world concept is inherent in marxist-leninist theory, at the beginning it did not find expression in the Soviet press. In the 'twenties the Soviet press was still comparatively able to give a balanced picture of life in the Soviet Union and an undistorted picture of the outside world.

But from the 'thirties on, when the construction of socialism began, the press had to write about 'successes' about the 'new, happy life', because the situation was quite the contrary. Millions of peasants were uprooted and deported to Siberia or the northern parts of the country because they refused to join the *kolkhozes*; millions of workers were sent away from their families and homes to build factories and dams; and literally millions of people were starved to death in the great famine which swept the Soviet Union as the result of the collectivisation of agriculture.

In those grim days, as A. Kotlyar, a former Soviet journalist, notes in his recollections[1], newspapers were forced to write about 'positive things in the Soviet reality', and since then the practice of writing only about positive things, giving only a rosy picture of life in communist society, has become a *conditio sine qua non* of the press. The dreary and difficult aspects of life were glossed over; existence of contradictions or conflicts was denied.

After Stalin's death, journalists and especially writers revolted against the theory of 'no conflicts' in communist society, and for a time conflicts, and the grey, even bleak sides of life were referred to in the press. But after 1958–9 these tendencies were tacitly either suppressed by the authorities or dropped by journalists and writers as they ran into serious trouble and obstacles. The picture of communist life nowadays is somewhat different from that obtaining in the pre-1953 period, but the bright side must still be emphasised and the darker sides are only allowed as a background to a general improvement.

To distract attention from the low living standards in the Soviet Union and in other socialist countries—chronic shortages of food and consumer goods, absence of personal and political freedoms—the logical thing was to depict the life of working people in the 'capitalist' countries in the darkest colours as the complete opposite of the idealised image of communist society. At first, the Soviet press did this cautiously, with a sense of proportion, but later this sense—and the sense of shame or lie—was lost. A schematic image wholly shaped to the requirements of party agitation and propaganda became established as an integral part of the communist press.

This dualistic concept of the communist and non-communist world was strengthened in 1946 by the introduction of the cold war and the division into two camps of peace and war by Stalin and his associates, Zhdanov, Molotov, Vyshinsky, etc.

Characteristic of this cold-war division of the world was the official sanction it received from one of the chief ideologists of that time, A. A. Zhdanov.

Speaking in Warsaw in 1947, Zhdanov declared that the world was sharply divided into the camps of socialism and capitalism. There was no common ground between them, only irreconcilable contradictions, he said. The camp of socialism, with the Soviet Union at its head, was the camp of peace, freedom, happiness, progress and the defence of human rights. The other camp was the camp of imperialism, oppression and exploitation of their own people and foreign nations, and preparation for aggressive war. At the head of this camp stood the United States of America.

Zhdanov's theses, which were reflected in the practice of the Soviet press from 1945–6 onwards, became the official guiding line for all satellites. The agitation and propaganda line followed this concept absolutely literally: everything was either black or white, bad or good; there were no half tones.

THE IMAGE OF LIFE IN THE WEST

Though the new rulers of the Soviet Union began, after Stalin's death, to preach 'peaceful coexistence', nothing changed in the line for press treatment of the 'capitalist' and 'imperialist' world. Some small changes and short-lived phases of comparative 'objectivity' in reporting events from the United States and other western countries were of a purely tactical nature either to give a semblance of 'liberalisation' as a concession to the general pressure or as support for Khrushchev's visits to western countries such as Britain, the United States or France.

The continued propagandist line of giving readers a completely distorted image of life in western and other noncommunist countries is shown by comparing and analysing the contents of the press in various communist countries at different times.

In 1947 the results of two American investigations into this subject were published. One analysed the contents of Soviet newspapers in relation to the United States, and the other—independent of the first—made a comparison of contents of the Berlin press licensed (and censor-directed) by Soviet authorities. Both investigations came to the same conclusion:

that life in the US and in the west generally was so distorted as to create an image suited to the requirements of official propaganda and agitation.

Alexander Dallin in his study, published in *Public Opinion Quarterly*,[2] found that 80 per cent of news about the United States printed in *Pravda* could be divided under the following headings:

1 Militarism and imperialism in American policy; 'atom-bomb diplomacy' and 'dollar dictatorship';
2 Pro-Soviet points of view and utterances in America itself which argued critically against British-American policy;
3 Reactionaries, fascists, racial discrimination in the United States; 'monopoly capitalism' and 'exploitation';
4 Wage disputes, unemployment, inflation, and the 'inevitability of an imminent economic crisis'.

W. P. Davison and his associates undertook a similar research with a different approach on the press published under different conditions. They compared the press of East Berlin, licensed by the Soviet occupational authorities, with that of the western world. The results, published in *Public Opinion Quarterly*,[3] were practically identical with those of Dallin's research. All four papers investigated showed the same attitudes to the west, and gave the same picture of life. News was selected not for its news-value but to support communist policy and doctrine.

The authors of the study, who did not base their work on ideological or theoretical considerations, found that 55 per cent to 70 per cent of news about the United States and Britain appearing during the period studied was unfavourable to those countries, and only 10 per cent to 30 per cent could be regarded as favourable or neutral. The pattern of reporting was:

1 The American economy is constantly in a state of crisis.
2 Policy-making in Washington is in the hands of reactionaries.
3 The United States' 'dollar diplomacy' pursues imperialist aims.
4 All reasonable Americans want to co-operate with the Soviet Union.
5 The British Empire is disintegrating.[4]

Since they did not consider the subject in its ideological context, Davison and his research team attributed this uniformity almost entirely to the principles applied by the censorship.

Three of the papers examined were, in fact, communist, namely the official organ of the SED (communist) party, the official organ of the Soviet occupation authorities, and an 'independent' newspaper run, of course, entirely by communists who occupied all leading staff positions. The fourth newspaper was that of a 'bourgeois' political party which was forced by the Soviet censoring and directing organs, and also by the absence of other than communist-selected news, to conform to the communist line. For the other three newspapers, however, there was no need to impose the line; the ideological and partisan approach to the problems was sufficiently built-in to their whole organisation to ensure conformity and uniformity.

Some ten years later, in 1957, another analysis of the contents of representative East German newspapers confirmed that the identical line in reporting events in the west was still followed. It must be stressed that this time the analysis was made at a time when 'liberalisation' and 'peaceful coexistence' were the official line of the Soviet orbit. The results are, therefore, even more valuable and instructive.

This investigation examined six East German newspapers, representative of the main groupings in the press of the country. It was conducted in January 1957, and later in the same year, by the Infratest Institute, Munich. The analysis of non-political news items showed that 40 per cent presented the west in the worst possible light by skilful selection of news.

Comparing news reporting on events in West Germany with the findings of the two American surveys, one of the authors of the Infratest investigation said:

One need only exchange personal names, places and dates to obtain the very same picture that we had to present as the result of our own investigations into the East German news service about the Federal Republic. . . . It is a sign of extraordinary rigidity in the East German press that the picture of its reporting of news about the Federal Republic is covered, down to small details and the relative emphasis, by the findings of the Americans in the news about their own country at that time.[5]

The picture of the Federal German Republic in the six East German newspapers was based on the following themes:

1 Bonn conducts a militaristic policy.
2 German youth refuses to do military service.
3 Fascism is once again raising its head.
4 Workers are exploited.
5 Monopoly capitalists reign supreme behind the scenes.
6 'Good patriots' are imprisoned.

Summing up the news about the Federal Republic, the authors say that

> reporting is entirely directed towards ideological objectives, schematically presented, with preconceived ideas and conclusions, and working with only a modest catalogue of contents that fit into the ideological concept. Strike actions are praised as acts of solidarity with the world proletariat, the general economic news lays emphasis on crises, price increases, and a general recession in investment activities; the marxist theory of economic crises are dealt with as in a textbook. . . .[6]

The section on 'topical, non-political news' is a good example of how one can 'make politics' without the reader being aware of it, the authors say. (Though the reader is not deceived by this one-sided communist selection of news in East Germany or elsewhere as the mass exodus of people to West Germany, and the reaction of people in other communist countries, Poland, Hungary, etc., confirm.) The samples examined showed that nearly every other piece of news contained a report of some unfortunate happening in western countries. 'Capitalism' is 'unmasked' by a selection of news of suicides through economic distress, industrial accidents, abuses by western troops, immorality pointing to failing western values, chaotic conditions of road traffic and other similar unpleasant things.[7]

This description of the type of news selected to distort the image of life in West Germany entirely conforms with the news about the west in general which can be found in the press of other communist countries. This is confirmed by a brief survey of what and how two communist newspapers reported about the United States in November 1962.

The survey covers *Pravda*, organ of the Central Committee of the Communist Party of the Soviet Union, and *Rudé právo*, organ of the Central Committee of the Czechoslovak Communist Party, in the period, from Monday to Sunday, 12 to 18 November 1962, and includes all—even short one-sentence items—news, comment, articles and features. The day by day account is as follows:

Monday, 12 November:

Pravda: Huge profits of US companies from their investments in Latin America in the years 1946–59: an article from Academician E. Fyodorov (who was visiting the United States during the Cuban crisis) which tries to create the impression that American official circles conduct war propaganda and preparations, but the American people do not approve of and do not support the policy and measures of the administration. The article also complains that American newspapers, radio and television do not give a truthful picture of Soviet policy and life.

Rudé právo prints the same (TASS) item on profits and reprints the interview of the same academician on Moscow television giving the same picture as the article in *Pravda*. A short item quotes the report of the US Congress on the disappearance of smaller firms and the concentration of industrial enterprises in the hands of monopolies. The paper's New York correspondent writes an article about 'increasing general pressure' on the US administration to end the blockade of Cuba.

Tuesday, 13 November:

Pravda prints only two short items: one on the consultations in the White House on the Cuban situation (factual), and another based on the official American announcement about the successful firing of the new 'system of Atlas-Agena rockets', which is exploited agitationally by the headline 'A New Sputnik Spy!' and by adding the speculation that it fired a Midas or Samos satellite.

Rudé právo has a report by its New York correspondent headlined 'Some Lessons from the American Elections' stressing that the results of congressional elections had shown popular disapproval of the extremist, ultra-rightist elements, and considering the chances for the presidential elections in 1964. The article concludes by citing the communist *Worker* that the qualitative composition of the Congress might very slightly improve and thus, perhaps, be slightly more able to express the will of the American people for peace, peaceful co-existence and a juster solution of the problems of civil rights, etc.

There is also a short TASS item on President Kennedy's consultations on the Cuban crisis (as in *Pravda*) and a one-sentence item: 'The Columbian President commented on the American program of Alliance for Progress—"The shop-window is ready, but there is nothing to show".'

Wednesday, 14 November:

Pravda: There is a short TASS item on Kennedy's con-sultations on Cuba. An 'International Commentary' presents the United States as a 'champion of racialists in the United Nations'. A TASS item from New York speaks about the 'defeat of the reactionaries and warmongers' who tried to 'distort the sense and meaning' of the messages exchanged on the Cuban problem between President Kennedy and Premier Khrushchev. A further TASS item quotes Associated Press that the 'concentration of military forces in Florida continues'.

Rudé právo: The United States has the highest rate of road accidents. A long round-up of western agencies' reports (by the Czechoslovak New Agency) stresses that the United States insists on its unilateral demands regarding Cuba, that the provocative actions against Cuba continue, that American saboteurs had been caught in Cuba, and that the large shipping companies have refused the American demand to stop trans-ports to Cuba.

Thursday, 15 November:

Pravda: A TASS report that the government of Argentina had decided to send military units to the Caribbean area is headlined 'At the Pentagon's Command'. A lengthy TASS report describes the arrest of an 'important American agent' in Cuba with details of 'American subversive and sabotage plans'. Another long TASS story is significantly headlined: 'Guantan-amo—the Base for Aggression'. The newspaper's Washington correspondent reports on the great success of the Bolshoi Ballet.

Rudé právo: A long item by CETEKA on the US budget gives only figures on military expenditure and stresses the total deficit, under the headline 'Over 60 per cent of US Budget for Military Expenditure'. (No comparison is made, of course, with the relatively much higher Czechoslovak and

Soviet military budgets, and the reader is deliberately, as always on such occasions, misled to believe that the budgets in the US and communist Czechoslovakia are of the same structure and that they can be therefore compared.) Another CETEKA item reports on President Kennedy's talks with the West German Chancellor, stressing differences and difficulties. A long article is headlined: 'Facts about the American Military Bases Abroad. A Constant Source of International Tension.'

Friday 16 November:

Pravda: V. Mayevsky, the semi-official commentator, presents the 'militarist circles of the United States' and American bases in foreign countries as the main danger to world peace and as the main obstacle to world disarmament. A TASS item, datelined New York, on the twenty-ninth anniversary of the establishment of diplomatic relations between the United States and the Soviet Union asserts that the anniversary is remembered and fêted in the United States, pointing out that a special issue of the *New World Review* was published to commemorate the event, but, of course, omitting to say who publishes the review and what is its readership. A short item reports on the reception of the Soviet ballet dancers by President Kennedy.

Rudé pravo: An agency report under the headline 'The US is Damaging Chile's Economy' quotes the vice-president of the Chilean National Mining Corporation as saying that the United States is directly responsible for the present difficulties of the Chilean mining industry. There is a report on Bertrand Russell's interview in *The Vancouver Sun*, in which the British philosopher questions the right of the United States to maintain military bases in foreign countries.

Saturday, 17 November:

Pravda prints only two short items on Dr Adenauer's talks with President Kennedy and his statement to the press.

Rudé právo, on the other hand, prints many unfavourable reports. An item from Washington stresses that 'the US does not intend to stop its provocative flights over Cuba'. An item from Brazil points out that 'American "Aid" mainly helps the US'. A CETEKA report on the conclusion of Chancellor Adenauer's visit underlines that the talks between him and President Kennedy did not end so happily as the communiqué pretends. The report on the meeting of NATO parliamentarians in Paris says that 'the US exhorts its partners to increase their armaments' and contains passages from the statement by the American Under-Secretary selected in such a way as to present American actions as a preparation for a huge military and nuclear build-up in Europe.

Sunday, 18 November:

Pravda prints under the headline 'Humanity à l'Americaine' a typical anti-American agitational piece about an accident in which a tank-vessel of the 7th US Fleet collided with a small Japanese fishing boat. The TASS report, 'The US and the Common Market', says that the American delegation intends to exert great pressure at the forthcoming Brussels talks upon west European countries to comply with American wishes, and that the United States wants to shape the EEC so that it suits American and not west European interests. 'Unlawful Action of the American Authorities' is the headline to a distorted account of the arrest of Cuban saboteurs in New York.

Rudé právo uses the speech of Zorin, the Soviet delegate in the United Nations General Assembly, for propaganda against the United States. The report concentrates on anti-American passages which are further stressed by sub-headlines: 'The US does not want to stop provocative flights over Cuba', 'Zorin refutes the arguments of the American delegate' (the arguments were not published). The trend of another story is implied by its headline: 'Provocative American Manoeuvres near Florida'. The paper also prints the same distorted report as *Pravda* on the arrest of Cuban saboteurs in New York.

This brief survey shows the same ingredients or themes which were noticed by research and analysis in 1947 and 1957 already cited. It will be seen that press reports completely misrepresent events in the United States, stress 'dollar-diplomacy' and its exploitation of foreign nations, rule by monopolies, militaristic policy, military bases, warmongering and so on. Instead of important events, communist propaganda, which clearly pervaded all items and even the headlines, exaggerated marginal events, and magnified unimportant utterances or happenings to assume world-wide importance, as Dallin noted.

The image of the United States presented to the readers of the communist press who have no other means of verifying or supplementing the information given to them, is unmistakable.

It must, at the same time, be remembered that the central organs, such as *Pravda* or *Rudé právo*, give more space to foreign news than other newspapers, and that the vast majority of readers of the latter therefore have even less information about the outside world. The little they get is, due to editorial cuts, even more distorting.

It is understandable that communist propaganda should concentrate mainly on the United States as the head of the 'imperialist camp'. But the rest of the non-communist countries, with the modified exception of neutralist, non-committed nations, is treated with the same dualistic method. This is confirmed by reports from *Rudé právo* surveyed in the same week as above.

On *Monday*, 12 *November*, the newspaper tried in a selection of items from Oslo, Ottawa, London and Bonn to persuade the reader that the whole world was supporting the communist appeal 'Against Militarisation and Nuclear Weapons', while in fact the Norwegian communist front organisation, without any real backing from the public, only published a brochure. The item from Ottawa was a mere statement that Canadian 'Peace Week' had been concluded, without giving any concrete figures about meetings, participation etc. The London story spoke about a small demonstration in Manchester, and the Bonn item distorted the proceedings of the trial of a German convicted by the federal court of espionage, and presented the spy as a 'peace fighter'.

On *Tuesday*, 13 *November*, *Rudé právo* reported that the French government was intensifying its nuclear armaments drive, and also printed a lengthy report on the election program of the French communists. Next to it was a statement of the British Communist Party attacking the foreign policy of the United States and Britain, and also the British government's announcement of its intention to conduct a nuclear underground test. (A long series of intensive Soviet nuclear tests in October and November was not reported by the paper.)

Two commentaries dealt with differences and contradictions between the United States and West Germany, and inside the French African Community. A news item on events in the Yemen was slanted against 'British colonialists and imperialists'. Widespread strikes were reported from France and Italy. Prominence was given to a several-weeks-old statement by the Central American communist parties, professing loyalty to the principles of Soviet policy and attacking the governments of the Latin American states and the United States.

On *Wednesday*, 14 *November*, reporting on the Geneva disarmament talks, *Rudé právo* said 'the western powers had no interest in reaching an agreement on banning nuclear tests', and that only the Soviet Union was pressing for the ban. A statement of the Belgian Communist Party informed the reader that the 'policy of the Belgian government is more and more in conflict with the wishes of the people', and the picture of general oppression, and of resistance by the people in 'capitalist' countries was underlined by reports from Spain and Portugal about protests against police terror.

On *Friday*, 16 *November*, the election program of the French communists was again prominently featured, followed a day later by an item from the communist *L'Humanité* that the budget did not provide sufficiently for the health service. Japan was represented by only one report in the whole week on the 'increasing fight of the workers for their rights'.

THE IMAGE OF LIFE IN COMMUNIST SOCIETY

The image of life in communist countries is presented quite differently and can be dealt with more briefly. According to reports published both in *Pravda* and *Rudé právo* during October and November 1962, the communist countries as a whole presented the picture of a life filled with enthusiastic work in the construction of communism and brimming with enjoyment of the fruits of socialism. True, individual countries did not, since they could not, entirely hide their difficulties from their people, but the difficulties were minimised and glossed over. There were hardly any dissonant tones in the general symphony of socialism. The food shortage widespread through the whole camp which led to steep price increases and in some places even to rationing; panic among the population during the Cuban crisis; popular dissatisfactions; flight of citizens to the west etc., were not reported.

The public was also kept in the dark about the rapidly deteriorating relations between the Soviet Union and China. (It was only later, after December 1962, that the press began to imply that the real differences were not with Albania, but with

L

China. At that time only Albania was depicted as the chief centre of leftists, dogmatists, war adventurists, etc.)

In reports about their own and other communist countries, *Pravda* and *Rudé právo* put the stress on showing the successful fulfilment and overfulfilment of economic plans, high living standards, blossoming culture, and the growing military and economic strength of the camp as a whole.

In this connection the greatest possible capital was made of Soviet astronautical successes which were reported in multiple bold headlines, often even in red, to an extent which dwarfed even the western sensational press.

The picture of progress was spread over the individual branches of the economy: industry, agriculture, construction and mining. Even the inevitable criticisms and exhortations about not fulfilling quotas were kept in proportion so as not to mar the general favourable impression.

PLANNING THE IMAGE OF LIFE

This conformity in the image of life presented by the communist press in various countries is the result of careful news selection and an equally careful preparation of regular articles and features based on the so-called perspective editorial plans, drawn up according to directives issued by the Agitprop departments through their press sections. These directives give general guidance for the co-ordination of reporting and comment on a long-term basis, the details being fitted into the broader frame according to the political and economic needs of the moment.

In Czechoslovakia the propaganda and agitation department of the Central Committee began to issue such general directives from the end of 1949 or beginning of 1950. They remained basically unchanged until 1961, though details were sometimes changed. Such was the case of Yugoslavia, which, originally treated as 'Enemy Number One', more disreputable even than the 'American imperialists', was later regarded as 'just another capitalist country', and more recently has been moved into the category of 'neutralist, friendly states', whence it is only a small step back into the fold of the 'big family of socialist states'.

From time to time, directives shifted the emphasis of attack from revisionists to dogmatists, from social democrats to fascists and neo-nazis. Attacks on Britain, France or the United States would be temporarily toned down or suppressed according to diplomatic requirements. But the outline and main points in the general directives issued to the Czechoslovak press for presenting the image of life remain valid. These may be summarised as follows:

1 Home affairs. Life in socialist Czechoslovakia is full, rich and truly democratically free. The people have the right to govern their state. The economy is constantly expanding; economic plans are, and must be, fulfilled and overfulfilled thus assuring further social progress and the construction of socialism. These economic plans are the best guarantee of the future high living standards of the population.

2 The socialist camp, headed by the Soviet Union, is stronger than the imperialist camp and its power is constantly on the increase. The uncommitted nations are joining the camp or following its policy. There is full equality between the states of the socialist camp. Their fraternal co-operation is based on unselfish mutual help.

  The Soviet Union is the most trustworthy friend of Czechoslovakia and this friendship, a matter of life or death for Czechoslovakia, finds its expression in the slogan: 'With the Soviet Union Forever!'

3 The existence of Czechoslovakia is directly endangered by the West German revanchists and militarists who occupy leading positions in the German Federal Republic, aided by American, British and French reactionary ruling circles. The people must be thoroughly informed about the militarist and revanchist plans of West Germany. The existence and strength of the Soviet Union is the only safeguard against West German aggression. Not all Germans, however, are alike: Germans in socialist East Germany are friends of the Czechoslovak people.

4 The unity of the socialist camp and the unity of the ranks of the Czechoslovak communists, their union with the masses, as well as the purity of ideology, must be protected against all attempts at disruption by dogmatists, revisionists or social democrats.

5 The imperialist camp is plotting against the socialist camp and Czechoslovakia, and is preparing aggression and war.

The people must be warned against imperialists, and the press must unmask their plans. The United States, as leader of the enemy camp and as the propagator of the harmful 'American way of life', must be sharply attacked and discredited in the eyes of the people, who must also be protected against the influence of decadent western culture in general.

6   Life in socialist Czechoslovakia is in sharp contrast to the life of workers in 'capitalist' countries. There the people are exploited, their living standards deliberately lowered by a policy which creates a pool of unemployment.

7   The imperialist and exploiting nature of the United States and other western colonialist countries must always be stressed to colonial and non-committed nations. Their only friend and ally is the socialist camp.

These main points form the basis of directives and perspective and operational plans for individual newspapers, radio, television and news agencies; they have been elaborated on the Soviet model. Soviet 'experience' in planning the image of life is applied equally in other satellite states, which explains the obvious conformity of propaganda. In East Germany, as Richert points out, Soviet authorities insisted as early as 1947-8 that Soviet methods must be applied in the East German press.[8]

Since 1950 the East German press and radio have been given five main directives by the party's Agitprop department. These concern the line of reporting and comment on events within the country, in the socialist camp, in West Germany and in the 'imperialist camp' in general. They tally basically with those for the Czechoslovaks and direct the press to:

1   Emphasise the role of the 'peace camp'—the leading role of the Soviet Union in it, the necessity of German-Soviet friendship, the Oder-Neisse line as the border of peace.

2   Stress the 'peaceful' fight for the renewal of German unity.

3   Popularise economic planning, the necessity to fulfil and overfulfil economic plans as a means of strengthening the 'peace camp'.

4   Stress the social progress achieved under the government of workers and farmers.

5   Elucidate the role of the 'hostile bourgeois camp', especi-

ally the militancy of Wall Street imperialism; unmask the 'American un-culture' and exhort the people to constant vigilance against spies and saboteurs sent from West Germany by the imperialists.

The general directives are, in all communist countries, constantly adjusted to keep pace with changes in the Soviet line, thus assuring the best possible co-ordination and conformity in propaganda.

THE COMMUNIST CONCEPT OF NEWS

NEWS WHICH GIVES THE READER true information on
all important events and aspects of life does more than anything
else to influence his mind, and create images and attitudes which
are resistant to subsequent efforts at change by propaganda and
agitation. News and general information which are objective,
accurate and comprehensive, enable the reader to draw conclusions according to his own personal, political, religious or ethical
convictions, independent of the pressures of propagandists.

Naturally a flow of news in this sense would clash with
propaganda's aim to give a one-sided, preconceived image of
the world and to mould the minds of readers—public opinion
—in the desired way. Communist propaganda, therefore, found
from the very beginning that it would be imperative to curtail
the extent and flow of news, to suppress unwanted news and
to doctor the rest.

The latter being the communist attitude towards news, it
becomes one of the least important ingredients of the communist press. A brief analysis of the pages of the press shows
that news forms less than a third of the contents. And even
out of this small proportion, almost half consists of communications from official bodies. The bulk of the remainder is foreign
news and only a small proportion is news about the particular
country itself. Yet even such home news as is published would
rarely be considered newsworthy by journalists or readers in
non-communist countries. It mostly consists of production
targets, records achieved by individual workers and farmers,
factories or collective farms, districts and regions, or socialist
emulation, shock workers or 'innovators' movements and such
matters.

OFFICIAL RELEASES AS NEWS

The large proportion of official communications in the
news sections is the result of several factors characteristic of the
communist press and of communist society in general. The
bureaucratic structure of society; the dependence of the press
and journalists on the appropriate echelons of the party and
government machine; the necessity to print and propagate every

political and economic decree and decision, all speeches of leaders, diplomatic notes and documents, economic plans and regular statistical reports; and the 'organising' task generally— all this is inescapable. Certainly journalists have little choice for even today, the Agitprop department decrees where and how newspapers are to print, for instance, Premier Khrushchev's latest speech, drafts of the Five or Seven Year Plans, reports on their fulfilment, government statements on international problems and similar documents.

Among communist journalists there is a general aversion and revulsion against such material which is seldom read by the ordinary public. The quarterly periodical of the Czechoslovak Union of Journalists admitted the negative attitude of the average reader when it wrote: 'How many people might have read the lengthy report of the State Statistical Office? It is difficult to say, but the journalist knows well that there are too many people who do not read it.'[1] Journalists, especially in Poland, Czechoslovakia and Hungary, demanded a new policy which would allow them to drop, cut or summarise this massive official material.

Under their pressure some small improvements were achieved in the east European press after 1953. The Polish, Czechoslovak, Hungarian and, to a less degree, East German press began, before the climax of 1956, to omit the less important speeches of party and government representatives, but of course, only on the instruction of party authorities.

In the Soviet Union progress was slower and the subservience of the press not only to the party but to all kinds of officialdom persisted. But in June 1956 the newly founded organ of the press, *Sovietskaya pechat*, criticised journalists who were writing not for the benefit of their readers but for the benefit of the authorities of which the paper was the organ, and who were concerned with making a good impression on bureaucrats and not on their readers.

Yet the process of 'de-officialising' the press was slow, even after such official encouragement. *Sovietskaya pechat* again returned to the problem in 1958. In an article 'On so-called official material' it attacked the Soviet press's excessive use of speeches by officials at various administrative levels, and government decrees. It urged editors to 'publish such material moderately and only in extraordinary cases', and not to let it replace local news.[2]

The insistence of the highest authorities on the publication of their official texts makes any radical change impossible. They still consider that publication of the full text of, for instance, Khrushchev's speeches, and of party decisions, alone achieves the desired propagandistic effect. Publication of official announcements, such as decrees on the proclamation of election to Soviets, the division of electoral districts, or the schedule of pre-election meetings, is still obligatory. In January and February 1963, the entire Soviet press at republic and regional level assumed the character of official gazettes and devoted three and sometimes four whole pages to gazette material.

The same attitude was manifest on the occasion in December 1962 when the Soviet newsagency *Novosti*, at the behest of the Central Committee's propaganda department, bought in the London *Daily Express* and in the Paris *L'Express* advertisement space, publishing the whole text of Khrushchev's speech at the session of the Supreme Soviet. In the *Daily Express* the agency bought four full pages at the full rate. Probably only a handful of the 14 million people who read the *Daily Express* because of its concise, brief and striking news reporting and features, perused this cumbersome and tedious article.

COMMUNIST CONCEPT OF NEWS AND INFORMATION

Communists do not subscribe to the view that news and information should give an accurate, objective and comprehensive account of events as formulated, for example, by journalists and other related bodies in the discussion on freedom of information at the United Nations Organisation in November-December 1959. Neither do they recognise the primary task of newspapers to print news and inform their readers. They regard such an approach as the negation of leninist principles about the basic functions of the press.

In several pamphlets on the press, Lenin maintained that bourgeois papers misused news and information to deceive the masses in furtherance of the interests of capitalists, and that only in the communist press, freed from such interests, could news and information become truthful and objective. Since the task of the communist press was to educate (that is to propagate and agitate) and organise, information had to be subordinated to these tasks and help to serve them.

News and information, Lenin maintained, were necessary because without them it was impossible to make propaganda and agitation. But if they did not serve this purpose, if they only informed for the sake of informing, they were useless and could be more damaging than useful. In his conception all news, every piece of information, must have an inner tendency, must point to a certain goal, and must agitate for something.

Having in mind that marxist-leninist theory considers that economic (production) processes are the most important factor in the development of society, these, in the communist conception, must form the basis of the informative part of the press. In fact, Lenin pointed out in his draft article, 'The Next Tasks of the Soviet Rule', one of the most urgent tasks in socialist construction was to 'change the press from an organ which is for the most part merely announcing political news into an important organ of economic re-education of the masses'. He also said that 'our press must from now on give first place to production questions in their immediate, practical formulation', because the organisation of work in factories, farms and elsewhere was, through the socialist press, becoming the public concern of all citizens.[3]

Lenin's negative attitude to the informative side of the press was also clearly expressed in the following passage of the same article:

Let us have ten times less news (perhaps it would be better if there were a hundred times less) related to so-called actualities, but let us spread in hundreds of thousands and in millions of copies such a press as would acquaint all the population with the model work of several communes which surpass all other communes in the state.[4]

Lenin's claim that news serves class interests and his demands that news and information must suit the educational and organising tasks of the press and that (home) news must be predominantly of economic character, are the guiding principles in the theoretical treatment of this question. Thus, one Soviet journalistic theoretician, D. Kuzmichev, defined information in the following way:

The purpose of information is not that of commercialising news, but of educating the great mass of the workers, and organising them under the exclusive direction of the party according to clearly defined objectives. . . . Information is

one of the instruments of the class war, not one of its reflections. As a result, an objective concern with events
prevents information from being used to its true purpose,
namely to organise the workers.[5]

In the early 'twenties and later, the necessity to combine
in news reporting the two demands of the class (i.e. agitational)
character and of the informative character led to a dualistic
conception distinguishing between two different types of information: factual and creative. Into the category of factual
information fell all news in which the fact itself spoke clearly to
the reader and conveyed the desired message without any
need for further explanation, or such news as had to be reported
because of its intrinsic importance regardless of any agitational
or propagandist effects. Creative information included such
news as was by its nature especially suited for 'creative' agitation or in which facts, not important or revealing in themselves,
could be 'creatively' elaborated into an effective piece of
political persuasion or agitation.

This concept was, however, abandoned. It was denied, for
instance, together with the 'bourgeois' concept of the purely
informative function of news, by N. G. Palgunov, the former
general director of the Soviet news agency TASS. Palgunov
lectured, in 1954, at Moscow University's Faculty of Journalism,
and summed up the essence of his lectures in a booklet, *Principles
of Information in the Newspapers: TASS and its Role.* Palgunov's
conclusions on information and its role in the communist press,
based entirely on leninist principles, and also his reflections on
TASS as the prototype communist news agency, have become
the authoritative textbook for all communist journalists concerned with news reporting both in the Soviet Union and in the
satellite countries.

Palgunov's definition says that 'information is the literary
reflection of a fact or facts concerning any sphere of life,
knowledge, politics, culture, economics, science or technology'.
Being a reflection, it excludes creative approach, because it
must reflect the reality or fact truthfully, with absolute accuracy
(which is allegedly the characteristic feature of communist or
TASS information), without embellishment, addition or distortion.

The attributes which Palgunov further attaches to good
communist information and news dispel, however, any possible

notion that they should be truly objective and primarily serve, even with partial interpretation, the task of informing the public. He says:

> News must be organised; otherwise it is a mere account of events and happenings. . . . News should not be merely concerned with reporting such and such a fact or event. News or information must pursue a definite goal: it must serve and support the decisions related to fundamental duties facing our Soviet society, our Soviet people marching on the road of gradual transition from socialism to communism. Information is agitation through facts; it must educate and instruct. . . . In selecting the object of information, the author of an informative report must, above all, abandon the notion that just any fact or just any event has to be reported in the pages of the newspaper. The aim of information must be to present selected facts and events. . . . [6]

The selection must proceed, in Palgunov's words, from the viewpoint of the needs of building communism, that is, the political and economic viewpoint determined by the communist party. He does not forget dutifully to add, as Kuzmichev did, that information thus conceived—Soviet information—'differs radically from bourgeois information. . . . In the capitalist world the press is used by the bourgeoisie to deceive the ordinary people so that the capitalists can impose their will upon the workers.'[7]

Apart from this political aspect, Palgunov is ready to admit that information and news, as spread by news agencies in general can have, in their technical or professional aspect, an almost universal character, making them commonly acceptable. This common technical aspect of news, facilitating the exchange of information between capitalist and socialist news agencies, has its root in the common task: speedily supplying the press with news characterised by brevity, concentration on moments of general interest, and omitting superfluous details.

Despite all his efforts, Palgunov is not able to explain satisfactorily how it comes about that the communist news agencies and press can use 'bourgeois' information which has been spread by capitalist news agencies and press with the alleged sole aim of deceiving the people. Eighty to 90 per cent of TASS material about foreign countries is taken either from the services of international news agencies such as AP, UPI, Reuters, Agence France Presse, and smaller national agencies, or from western newspapers. It is difficult for Palgunov or for other journalist experts to admit that the large news agencies and the responsible press in the west are guided in their work by a wish to inform the public as widely and objectively as possible within the limits of specific conditions and requirements such as national viewpoint, interests of subscribers, readers, etc.

They try to explain it away by the existence of sharp competition which, in their view, alone contributes to the variety of news and the appearance of objectivity in information and the isolation of facts from editorial comment.

Thus, a Czechoslovak specialist in journalism, analysing news reporting of the Suez crisis during the autumn of 1956 in the *New York Times*, *The Times*, *Pravda*, *Trybuna ludu* and *Rudé právo*, had to admit that in scope, variety and objectivity of information and coverage of all interested parties, to say nothing of speed in reporting, the two western newspapers were far ahead of the three communist organs. The latter, he added for the comfort of his readers (his article was in the theoretical journal of Czechoslovak journalists), had, however, 'won decisively on the ideological front'.

He attempted to minimise the position, generally known among communist journalists, by this typical argument:

> It is true that the efforts to have many sided information and the publication of documents and news with which the editors apparently do not agree, create in a superficial reader the impression of objectivity. In reality, however, every correspondent of the capitalist newspaper, even of the 'ultra-objective' *New York Times*, colours his reports with his subjective viewpoint. ... Of course, the capitalist press must publish news unfavourable to its political line. It must do so because there is always the danger that if such news were not published by one editor, subordinated to the private owner of the newspaper (or to a group of monopolies), it would be published, for competitive reasons, by another editor, subordinated to another private owner of another newspaper (or another group of monopolies). The competitive fight is the *ultima ratio* of the capitalist press. But it publishes every such report with a sour face and in every way makes this apparent.[8]

News and information raise serious problems for communist propaganda organs and journalists. Various methods are used for the co-ordination of the tasks of 'educating' and 'informing' the masses: suppressing some news and delaying others until a more 'suitable moment' for publication; one-sided selection or deliberate omission of portions of otherwise comprehensive information; adapting, slanting and, in the last resort, outright falsification of inconvenient news which, because of its significance, cannot be suppressed.

Falsification of embarrassing news is comparatively rare, since alternative methods usually prove adequate, and it is used only in exceptional cases such as the revolt in East Berlin in June 1953 or the Hungarian Revolution in October 1956. Both these popular risings against communist regimes were presented, after considerable hesitation and delay, to Soviet and other communist readers, as attempts by a few reactionaries and fascists, sponsored and aided by 'American and western imperialists', to restore the old regimes of the landed gentry and capitalists. In both cases the workers, fighting for freedom first against the local communist regime and police and later against the intervening Soviet Army, were described as 'counter-revolutionaries, reactionaries, agents of Wall Street, fascist incendiaries, pillagers', etc.

All these methods of news manipulation are part and parcel of the direction and censorship of the press referred to in previous chapters. Examples could be quoted *ad infinitum*. The IPI Survey *The Press in Authoritarian Countries* shows how some of them were applied by the Soviet authorities:

The news of the capitulation of Italy in 1943 was held up for a considerable time.

Britain's decision to grant independence to India was never published as news.

In 1944, the autonomous republics of the Crimean Tartars, the Kalmouks and two smaller nationalities in the Caucasus area and their population were deported in reprisal for their anti-communist attitude shown during the German occupation. Only in 1946 did *Izvestia* mention the event in an article.

Mass deportations from the Baltic states in 1941 and 1949 have never been reported.[9]

Though this attitude to news was most pronounced in the

stalinist period, it has not changed radically since 1953 or 1956.
Party authorities in the Soviet Union and some other communist
countries proclaim the necessity to 'inform the public better'.
Some changes have been made, but in principle old practices
still continue. Thus in 1956 the Soviet press held up for five
days, from 29 January till 3 February, President Eisenhower's
reply to Premier Bulganin's proposed non-aggression pact. In
1957 the decision of the Central Committee to dismiss Molotov,
Kaganovich, Malenkov and Shepilov was held up for four days.
Poland's acceptance of American economic aid was not published
in any communist press except that of Poland.

A most blatant case was the great flood disaster which
occurred in Kiev on 13 March 1961 when a river dyke collapsed.
One hundred and forty-five people died and as many were
seriously injured, and many homes and public buildings were
destroyed in the suburbs of the city. By order of the authorities
the local and central press remained silent. *Eighteen days later*,
on 31 March, a short announcement, in dry 'officialese', devoid
of any feeling, was issued, giving the extent of the catastrophe
and saying that an official commission found that the disaster
was caused by negligence on the part of the engineers constructing the dyke, and that the guilty had been arrested and
would be prosecuted.

The behaviour of the authorities, first in suppressing the
news and then in issuing (under pressure of wild rumours)
nothing but a heartless, dry announcement of the tragedy,
caused deep resentment among the public and especially among
Soviet journalists, as Soviet correspondents who arrived at
London during 1961 privately reported.

The same attitude was shown by the Czechoslovak communist authorities on a parallel occasion. On 14 November
1960, at about 18.00 hours, two trains collided near Pardubice,
about 100 kilometres from Prague. One hundred and ten people
were killed and one hundred and six injured. The radio and
CETEKA, the official news agency, did not report the disaster
until the following day, and only on 16 November did the press
report it, despite panic rumours that many hundreds of workers
had been burnt to death in the collision, which occurred near an
oil refinery. The press was forbidden to send special reporters
or to write anything about the tragedy. General indignation was
further increased by the official release consisting of sixteen lines,
including the names of party and government functionaries who

visited the place. It was broadcast on the radio as a news item of minor importance and (by order of the Agitprop department) was tucked away at the very bottom of the front page of newspapers.

The announcement itself was a masterpiece of official heartlessness in approach to a moving tragedy. It was published by the news agency in the following way:

ANNOUNCEMENT OF THE
GOVERNMENT OF THE CZECHOSLOVAK SOCIALIST REPUBLIC
ON THE RAILROAD DISASTER NEAR STÉBLOVÁ STATION

Prague, 15 *November* (*CTK*) The Government of the Czechoslovak Socialist Republic hereby announces with regret a great railroad disaster on a side-track near Stéblová station, near Pardubice.

In the evening hours of 14 November 1960, the collision of two trains occurred, in which 110 people lost their lives and 106 were injured. The injured were taken to hospital at Pardubice and Hradec Králové. Some were released for home treatment.

According to a yet unfinished inquiry the cause of the disaster was gross violation of the fundamental rules of railroad traffic.

Minister of Transport and Communications, comrade F. Vlasák, head of the department of the Central Committee of the Communist Party of Czechoslovakia, comrade Hruška, First Secretary of the region committee of the CPC, Fr. Pecha, deputies of the ministers of the Interior and Health Service and other comrades immediately visited the scene of the disaster.

The government of the Czechoslovak Socialist Republic has appointed a commission with the Minister of Transport and Communications at its head to help the members of the families of the dead and injured and to conduct further inquiries.[10]

Independent reporting or probing by the press of the wider circumstances of the disaster was forbidden since it would have brought into the open the real causes, namely the low standards of railroad equipment and safety measures, and the overworking of both train crews who, as other railwaymen in general at that time, had been working for the last weeks daily shifts of 12 or even 16 hours in a whipped up 'socialist emulation' drive for overfulfilment of transport plans for deliveries of beet to the sugar factories. The low standard of railroad safety measures and gross overworking of railroad personnel was common knowledge, and only a year previously *Rudé právo*, the party central organ, had printed several letters and an editorial on 'bad organisation' after the crash of an express train which had been hushed up.

Journalists in all communist countries are forbidden to gather or seek news on their own initiative since it might not be approved or released by the party or government authorities.* Thus only news and information which the party wants to publish reaches the newspapers and radio. Needless to say, this type of official news is dry and dull, its language and style is devoid of journalistic quality and totally lacking in human approach and interest. Newsworthiness is judged in principle by the party, not by journalists who would be swayed by the interests and tastes of their readers.

The official attitude to news and information in the stalinist period was that nothing should be published which could detract from the idealised picture of socialist life. The second maxim was that individuals were not important in themselves, only because of their official position or social achievement, and no news-stories about personalities were allowed. These principles led to the situation where no accidents, disasters, crimes or cases of hardship were reported in the press.

Communist experts on journalism tried to justify this absurd situation by elaborating a theory of the absence of 'sensationalism' in the socialist press. Supporters of this theory, who have still, and especially since 1959–60, the upper hand in the shaping and directing of the press, base their negative attitude to publishing news of calamities in the following way: 'What sense is there in announcing such a catastrophe in a sensational manner? This would mean that we would only make thousands of families terribly anxious . . . !'[11] In their view the press may only be concerned with such topics on one condition: to help the authorities to eliminate them.

CHANGES IN NEWS REPORTING SINCE 1953

Since 1953 and particularly since 1956, the situation in news reporting has slightly improved. The communist press as a

* For the activities of reporters and correspondents, see chapter 12.

whole is now printing more news and information from foreign countries, though still slanted from the ideological and partisan standpoint. Information and news on important events, which would previously have been suppressed, is now published, sometimes in a straightforward factual manner as, for example, is news of American space achievements or Nobel prize awards.

There is also some increase in the amount of home news which now reaches readers. Crime is reported in varying degrees in individual countries. Newspapers in countries like Hungary or Czechoslovakia where the public previously favoured 'stories from the courts', now have regular sections of vivid reports of trials of 'hooligans', 'anti-social elements', speculators, pillagers of 'socialist property', or those who generally transgress 'socialist legality'. Road accidents, fires and the like are also often reported.

All this, however, is not done on the initiative of the news-papers, but through the official policy that the press is useful in combating social evils. The planned and directed character of such reporting is manifested in the fact that it disappears completely from the pages of the newspapers for weeks or even months in times of pre-congress discussions, preparations for important anniversaries, festive occasions, elections, etc.

In principle, the present official attitude to news and informa-tion is that the task of the press is to record and report only 'im-portant, meaningful daily events and information' which reflect properly the new way of life—communist society. What the 'meaningful events' in fact are, is decided again by the propa-ganda and agitation department of the party and not by the journalists. 'Important, meaningful daily events and informa-tion', in the view of leading communist propagandists, are still only those from the most important aspects of the economy, in-dustrial and agricultural production, as Lenin saw it some forty-odd years ago. Such events, together with successes of socialist science and technology (for example, Soviet astronautical achievements), deserve a 'sensational' treatment in the press. One Rumanian journalist, dealing with what is 'sensational' for the communist press, explained:

It is completely different if we speak of the need to trans-mit news or events which are important for the people. I believe that sensational events occur in our country also. For instance, when . . . the atomic reactor was put into

M

operation I considered it a sensational phenomenon, but of a just and nice kind, which fills the people's heart with joy. Of course, when a furnace starts operations in our Hunedoara plant, this fact should be made known immediately and developed in editorials, so as to show the working people how we can work, how we fight and contribute to the cause of peace, to man and his life.[12]

The bureaucratic attitude of communist authorities to news and information, lacking in human touch and deliberately suppressing the truth about real life, met with more or less open opposition from journalists in practically all communist countries with the exception of the Soviet Union. East Germany provided the first signs of indicating that the old methods had become discredited and that a new approach to informing the public more comprehensively and truthfully was needed. The shock created by the workers' uprising on 17 June 1953 in East Berlin and elsewhere in the country led the editor-in-chief of the communist organ *Neues Deutschland* to demand: 'Our newspapers should inform the public more comprehensively if they are to be read with interest. . . . Our newspapers must give better commentaries, with less phrase-mongering and without glossing over [reality]. . . . It is completely useless to sit in an ivory tower and wave the red flag.'[13]

Some courageous East German journalists also criticised the communist hacks in the press who 'with all their strength fought against the instigators [of the uprising] but spoke of the failings of the government and the party only on the margin'.[14] The courageous criticism of journalists in revolt against the misinformation of the public was, however, soon suppressed. The editor-in-chief of the above-mentioned paper had to exercise 'self-criticism' in an article entitled 'Towards a Consistent Attitude of the Press' for his failure to make his rebellious article 'the subject of a collective discussion of the whole editorial board'.[15]

Though the East German press, after this short outburst, submitted to official party guidance, the demand for more and better news reporting on the life in the country and abroad persisted. Walter Ulbricht, the general secretary of the ruling communist party (SED), had to acknowledge such undercurrents among the journalists and the public, and made concession to them by declaring that the public does not buy the newspapers for the sake of agitation but because it wants to be informed. An extension in the range of information provided by the East German press has been noticeable since 1953, but it has, however, been kept strictly within the new demands of propaganda.

The revolt of journalists against the suppression of news by the party and government was, of course, most prominent in Poland. The press began its criticism cautiously, first by letting readers speak their mind about the way the press had informed them until then, but gradually, with the changing atmosphere, the criticism was expressed more frankly and sharply. Thus in November 1955 the newspaper *Życie Warszawy* published the results of an enquiry into what readers thought of it. The replies were more concerned with the Polish press and its problems in general than with the paper itself.[16]

One of the readers wrote: 'Up to now, the "chewed up" and "digested" news has been published in a manner far too one-sided (and often neither very cleverly nor convincingly). It is high time to let readers draw their own conclusions on the basis of information which is honest, objective and as complete as possible.' Another anonymous reader said: 'More objectivity is needed in international reporting and in editorials. Exact factual information is lacking on the life of west European countries and America.' Another reader from a provincial town remarked: 'It is a shame that the Poles know so little of the outside world; but this is chiefly the fault of the press which has so little to offer that the citizen who wants to be informed must listen to Radio Free Europe.'

Several similar readership enquiries and editorial articles by other newspapers followed, and the problems of news reporting and informing the public became the subject of lively debates in the Polish parliament which had no parallel in any other communist country. A prominent Polish journalist and catholic deputy, Edmond Osmanczyk, had the following to say about the methods of administering the news and truth by the authorities:

A considerable amount of interesting news from the highest sources of the community manages to find its way into the columns of newspapers only after having come up against unimaginable difficulties, and when it does appear it is, from a psychological point of view, too late as well as

being disagreeably laconic in style. . . . The only form of contact between the authorities and the press and radio that
survived took the form of instructions given to editors-in-
chief concerning subjects which, at certain moments, had to
be dealt with in the form of long voluminous articles. . . .
Things had developed to such a state that newspapers,
especially those of the provinces, had to renounce the very
'raison d'etre' of a daily newspaper, that is the reporting of
news. . . . It was no exception to find one of the papers of
the coastal region publishing the following statement in 1952:
'The Polish Press Agency informs us from Warsaw that the
day before yesterday a heavy storm raged on our coast.'[17]

Osmanczyk deplored that in 1956 'the anachronistic forms
of propaganda should still be in vogue; as in the old days, truth
is filtered through a dropper, the calibre of this varying according to the circles concerned; the larger these circles the smaller
the drops'.

Not only non-party deputies, but also a communist deputy
supported the demands of journalists by declaring: 'It seems to
me that things have reached the point where the entire responsibility of the press should, from now on, rest on the shoulders of
the editors alone. For until now, the Chief Press Control Office
has in certain respects borne this responsibility.' The communist United Workers' Party and the government had to give
in. Prime Minister Cyrankiewicz promised to 'keep the press
and the radio better and more widely informed of the decisions,
activities and plans of the government, perhaps also passing on
this information more rapidly'. He also admitted that the state
officials were overdoing the need for keeping state secrets and
state safety under control, and said that the suggestion that he
should hold regular press conferences was justified in principle.

After that the reporting of news from Poland and from
abroad improved very much. Though the communist ideological
and partisan angle became after 1959 more prominent than in
the period 1956–8, the coverage of events was more complete
and objective than in other communist countries, except Yugoslavia, as has been shown in the previous chapter in comparing
Soviet, Polish, Czechoslovak and Hungarian party organs.

Polish journalists were also permitted—as in no other communist country of the Soviet bloc—to seek and gather information on their own initiative. But party and government authori-

ties, who since 1959 have been imposing one curb after another on the press, tried to cut the volume of such news in February 1963. The government issued an order requiring persons seeking information from organs of state administration and other state offices to submit their questions in writing. By this order, the application must also outline clearly the purpose for which the information is required. The reply, if given, must be in writing, with two copies. One copy must be kept in the office files. This means there is to be an official record of who told whom what. The reply must contain also a warning that the use of the information for purposes other than those stated in the request will be an infringement of a decree of 26 October 1949, concerning official secrets.

The decree of February 1963 means that Polish journalists will be able to get hardly any information at all (except that which the authorities—as in other communist countries—want to release) since almost every form of activity is state-controlled. Few bureaucrats are likely to be caught giving out any information if they are to be officially accountable for what they say. The decree gives a 'let-out' for such bureaucrats by stating that giving information cannot be allowed to interfere with the normal work of the office.[18]

Aversion to the suppression of news and truth was manifest also among the Czechoslovak journalists. The discussion on the necessity of wider and more objective news coverage was already starting in 1954 in the editorial rooms of the newspapers and was later transferred with much greater intensity into the journalists' clubs in Prague and Bratislava and into the regular meetings of the provincial organisations of the Union of Journalists. Though the party control and censorship mostly succeeded in suppressing their publication, critical voices and demands came from time to time to the surface.

Thus in the spring of 1956 the editorial board of a provincial newspaper *Pravda* in Plzeň wrote: 'Our press has kept quiet about things that were common knowledge. For example, last year Plzeň suffered from a flood that even reached our offices; but there was not a word of this in the paper!'[19] Demands for more and truthful news were gaining in strength throughout 1956, but after the events in Poland and the October uprising in Hungary party authorities clamped down on such 'liberalistic' tendencies.

Yet despite all efforts of the party, the discussion among journalists continued into 1957, and even at the well-managed Congress of the Czechoslovak Union of Journalists in June 1957 demands for better information policy were still evident. A large number of journalists claimed that the foremost task of the newspapers was to print news and to inform the reader truthfully. They maintained that the main cause of the general decline of the Czechoslovak press and of its readers' mistrust was the lack of 'vitamin I', that is information. All other functions of the press should be, therefore, subordinated to the overriding one of being an objective public informant. The defenders of these views supported their claim by saying that Lenin considered the informative function of the press as self-evident, and therefore did not refer to it, stressing only the functions of the party propagandist, agitator and organiser.

A spokesman of the communist party attacked such views at the Journalists' Congress and at the end of the year the theoretical journal of the union again dealt with the problem.[20] The views that the primary function of the press is to inform and not to make propaganda were labelled as 'distortion of leninism', as 'one of the manifestations of revisionism in journalism, a negation of the leninist principles and basic functions of the press'.

The article in the journal emphasised that the function of the press is to educate (propaganda and agitation) and to organise, and that information must serve this purpose:

All information must . . . pursue a definite goal, must agitate for something. In any case, no information in bourgeois news reports is 'supra-class'; they all have their tendency, they serve the bourgeoisie, they fool and disorientate the people. . . . Any notions about the objectivity, comprehensiveness and accuracy of bourgeois news reporting are without foundation. Similarly without foundation is the objectivist 'vitamin theory' which would like to place the informative function of the press in the dominant position and subordinate to it the true mission of the socialist press. . . . If we would admit that the primary function of newspapers is to inform, and applied this principle thoroughly, then it is difficult to imagine to what suicidal consequences such a theory could lead.[21]

Gradual reimposition of 'stalinist' methods of suppressing

or slanting home and foreign news, especially in the period 1959–62, gave rise to widespread dissatisfaction among journalists. At journalist congresses in Prague and Bratislava in April and May 1963, during the new wave of pressure against the continuation of the 'cult of personality', many journalists criticised the official information policy and demanded radical changes. The congresses even voted resolutions on this problem.

Party authorities were, however, still reluctant to adapt their line to such demands, and the weekly *Literární noviny* in June came forward again with the same demand. Recalling that the journalists' congresses had criticised 'the impossible practice in our foreign news service', the paper said that the congress in Prague had greeted with enthusiastic applause the remark of one speaker that 'it was necessary either to give information about important speeches by foreign leaders in such a way that the people could know what had been said, or not at all'.

It pointed out that President Kennedy's speech of 10 June at the University of Washington, in which he announced the coming Moscow talks on a nuclear test ban and called for a new approach to the cold war, had been reduced by most Czechoslovak newspapers to a few lines, although it was a speech 'the like of which had not been made by any US President for many years'. (The speech had been praised in the Soviet press, and *Pravda* reproduced it in full.) To do this, the journal added, at a time when (foreign) radio and television existed, was 'neither journalistic nor wise nor good for anything'. It then concluded drily: 'If so, it would have been better not to have applauded at the congress but instead to have booed.'[22]

The journalists' pressure, however, had some effect. Later in 1963 it became obvious that the party authorities had changed their attitude and reporting on life in foreign countries became wider in scope and more objective than in previous years. It was noticeable that a general trend had been slowly set into motion to bring the Czechoslovak press nearer to the practice of the Polish, but under stricter party control and direction.

THE COMMUNIST NEWS AGENCY

TO KNOW what is happening in his own country and in the world is considered today to be a primary need of man. In democratic society it is also considered to be his right. Satisfying this need and right in the conditions of the modern world has become a complex business which can be performed satisfactorily only by a specialised organisation—the news agency—whose main occupation is gathering and disseminating news.

News agencies in democratic countries, whether large international organisations or smaller national ones, have not only been faced with technical but also with professional and ethical problems. In most cases the principles on which their work was to be based evolved gradually. Having home subscribers (newspapers) of varying political convictions and foreign subscribers with differing national or religious outlooks, news agencies had to stress the principle of impartiality and truthfulness in their work and to concentrate on communicating facts and withholding comment which might introduce subjective elements into reporting.

These principles in essence are accepted in the democratic world today—that news and information should be objective, accurate, and comprehensive. This, of course, is an ideal which is difficult to achieve in the everyday work of news reporting. Inevitably the content and quality of news coverage is affected by certain considerations among which may be mentioned: the element of individual and national subjectivism; specific interests and the need to consider the views of the majority of subscribers; commercialism and competition with other agencies; pressure of time and the resulting tendency to sensationalise and sometimes publish news not properly verified. But to try to report truthfully, impartially and comprehensively within practical limitations remains the underlying aim.

The approach to news reporting which maintains that mere objective and faithful reproduction of facts is not enough and that, for the reader to understand them, he must be helped by expert interpretation, cannot alter the above principles. Facts and events have to be reported accurately first, and only then can they be interpreted, thus giving the reader a chance to compare both facts and interpretation and to form his own judgment.

Communist news agencies subscribe to no such principles. The negative communist attitude to an objective, accurate and comprehensive news coverage, as has been shown in the previous chapter, with all the demands as to the ideological, class, partisan, militant character of the press are also fully applied to the work of a communist news agency. It has to make propaganda and agitation for the communist policy at home and abroad, and all other aspects of its activities, including news reporting, must be subordinated to this political task. The news agency is fully integrated into the propaganda system and, in fact, occupies a prominent place there since its position and monopoly of news reporting make it a very suitable instrument for the direction of the press.

Outwardly the news agency in every communist state is an official organ of the government, usually attached to the Office of the Prime Minister. In this respect the communist governments of the Soviet Union and east European countries continue the practice established by their predecessors.

THE SOVIET NEWS AGENCY TASS

When the bolsheviks seized power in October 1917, they took over the former Petrograd Telegraph Agency, but at the same time created another news agency in Moscow with the unwieldly name of the Press Bureau of the All-Russian Central Executive Committee of the Councils of Workers', Peasants' and Soldiers' Deputies. The two agencies lived side by side for only a short period. By a decree of the Central Committee of the party of 9 September 1918 a new agency was established, the Russian Telegraph Agency (Rossiyskoye Telegrafnoye Agentstvo), known as ROSTA.

ROSTA united under one roof the news reporting and propagandist activities of its predecessors. It had two sections: one for news, the other for agitation and propaganda, called Agit-ROSTA. Lenin's demands that news should be agitation, and the civil war from 1918 to 1920 and its consequences, apparently forced the bolsheviks to concentrate ROSTA's activities almost entirely on agitation. News reporting became just a side line, because the newspapers of that time were published mostly as sheets of two pages only, due to desperate shortage of newsprint and the collapse of industry and transport. They only had room for the minimum of news.

Agit-ROSTA, so called after the name of the bulletin it issued for party workers, attracted as contributors many writers, poets, prominent communist publicists, artists and caricaturists. From October 1919 until the end of 1921 it published posters called 'Okna ROSTA' (ROSTA's Windows) in which artists, caricaturists and poets (Mayakovsky was the best known among them), using sharp, poignant, easily memorised verses and drawings, appealed to the population to fight counter-revolutionaries, army deserters, hunger, drunkenness, illiteracy and other evils of the period. Each poster had one theme, conveyed through a series of twelve drawings with captions.

By 1922 the agitational section of ROSTA had outlived its usefulness and was abolished. News reporting became the main preoccupation and the agency was run more on the technical lines of a western news agency. But the theory of 'creative news', embellished and adapted to suit the needs of communist party propaganda and agitation, persisted and the agency also served the party with a feature service.

In 1925 ROSTA was replaced by a new all-union, Soviet news agency, the Telegraphic Agency of the Soviet Union (Telegrafnoye Agentstvo Sovietskovo Soyuza), TASS. ROSTA continued to function as a news agency of the Russian Federal Republic until 1935 when TASS took over the republic's news agency.

TASS is an official news agency, attached formally to the Council of Ministers of the USSR. In practice, however, it is directed by the secretariat of the Central Committee of the party, by its propaganda and agitation department. TASS's general director and his deputies are appointed directly by the presidium of the Central Committee and the editors by the propaganda and agitation department. All major decisions concerning policy, organisation, contacts and contracts with foreign news agencies, or establishment of bureaux abroad have to be approved by the party and co-ordinated with the general policy of the Soviet Ministry of Foreign Affairs.

According to its constitution TASS is not financed by the state. Its finances are supposed to be fully covered by subscription fees which Soviet newspapers, radio and television (and theoretically also foreign subscribers) have to pay. It is, however, obvious that the extensive network of correspondents and the free distribution of its services to foreign countries could not be financed from subscriptions from the Soviet newspapers since they need state subsidising themselves. Their prices are too low to cover even basic production costs and they have practically no revenue from advertising.*

The task of TASS is to 'disseminate in the USSR and abroad political, economic and other information and official documents characterising the situation in the Union and in foreign countries'. TASS is concerned, apart from foreign news, with gathering and disseminating news of all-union character and has to fulfil the same tasks also in the territory of the Russian Federative Republic—so it operates only as the all-union and Russian news agency. Each of the other Soviet republics has its own republican agency which gathers and distributes news only within the republic and passes it on for all-union and foreign distribution to TASS. News from foreign countries is distributed only by TASS.

The work of the news agencies of the republics is in general managed by TASS, though formally they are attached to the republican councils of ministers.

During the Stalin period and until 1956, the general director, acting under instructions or advice from the propaganda department of the Central Committee, managed the affairs of TASS almost single-handed, in line with the stalinist conception of one man's rule. With the introduction of 'collective leadership' in the communist party, the system of management was changed.

TASS now, in fact, has two collective bodies. One, called the editorial collegium or editorial board, consists of the general director, his three deputies and the chief editors of the editorial departments. It meets regularly, usually once or twice a week, and discusses and decides all matters directly concerning editorial work. The other body, consisting of all members of the collegium and also heads of other, non-editorial departments, like technical, economic and personnel departments, deals with matters concerning the management of the whole agency in other than editorial aspects.

Until 1954 TASS was organisationally divided into the following departments:

> Union news
> Foreign News
> News for distribution abroad
> Commercial news from abroad

* See chapter 13.

News for the local press
Feature service
Picture and block service

After 1954, reorganisation amalgamated the former editorial departments (called in Russian *redaktsia*) for union news and news for the local press into the Department for Soviet Information (RSI) responsible for gathering and distributing internal news within the Soviet Union. At the same time the departments for all incoming news from foreign countries and all outgoing news for distribution abroad were merged into one editorial department called INOTASS (from *inostranny*—foreign). So the present editorial structure of TASS is:

Soviet Information Department—RSI
Foreign Information Department—INOTASS
Feature Service
Picture Service—FOTOCHRONIKA TASS

The Soviet Information Department is divided into sections for individual republics, for industrial branches, transport, agriculture, culture, sport etc. It also has a special section of reporters covering events in Moscow and other places in the Union. INOTASS has sections for eastern Europe (socialist countries), south-eastern Europe, central Europe, western Europe, Middle East, Far East, Africa, northern America and south America. Both RSI and INOTASS have chief editors and several assistant editors.

Dissemination abroad of news and information about the Soviet Union and of carefully selected and adapted news from foreign countries has been one of the main tasks of TASS from its very beginning, but it was not able to get a foothold in any foreign country before the last war. Immediately after 1945 in countries like East Germany and Rumania, which were under Soviet occupation, TASS was installed as the sole source of news and information from abroad. In other east European countries—Poland, Czechoslovakia, Hungary—TASS had still to compete with western agencies whose news was distributed by the local agencies.

After 1947–8, when the communists seized power in a series of parliamentary *coups*, TASS dominated the field in all east European and Asian communist countries (with the exception of Yugoslavia where the process of 'derussification' began after the break with the Comintern in 1948). This domination was not achieved by purely expansionist or bullying tactics on the part of TASS. In fact, TASS never tried to force its services on subscribers in the manner of those former international cartel agreements which made the smaller national agencies fully dependent on Havas, Reuters or Wolff, and prohibited their maintaining contacts with other international news agencies. TASS demanded no payment for its services from other communist agencies and was anxious to give all possible technical and editorial assistance within its limited possibilities.

The domination of the news field in communist countries by TASS was the natural outcome of the deliberate policy of local communist parties bent upon destroying all ties with the west and relying totally upon the Soviet Union. Pressure and even direct orders from Moscow—and often from Stalin personally—played, of course, the most important part in such policy of east European countries.

The phase of TASS's domination was short-lived. The emergence of the Chinese communist news agency *Hsin-Hua* after 1951 and the new spirit after Stalin's death in 1953 brought it to an end. *Hsin-Hua* soon took first place in North Korea, North Vietnam and also in the communist or leftist press of other Asian countries like Indonesia, Burma and elsewhere. Now it freely distributes its news service almost all over the Middle East, south-east Asia, Africa and Latin America, sharply competing with TASS in the effort to win over the nationalist, communist or leftist press.

After 1953 the east European communist news agencies began to use material from western news agencies, with which they had previous exchange contracts, for their news bulletins. (Until then they were using them only as reference or 'confidential' information for party and government officials and for editors.) They began also—especially after 1955–6—to expand their contacts and agreements adding more international and national agencies as sources of news. For example, the Czechoslovak news agency CETEKA had a list of 14 agencies in 1956 whose material was used almost daily as sources for news bulletins.

The degree to which satellite agencies have done away with their former almost total dependence on TASS's material varies from country to country. The Polish agency PAP uses western agencies more than anything else, and the East German ADN and Hungarian MTI make very liberal use of these materials. The wide scope of non-communist material used by CETEKA was indicated by the above list of sources. But the Rumanian agency Agerpres and the Bulgarian BTA were still relying on TASS as their main source of information in 1962–3.

Progressive emancipation of east European agencies from dependence on TASS has been helped considerably by the establishment of permanent bureaux or correspondents in all important, and sometimes in less important (from the reporting, but not from the communist political standpoint) places all over the world.

There are several reasons for the considerable decline of TASS's influence and share in the satellites' news agencies. The national agencies in Czechoslovakia, Poland and East Germany had to counteract western influence and propaganda media, like Radio Free Europe, Voice of America, BBC, RIAS and other western radio broadcasts in general; they had to shape their news services in their own way to specific national problems, and also to cater for the specialised interests of a public grounded on different cultural, technical levels and traditions, and with strong past ties with the west.

TASS, with its simple approach and limited selection of news and information, was unable to provide sufficient suitable material for the sophisticated and specialised needs of the more advanced and more west-oriented countries. But above all, TASS was lacking in the most essential attributes of a news agency: speed, promptness and reliability. The satellite news agencies could never fully rely on TASS's supplying them with the most important world news of the day. And when it supplied it, there was often a delay not only of hours but (even after 1953 and 1956) sometimes of several days.

With such service, the revitalised propaganda apparatus of east European countries could not get very far. In Czecho-slovakia, for instance, it was soon realised that speed in news reporting is one of the most important assets of propaganda.*

* Despite the realisation of the shortcomings, only slight changes were made in Czechoslovak news broadcasts in 1957–8. Radical improvement was effected in 1963 when an 'independent chief news-editor' was appointed and direct teleprinter links with western news agencies installed. Commenting on these improvements, the weekly journal *Kulturní tvorba* wrote on 13 September that 'minutes will now begin to count' in the newscasts and 'such phrases as "a few days ago" and "yesterday", used until now, will be dropped' in an effort to beat the influence of western radio stations.

An expert on problems of news reporting wrote in *Novinářský sborník*, the journalistic theoretical organ:

> Our rivals in the speed of news reporting are the foreign broadcasts. Czechoslovakia is a country with widespread radiofication. Almost every family has a radio set on which dozens of foreign broadcasting stations (very often hostile) can be received. Both in Czech and Slovak there are broadcasts from Radio Free Europe, BBC, Voice of America, Paris, Rome, Vatican, Canada and Madrid. These stations have some 50 news broadcasts per day. If we add dozens of news broadcasts in German—in our country there are, of course, very many people who understand German—from west European stations, we see how strong is the opposition. We must realise that he who informs first about a certain event, most easily gains the attention of the listener, and can most easily influence him. Later reports of an event, about which the listener has been already, even though falsely, informed, are accepted with much less attention and can even clash unfavourably with an attitude or view already formed by previous information.[1]

Editors and journalists in general in most of the east European countries criticised the tardiness and sluggishness of TASS, and their national agencies for slavishly waiting for TASS instead of using the prompt and speedy services of western agencies in a marxist way. This further hastened the deterioration of TASS's position as mainstay of other communist agencies. This situation became particularly striking after the early months of 1956. Since then TASS has been discreetly criticised at regular meetings of the communist news agencies.

The inability to supply news without delay and in a wide enough variety was the main reason why TASS failed to become the fountainhead of information for the numerous and sometimes strong communist and leftist newspapers in the noncommunist countries, though it was giving its news bulletins (and very often also equipment for the reception of broadcasts) without demanding any payment.

A frank criticism of Soviet news and information services, aimed primarily at TASS, though without mentioning it by name, was contained in the Soviet monthly *Novy mir* in the form of a discussion between the writer Viktor Nekrasov and Gianni Rocca, editor of the Italian communist newspaper *L'Unità*:

The first question I (Nekrasov) asked was: 'Do the Italian communist newspapers get their information from the UP, AP, AFP, or do they get it from our press?'

'No' (not from the Soviet press), Rocca replied.

'Why?'

'We don't have the time to wait for it. We are surrounded by the bourgeois press. If we are an hour late with current news, people will not buy us. And it is, unfortunately, difficult to say that your people are excessively co-operative. Judging from your papers, there aren't even any natural disasters there, not to mention such things as railroad accidents.'

Rocca listened carefully to my arguments, and then said: 'All these are good things, I have no doubt, and these are things we learn from you: the active participation of the paper in the life of the people. But we are talking about something else—about information. And this is where our situations differ. I don't know who is in a more difficult position. If I do not write about accidents and murders, I lose circulation to some Giorno. You will not lose circulation, but the same thing will appear which appears whenever there is a lack of information: rumour. And it is not easy to fight gossip. Besides, you are awfully verbose. Your papers appear in four or at most six pages which, compared to our particularly wealthy bourgeois papers, is not much. And yet, you have such quantities of needless and useless words. The next sin is scanty information and its unforgivable tardiness. Do you not spend too much time over sending each piece of material to the press? Speed means everything in journalism. I have no right to be one hour, one minute late.'

Oh the truth of many of Rocca's words! How boring our papers often are, how heavy, how dead! How late the news reaches us! And Rocca said this all, not to boast, but simply because as a communist and journalist he wants our papers to be an example to them.[2]

It must be remembered that this devastating criticism of the Soviet news and information service and policy was delivered and printed in 1958, at a time when, according to many western press experts, the news coverage in the Soviet Union did improve to a considerable degree.

The printing of this criticism in a Soviet publication was not accidental. It coincided with increasing dissatisfaction of journalists with the inefficiency of TASS which culminated in veiled attacks on the agency at the Soviet Journalists' Congress in Moscow in 1959, and led to the replacement of the general director, N. G. Palgunov, by D. P. Goryunov in the summer of 1960.

In December 1960 a conference of TASS correspondents and photographers from the Russian Federal Republic was held in Moscow. It was pointed out there that in some ways TASS had improved of late, that there were now appearing in its news bulletins more lively reports (although only on agricultural and industrial problems). But generally, it was stated by a representative of the Central Committee's propaganda and agitation department, there was still much dull and unimportant material in the information transmitted. Many TASS workers were displaying a superficial attitude towards their work. Goryunov, the general director, admitted that some correspondents lacked understanding of the necessity to work with a proper journalist's approach and speed. He promised that measures would be taken to change TASS quickly into a genuine, operative centre supplying press and radio with substantial and interesting information.[3]

Despite some small improvements, mainly due to technical innovations, the basic inefficiency of TASS in supplying important news quickly and reliably still persists. Disappointing, for example, was TASS's performance during the Cuban crisis of October 1962, as can be judged from reports by east European agencies printed in the press. The Czechoslovak news agency CETEKA has, apart from normal equipment for the reception of Russian and foreign-language TASS news broadcasts, also a direct telex line with TASS and at the Prague end of the line uses the same printers with cyrillic letters as in Moscow (to facilitate the quick transmission of important news). Nevertheless CETEKA could not get from TASS the important statement of the Soviet government on President Kennedy's speech announcing the blockade and demanding the withdrawal of Soviet missiles and forces from Cuba. The statement had been distributed by TASS to the Soviet press and Moscow radio was broadcasting it, but TASS was still not transmitting it to foreign subscribers. So CETEKA had to monitor Moscow radio, translate the statement into Czech and publish it with the

N

introduction: 'Moscow radio broadcasts the following statement. . . .'

The same happened in 1961 and 1962 on several other
important occasions, such as the Soviet space flights, when
CETEKA (and other satellite news agencies) could not afford
to wait hours for TASS and so let the Czechoslovak radio and
press miss the news. In fact as in 1952 or in 1957–8, CETEKA
in 1962 was receiving in Prague important news from Moscow
at the same time as evening newspapers or first editions of the
morning papers were already on the streets of London with the
printed stories! Such deficiencies in TASS's service only add
to the disrespect felt among agency workers in Prague, Warsaw
or East Berlin towards TASS.

All too often western experts are inclined to ascribe such
failures to political censorships holding up publication of
certain news. Mostly, however, the failures of TASS are
caused by bad organisation of work, and the inefficiency of the
system. Political and 'safety' considerations of course, do play
their part even in the operation of the system. But the failure
to transmit, for instance, the Cuban statement of the Soviet
government or news on Soviet space flights in the Russian
foreign service almost simultaneously with the broadcast to
the Soviet Union can only be explained by the inefficiency of
the system.

An analysis of the system confirms this view. Normally all
news and information coming from Moscow sources or reporters, from TASS correspondents outside Moscow, and from
news agencies in the republics is routed into the corresponding
sections of RSI. The section then sub-edits the item and passes
it to the editing desk of the department where it undergoes
another technical and also a political sub-editing. It then passes
through further channels (described in dealing with the
procedure in INOTASS), and finally to the transmission
department which sends it by teleprinter to Moscow subscribers and by other means to agencies in the republics. A
special section of INOTASS for 'export' then selects from the
RSI bulletin such news and information as it considers suitable
or necessary for distribution abroad.

RSI has most of its staff in Moscow and a smaller section
in bureaux spread over the Union. It has a separate section of
about twenty to thirty reporters covering events in Moscow.
Sometimes they are used as general reporters, but more often

they specialise as political, industrial, cultural, trade union, youth, etc. reporters. They and their colleagues in other sections have to have specialised knowledge and many journalists are graduates from universities, technical and agricultural colleges.

As for work in INOTASS, the system is also divided into sections. All incoming material from foreign TASS bureaux and correspondents (mostly excerpts from foreign newspapers and written in foreign languages by local employees of TASS) and from other agencies are first channelled into the translation section. There they are checked for accuracy of facts, figures, names, dates etc., and translated into Russian. A special press section deals in the same way with incoming foreign newspapers in so far as these have not been digested by correspondents abroad. The material from these two sections then goes into two channels.

First a section produces a summary of all agency material on specific events or facts, which is then transmitted by closed teleprinter circuit as background or preliminary information to the editors of Moscow papers and to the selected government and party organs so that the political leaders are kept immediately and constantly informed about all important world events. All the material is then digested in a special, confidential bulletin. The essence and practice of preparing and distributing such bulletins will be discussed in detail in the section describing the Czechoslovak News Agency.

The second channel takes the material into the geographical sections which, after consulting the news editor, decide whether and how to rewrite the story for publication in the Soviet press. This in fact represents the first step of censoring news for the Soviet reader. The draft of the news item, made by one member of the section, is read by the section head and passed to the editing desk where it is again checked for possible stylistic, factual or political errors. From the editing desk the story passes into the typing department for retyping. Then it goes through the proof-reading department and the Glavlit* department. Only after final approval by Glavlit, which is almost always a formality, the item goes to the transmission department and is sent to subscribers in the Union.

The section for news service to foreign countries selects and

* See pages 140-4.

adapts its material from all cables coming in from other news agencies and TASS's bureaux abroad. This service is, of course, much wider than that for Soviet subscribers since the needs of Soviet propaganda are quite different for home and abroad.

The system is cumbersome and causes lengthy delays which are multiplied by the fact that there is no news-room. The cable reception, translation and geographical sections all have their own rooms, so have the editing, typing and proof-reading, Glavlit and transmission sections (some of them even on different floors), so that material has to cover considerable distances in the 'production' process.

Delays in TASS news service are also caused by sluggish reporting from foreign bureaux. Palgunov wrote in his booklet on TASS that the correspondent must send his dispatch not later than 30 minutes after the occurrence of any important event, and visitors to the head office of TASS are always reminded of this supposed speed and agency-like approach to news reporting. But the practice differs very much from the theory, and dispatches from correspondents arrive in Moscow with a delay of one hour or more after western agencies have transmitted the same news through their world service. So these materials and not those from TASS's correspondents are mostly used for 'hot' news.

These shortcomings and the necessity for streamlining the flow of news both in RSI and in INOTASS were fully recognised as far back as 1957–8. But under the existing system, whereby the management of TASS cannot decide upon any reorganisation on its own and has to submit plans to the press section of the party's propaganda department (in fact, they have to be approved by the secretariat of the Central Committee, and the presidium of the party has first to deal with them in substance before approval in detail is given), improvement can be but slow. It can be illustrated by the fact, for instance, that it was decided (and confidentially announced to other communist agencies) as early as spring 1959 to replace Palgunov, but the change was effected only in the summer of 1960.

Goryunov, the new general director, was given the task of reorganising TASS into an efficient international agency which could effectively compete with western rivals and thus spread Soviet communist propaganda in its news services throughout the world. A plan for reorganisation was prepared in 1962 but, judging from the present operation of TASS, it is obvious, even to experts from outside, that little has been effected.

Many drawbacks are inherent in the system. These prevent the agency from reacting on its own to important political events (when speed is most necessary) and force it to seek approval or advice of party and government authorities, involving bureaucratic procedures, and far too much checking and even censoring.

Some confusion was caused among western observers in 1961 by the creation of another press agency, called *Novosti*. It was considered by some as an attempt to downgrade TASS, or to free it from propaganda duties.

The agency now widely known under its logotype APN—*Agentstvo pechati Novosti* (Press Agency Novosti)—was founded on 21 February 1961 as the 'public information agency' at a joint meeting of representatives of the Union of Journalists, the Union of Writers, the Union of Soviet Societies for Friendship and Cultural Contacts with Foreign Countries, and the All-Union Society for the Dissemination of Political and Scientific Knowledge.

Its aim is not to compete with or to 'degrade' TASS; it is not a news, but rather a feature, agency for propaganda purposes. Its aims, according to an article in *Sovietskaya pechat* are 'to disseminate abroad truthful information on the Soviet Union and to acquaint the Soviet public with the life of peoples in foreign countries, and thus to help to develop and strengthen mutual relations, trust and friendship among the nations'.[4]

The rules of APN emphasise that it is not a government organ (like TASS) and that Soviet governmental organs and institutions are not responsible for its activities and that it is not responsible for any misconceptions which could arise about its non-official status. The highest organ of APN is the Council of Founding Members which nominates the management. It is said to be financed from fees received for the material issued and from revenue from its publishing activities.

The rules also state that the agency shall have the necessary network of correspondents in the Soviet Union and abroad; shall make contacts with foreign news and feature agencies, press, radio, television, etc.; shall widely attract the co-operation (as authors and consultants) of 'prominent representatives of Soviet society, literature, science, culture', well known at home and abroad.

The activities of the agency in its first two years indicate that it concentrates exclusively on propagandist features both on life in the Union and in foreign countries, and that it is above all intended as a supple, unofficial and uninhibited instrument of Soviet propaganda abroad. 'Through this agency', claims its general director, 'Soviet society can even more actively and fully assist in establishing and maintaining lively contacts and exchanges with the foreign public.'[5]

This fact, and its practice of paying large sums of money for whole advertisement pages in certain western newspapers for printing the full texts of Khrushchev's speeches and party documents, show that *Novosti* is just another organ of official Soviet propaganda, camouflaged outwardly, yet fully dependent on the party for instructions, subsidies and appointment of the management.

THE CZECHOSLOVAK NEWS AGENCY

A short sketch of the development of a small communist national news agency, like the Czechoslovak News Agency, is illustrative. It shows the gradual transformation from an independently reporting agency into a translating bureau of TASS in the period of 1948–53 and its subsequent emancipation into a fully fledged national communist agency, able to perform reporting duties in conformity with the requirements of general communist propaganda at home and abroad and with specific Czechoslovak needs in particular.

The Czechoslovak News Agency, known under its logotype CTK (Československá tisková kancelár), or as CETEKA, rose in 1918 out of the ruins of the Czech branch of the official agency of the Austro-Hungarian monarchy. It was also an official news agency, subordinated to the government, but in the democratic system of 1918–38 it maintained a high degree of independence and objectivity in news reporting. After 1945 CETEKA continued its independent and objective line, since the communists did not succeed in occupying any leading positions in it, and certainly not in the foreign news department.

After the February coup of 1948 the process of transformation began almost immediately. Communists took over all executive and leading editorial posts, but they could not replace all non-communist journalists immediately. News reporting from foreign countries, though adapted to the communist line, was based until 1950 mainly on Reuters, Associated Press and United Press services because of surviving traditions and mainly because the replacement of the staff in the foreign department was especially difficult. The agency also had its own correspondents in Washington, London, Paris, Bonn, Berlin, Vienna, Rome and Moscow, and in some east European capitals. In the home news department the process of taking over all journalistic posts by communists and reporting home events and developments fully from the communist point of view was an easy matter and was completed within a year.

By the end of 1950 the remaining non-communist journalists in the foreign department were eliminated in purges carried out by the Union of Journalists and replaced by the new, younger generation of communists and screened non-communists. At the same time all correspondents from abroad, with the exception of those from Moscow, were withdrawn. The use of TASS material increased constantly, and the proposal was to change the foreign department of CETEKA into a translation bureau of TASS.

The increased use of the TASS service by communist agencies was analysed by Vladimir Dedijer, a Yugoslav journalist and member of the UN Commission on Freedom of Information. Dedijer compared the material on foreign affairs published in the central organs of communist parties in east Europe in two periods: from mid-1947 to mid-1948, and in 1952. In *Rudé právo*, the Czechoslovak communist organ, during the first period 80 per cent of foreign news came from national, only 3 per cent from TASS and 17 per cent from other sources. In 1952 the proportion of non-TASS material fell to under 44 per cent while TASS news rose to 46 per cent. In Rumania the growth of TASS-origin news rose from 30 per cent in 1947 to 75 per cent in 1952, and in Bulgaria from 20·6 per cent to 75 per cent.

The proportion of Tass material in CETEKA's foreign news, and subsequently also in *Rudé právo*, was, however, much greater than is suggested by Dedijer's analysis which is apparently based on news credited to TASS. In fact, 70 per cent to 80 per cent of foreign news distributed by CETEKA in 1952 was a mere translation or rewriting of TASS. Hardly any other agency's materials were used, certainly not any western agency's. Even reports on important events in communist countries like Poland, Hungary and Bulgaria, were taken from

TASS and not from the national agencies. Moreover, all major international events and reports from the United Nations were always from TASS. The word TASS began to be so prevalent in the foreign news that newspapers and later also CETEKA started deliberately dropping the credit to TASS so as to create an impression of independence among readers.

Total reliance on TASS was resented by journalists on newspaper and agency staff alike, but it lasted until 1954. The beginning of 1954 saw the first timid attempts to use western agencies and press for CETEKA's own news and information. At that time the party secretariat had also decided the time had come for CETEKA again to have its own correspondents, first in the people's democracies, and then in non-communist countries.

At the end of 1955 the general director of the agency and his deputy were removed and the new management was given a comparatively free hand in using western sources for the news service. Also the former servile dependence of CETEKA on the press section of the Central Committee's propaganda department or on the Foreign Ministry was modified. The general director and the editors were encouraged, and also expected, to make independent decisions on the political line in reporting less important events. Reporting of important international events and developments had still to be referred to and approved by the party and ministry.

With these changes and an expanded network of foreign correspondents, the bulletin of CETEKA was showing in 1957–8 only about 30 per cent of news originating from TASS. But TASS remains the only source of information and guidance for the proper line to take in matters concerning the Soviet Union and the whole communist camp in relation to the United States, in major problems of international politics, and in relations between the communist parties and countries.

Continuing dependence on TASS in this respect poses many problems for CETEKA's reporting and for Czechoslovak communist propaganda in general. TASS or rather the Soviet authorities often react very slowly, and are often silent for several days or even weeks when it comes to deciding upon the attitude to important international developments. CETEKA has tried to overcome the difficulty by taking an independent attitude (after consulting the Czechoslovak party organs and the Ministry of Foreign Affairs). In most such cases, however, the subsequent Soviet line or TASS reports has proved to be quite contrary.

Thus in 1956 after the re-election of President Eisenhower, and again in 1960 after Kennedy's election, TASS or rather the Soviet government withheld comment for several weeks. CETEKA acted on its own and sharply criticised both presidents and their policies as aggressive and representing the interests of reactionary circles, or as being tools of such circles. The official Soviet policy, put out later by TASS, was more positive and conciliatory.

Much greater damage amongst the Czechoslovak people was done to the prestige of CETEKA and the national press and radio, as official media of propaganda, when the Soviet Union unexpectedly resumed nuclear tests in 1958 and in 1961. At the end of September 1958, the western news agencies and press reported that the Soviet Union had apparently broken its promise not to begin with the tests. CETEKA attacked the reports as 'imperialist lies' and Radio Prague used CETEKA's commentary for the following indignant broadcast:

A Japanese meteorological station angrily announced that according to its data the USSR (recently) carried out a thermonuclear explosion. It was unable, however, to ascertain the locality of the explosion. It would be much easier to ascertain with precision the place from which the wind blew this provocative news item to Tokyo. . . . Not just the Japanese government but even the meteorological stations and their apparatus collect only those impulses which come from Washington! Who else would be interested in blackening the USSR in the eyes of world opinion? . . . If the Japanese meteorological station has indeed caught some explosion it could only have been an explosion of fury by some Washington politician, because the USSR has once again demonstrated before the entire world its peaceful intentions.[6]

A few hours later, early in the morning of 3 October, Radio Prague broadcast a CTK news report beginning: 'According to a decision of the Soviet government, tests with nuclear weapons have been resumed in the USSR.'

Much worse was the resumption of Soviet tests in September 1961. CETEKA and the entire press and radio were at that time conducting a continuous campaign against the

United States on the line of Khrushchev's statement that 'only war criminals and enemies of mankind could now break the international agreement and resume nuclear tests'. The Soviet announcement on resumption therefore came like a bombshell. Leaders of the Czechoslovak Communist Party were immediately notified of the news. They decided to hold up broadcasting the news for many hours and set the entire party propaganda machinery into motion, organising first 'explanatory' meetings in factories, offices and villages, and only then releasing the announcement.

Still greater damage to propaganda media and party propaganda in general was done in connection with the Cuban crisis in October 1962. Lacking any guidance from TASS or from Moscow, CETEKA, press and radio were forced again to take their own line. At first they ridiculed reports about the forthcoming American blockade of Cuba, and then, after President Kennedy's statement, branded as 'imperialist lies' the facts about Soviet missiles and troops in Cuba. After Khrushchev's later admission and withdrawal of missiles even communist workers at factory meetings openly questioned the credibility of official propaganda and of CETEKA's and the radio's news services.

In cases like this it is not, of course, TASS who is to blame since TASS can only reproduce official party and government decisions and propaganda. TASS's failure lies in its inability to transmit the official announcement quickly enough when CETEKA and other communist agencies are feverishly waiting for the news, and finally have to resort to monitoring Moscow radio broadcasts. CETEKA's introduction to such news: 'Radio Moscow broadcasts the statement of the Soviet government . . .' instead of the usual: 'The Soviet agency TASS announces . . .' is a subtle rebuke to TASS. Complaints to the Soviet agency, supposed to be the model for other communist agencies, are not permitted.

The organisational structure of CETEKA is very similar to that of TASS. It consists of:

> Home news department.
> Foreign news department.
> Department for disseminating news abroad.
> Picture Service.
> Feature service.

The home news department works on the same lines as TASS's RSI. The foreign news department is divided into similar geographical sections as INOTASS (Anglo-Saxon section, Latin American Section, Far Eastern section, etc.). Incoming cables from correspondents and agencies go first to copytasters who make a short record of their contents for internal information. Then the dispatches go to sections which suggest to the shift-editor what should be published. The shift-editor decides whether and how the item should be rewritten. The section then works on the item (very often the draft is dictated to a typist in the typing room) and delivers the draft to the shift-editor or his deputies who scrutinise the news from political and journalistic standpoints. If approved, the draft is forwarded again to the typing pool for retyping. The clean copy is then checked by proof-readers for possible errors and after final approval of the copy by the censoring organ it goes to the transmission department. The news is then transmitted to newspapers and radio by teleprinters. Previously it was mimeographed page by page and delivered either by pneumatic mail or by messenger.

The system, like that of TASS, is inefficient and considerable time-loss is involved in covering the distances between the sections, editor's room, etc.

Like TASS, the organisation of the entire agency, and especially that of the foreign news department, was to undergo an overhaul. The reorganisation dragged on for many years, mainly due to frequent changes in the management of the agency. Within seven years four general directors came and went.

The foreign department has made some minor changes without waiting for the reorganisation to increase the speed of the flow of news. In some cases the department shows remarkable efficiency, equalling and sometimes even exceeding the speed of western international news agencies. But until the whole system is changed, a streamlined news-room and more modern equipment installed and a generally higher standard of work introduced, the work as a whole will remain defective. Most of the department's journalists are very efficient, highly skilled and well educated. Two foreign languages—generally Russian and English—are a minimum for journalists on the foreign staff, but three or four foreign languages are the general average. As far as knowledge of international affairs and journalistic skill or experience are concerned, CETEKA's foreign department staff in Prague or abroad is on the same level as any good foreign correspondent in western agencies.

The communist policy of suppressing most foreign news from publication in the home press soon made it necessary to provide a special bulletin containing full and unbiased information on world events and foreign countries for the use of the select circle of party and government functionaries and editors. The production of this confidential daily bulletin is concentrated in the agency.

News which is not approved by the shift-editor for the news bulletin distributed to the press is rewritten in the sections into an excellent digest of all available agency and other materials, including monitoring from foreign broadcasting stations. A special sub-editing desk is concerned with the sub-editing of such 'confidential' news and with preparing a special, mimeographed bulletin. The bulletin is divided into sections covering the main events and questions of the international scene, and into geographical areas such as Middle East, Latin America, etc. All news from western agencies, western press and broadcasts is grouped in these sections. The whole bulletin, consisting of a very concise and co-ordinated digest of all the important and latest news and comment, is distributed each morning to a list of persons provided by the party secretariat. It gives the communist leaders and officials a most comprehensive, readable and rapid summary of vital news. It is doubtful if even western statesmen receive such a good service as this bulletin provides for Czechoslovak and Soviet leaders. (TASS's confidential bulletin is produced on the same lines.)

But communist censorship is applied also in the distribution (though not in selecting or condensing its news) of the bulletin. The bulletin consists of three parts: the bulkiest contains information on the west and non-committed countries and is distributed to all persons on the list (about 200 in Czechoslovakia). The second part, containing news and information on difficulties, controversies, etc., in communist countries (except Czechoslovakia and the Soviet Union) goes to a much more limited circle; while the third part with confidential information from western and other sources on Czechoslovakia and the Soviet Union, and also any other subject chosen *ad hoc*, is distributed among only about thirty party leaders and top officials.

CETEKA is attached to the Office of the Prime Minister and is financed by the state. Its budget is part of the state budget, but it draws subscription fees from newspapers, radio and television. The system of management is very similar to that of TASS. The general director has three deputies in charge of the departments for home news, foreign news and news for dissemination abroad. They are all appointed by the party presidium. Since 1957 there has been an editorial collegium and a wider body, as in TASS, for the management of the affairs of the agency.

For a small national agency, CETEKA now has a very wide network of correspondents abroad which, if run strictly on economical and not political lines, it could never afford. By the end of 1962, it had bureaux or correspondents in twenty-eight places altogether: New York (for political reasons, a further post in Washington could not be established), London, Paris, Rome, Vienna, Geneva, Stockholm, Bonn, Rio de Janeiro, Havana, Beirut, New Delhi, Tokio, Conakry, Bamako, Accra, Rabat, Algiers, Baghdad, Belgrade, Moscow, Berlin, Warsaw, Budapest, Bucharest, Sofia, Peking and Hanoi. In some communist countries and elsewhere CETEKA maintains correspondents jointly with the party's organ, *Rudé právo*. In addition, it had in 1962 about twenty-five 'local correspondents' or 'stringers'.

NEWS AGENCIES AND PROPAGANDIST ACTIVITIES ABROAD

Propaganda of the Soviet bloc in non-communist countries has at its disposal a vast machine, and its operations are planned and co-ordinated to assure the greatest effect in influencing the people in favour of the 'unselfish and peaceloving' policy of the communist camp and against the 'imperialists' who 'exploit and threaten the world' with nuclear and non-nuclear wars. Radio, books, periodicals, films, delegations within the frame of cultural, scientific and sports exchanges, and thousands of press releases issued by diplomatic and commercial missions are some of the instruments in the orchestra of communist propagandist activities abroad.

In 1961, for instance, the Soviet Union broadcast 1,067 hours weekly to foreign countries, its satellites 1,163 hours and another 244 hours from clandestine stations operating from east Europe. The Soviet Union alone published 40 million copies of books in thirty-four languages, and the entire bloc (including China) produced 150 major periodicals in some twenty-two languages of the non-communist world.[7]

Communist news agencies have been playing an important part in this propagandist orchestra in the general communist expansion since 1945 and especially since 1953.

Activities of communist news agencies within the global propaganda abroad are directed and co-ordinated both in their contents and targets jointly by the party apparatus; in this case not only by the propaganda department but also by the international department of the secretariat of the Central Committee, and by the foreign ministries, with the Soviet Union as the conductor of the entire orchestra.

In this way, acting on instructions, the news agencies adapt their news broadcasts and feature services to the general line of extolling the communist policies and attacking the 'imperialists' and 'warmongers', and direct them to the specific demands of propaganda for individual regions and countries based on differing political, economic, ethnic or religious conditions. On instructions from the party and Foreign Ministry, the agencies also make contacts and contracts with national and international agencies and establish bureaux abroad or broadcasts of news services to special regions.

The first target in the expansion of TASS was south-east Asia. In the years 1953–6 Latin America came into the foreground, to be followed by the Middle East in 1954–8. The communist 'scramble for Africa' started rather late, after 1958–9 when the newly established independent African states began to present suitable territory for political penetration. This gradual shifting of emphasis does not, however, in any way mean that the interest of communists in previous areas has diminished. Once established, positions are always maintained and expanded, unless some political setback checks communist progress. The shifts of emphasis only mean that new spheres of interest and influence are added to the existing list.

In the penetration of the less developed countries several stages in the approach of the communist agencies can be observed. One, usually the first, is to establish direct and friendly contact with the local agency. This is followed by an offer of exchange of news services together with technical help consisting of free equipment for receiving and transmitting news, and of free training of technicians in the communist state.

Further, editorial help is offered: journalists from local agencies are invited to communist countries, or experts from communist news agencies are sent to local agencies. The actual needs of news-gathering or businesslike dissemination are subordinated in these operations to political tasks. The economic aspects of the expansion of agencies is of little concern since these are all activities financed by the government.

Under such conditions, expansion can proceed at a very high pace. In its efforts to become an agency with full international status and a useful instrument of Soviet foreign propaganda, TASS, by 1956, had established bureaux or 'correspondent points' in forty places abroad with a total staff of 200. In addition there were 800 personnel in INOTASS in Moscow. By 1962 TASS had established offices in about twenty more places, and the number of correspondents or editorial staff had risen to about 300 in 1963. TASS has made contracts with more than eighty national agencies and is distributing freely or on an exchange basis its world news service in Russian, English, French, German, Spanish and many local languages to about the same number of countries.*

Soviet propaganda abroad has received a great boost from the establishment of the previously mentioned press agency *Novosti* (APN), which is taking over from TASS certain functions, especially in the field of distribution of features and pictures. A review of APN's activities in *Sovietskaya pechat* in June 1963 revealed to what extent the agency is used for foreign propaganda.[8]

According to this article, APN has nine main editorial departments; they include departments preparing material for Soviet publications disseminated in foreign countries, for individual foreign countries and for the Soviet press.

In 1962, one year after its foundation, APN distributed 50,000 features and other forms of material in ninety countries for publication in 2,000 foreign newspapers, journals and magazines. The agency also provided features, pictures and other material for twenty-six Soviet magazines, five newspapers and fifty-three bulletins with a total one-issue circulation of 1.5 million copies distributed by Soviet official diplomatic or

* In February 1964 TASS announced that it had 100 'own correspondents' in 79 countries (i.e. Russian journalists, in addition to approximately 200 local assistants), and that the staff of the central office in Moscow now numbered 2,000. The agency is to build a new central office of 20 floors.

propaganda offices in sixty countries. APN usually sends its material to foreign newspapers in their respective languages. In one day its departments translate on average 500 pages of Russian texts. It also publishes twice daily *The Review of the Soviet Press* with three weekly supplements.

In Asia, Africa, and Latin America (and also to communist and pro-communist publications in 'capitalist' countries) APN is distributing its services free of charge or at a very low nominal charge, while it charges western newspapers, radio and television the usual fees for requested material.

Similar expansionist trends are shown also by the national agencies of Czechoslovakia, East Germany and Poland. The Czechoslovak news agency has since 1954 built up wide contacts with national agencies in about sixty countries. It has been gradually concentrating its interest on the same areas as TASS, using the same approach. Its news service, which tries to cover all the world, is now beamed by radio, morse, teleprinter or telex in English, French, Spanish and Russian. In its propagandist activities the agency is also extensively using its feature service known as 'Pragopress' which performs similar functions as APN. The articles and photographs are distributed free not only by the agency and its correspondents but also by the press departments of Czechoslovak diplomatic missions. This material is offered in English, Russian, French, German, Spanish, Polish, Hungarian, Rumanian, Bulgarian and Serbo-Croat.

The East German agency ADN now has correspondents in twenty-six places and is broadcasting its services to south-east Asia, the Middle East, Africa and Latin America in English, French and Spanish. Its main sphere of interest is in Africa. The Polish agency PAP also pursues propagandist activities abroad, but to a much lesser extent.

This brief sketch shows that there was no agreement between the communist agencies, as some western observers thought, which would have given international status only to TASS and limited other agencies in their foreign activities. In the overall expansionist drive in the years 1954–61, there were sometimes examples of lack of co-ordination, in some cases bordering on competition, between the smaller communist agencies for areas of influence in Africa and elsewhere. (There was real competition for influence between TASS and the

Chinese agency *Hsin-Hua*, especially after 1958 when China refused to submit to Soviet leadership and began to pursue its own political interests.) Only in 1961 was it realised that greater co-ordination was necessary because the underdeveloped countries with their limited communication media could not absorb the services of TASS, CETEKA, ADN, PAP and *Hsin-Hua*. The general trend towards closer co-ordination, now apparent in the Soviet bloc, will undoubtedly manifest itself soon in some way or other in this field.

But until now the activities of small national communist agencies have had some advantages over TASS. Smaller communist countries seem to be more acceptable to the newly independent countries since they are regarded as free of any imperialistic or power interests. Their political and propagandist activities also enable the communists to exert their influence from more than one direction, thus assuring easier and quicker penetration, as has been shown in the examples of Cuba, Ghana, Mali, Guinea and Indonesia.

HOW THE COMMUNIST NEWSPAPERS WORK

POLITICAL AND PROPAGANDIST tasks have so shaped
the system of work in communist newspapers that it differs
widely from that of American, British or any other non-
communist papers. News occupies only a minor part of the
column space so there is much less pressure of time in the
sections or desks, excepting those for foreign news which even
in the communist newspaper still retains its character of freshness and actuality.

The editorial structure, tasks of editors and journalists,
system of sections, columns, editorial meetings etc., are
adapted to specific political tasks. Home news desks and news
reporters, for instance, were non-existent until recently. There
are not, or at any rate were not till recently, any counterparts
of the British political and lobby correspondents, diplomatic
correspondents, defence correspondents, city editors, parliamentary reporters, labour or industrial correspondents and
leader writers.

In some cases the practice in communist newspapers is
changing; there are emerging, apart from the news reporters,
commentators on home political and economic problems, on
foreign affairs, and even columnists whose names appear regularly in the press and whose work in many respects resembles that
of their western counterparts.

But all in all, the system of work is basically different and
strange to a western journalist. The communist newspaper
still works according to strict plans: long-term or perspective,
and short-term or operational. The greater part of the contents is fixed for several days ahead; entertainment features
are few and infrequent since they must give place to propagandist, economic, political and ideological articles. Apart from
news, half the paper's contents consists of material written not
by the professional staff but by various kinds of external contributors. And most of the journalist's time is taken up with
working with these contributors and with other duties which
fall under the description of mass political work. The participation of non-journalists in editorial activities and the mass
political work are, indeed, the most prominent features of any
communist newspaper.

Different also is the approach to the problems of circulation, finance, advertising and other technical aspects of newspaper publication. In some ways the organisation, and also the terminology such as editorial collegium, secretary, departments and sections, is reminiscent of a bureaucratic institution rather than of a newspaper office pulsating with vigorous life and racing against time and competitors to give readers the latest and most interesting news.

EDITORIAL STRUCTURE

The system of editorial work, which varies only slightly in individual countries, can perhaps be best shown by several examples in which leading communist journalists themselves describe the operations and structure of their newspapers.

Rudé právo (Czechoslovakia)

A member of the management of Rudé právo, organ of the Communist Party of Czechoslovakia, gave, in Sovietskaya pechat in 1960,[1] a fully detailed description of how his paper is produced. It is very closely modelled on the Soviet Pravda. A 'delegation' from Rudé právo visited Pravda's offices in 1952 and in the following years there were frequent visits and exchanges between the two newspapers so that the entire system of organisation and methods of work of Pravda was applied, with some allowances for local conditions, in the Czech paper.

The newspaper is directed and managed by the editorial collegium (or editorial board). Its members are the editor-in-chief, his two deputies, the editorial secretary* and heads of the main departments. The collegium is convened regularly several times a week to discuss and decide perspective (quarterly) and operative (monthly or weekly) plans, new tasks resulting from decisions of the party organs, journalistic assignments and so forth.

The editorial collegium also discusses reports on the work of individual departments submitted by their heads. A group of journalists, called a 'commission' and appointed by the collegium, afterwards submits a similar, critical report on the same department. Conclusions made by the collegium meeting after

---

* The editorial secretary's nearest equivalent on a western newspaper would be the managing editor, but the duties are by no means identical. See pages 217–18.

this discussion are set out in the form of recommendations and tasks for improving the work of departments, and their fulfilment is checked over at the next meeting.

Rudé právo has the following editorial departments:

Party life	Agriculture
Propaganda	Literature and the arts
Home policy	Feuilleton and reportage
Foreign affairs	Information
Industry and Transport	Readers' letters
Sport	

The information department is responsible for news reporting from the capital and also directs the work of the paper's regional correspondents.

The editorial collegium deals regularly with problems of how to manage and make the best use of the *aktiv* of non-staff or non-professional collaborators, and worker and farmer correspondents. The collegium pays great attention to raising the educational level of editorial workers so that almost all journalists have completed some form of university-level education with a graduation diploma or have studied at the High Party School of the Central Committee which has a three-year course with university status.

An important place in the structure of the paper is that of the 'editorial secretariat' headed by the editorial secretary (managing editor), assisted by two deputies. The secretary is in charge of the production of the paper, reads the manuscripts and plans each issue. The daily production of the paper is supervised by his two deputies working in shifts. Apart from purely production problems the secretariat is also responsible for the financial side of the management of the paper.

The secretary has regular meetings with the editor-in-chief and his deputies. They form an editorial presidium and decide most problems relating to the editorial side, leaving only a few things to the collegiate meetings.

The management of *Rudé právo*, according to the article, is now endeavouring to give readers the very latest news. This had not previously been the case. Until 1957 the paper had two editions: the first for 'peripheries', i.e. places within 100–150 km radius from Prague, at 19.00 hours; the second (the Prague) edition at 1.30 a.m. Now a new edition has been introduced at 21.30 hours. It gives places within a 100 km perimeter a paper with even fresher news. To increase the 'operative work' the editors installed a teleprinter service to replace the old method of delivering mimeographed pages of the news bulletin by pneumatic mail from CETEKA.

The paper has regional editions in Brno and Ostrava printed from matts sent by air. It has now also a Slovak language edition printed in Bratislava. The entire contents of the second edition are transmitted by telex to the Bratislava office, translated from Czech into Slovak, and composed and printed there. The system still poses problems, even though the greater part of the contents are prepared several days ahead.

Plans for each issue of the paper are made at the daily editorial meeting called, as in Russian, *letuchka*. Letuchka at 10.15 a.m. is attended by the editor-in-chief, his deputy, heads of departments and also by all 'editorial workers' who can come. Plans are discussed and approved for three days ahead. The dummy of the current issue, submitted by the secretary, usually undergoes changes after suggestions by the participants in *letuchka*.

Before considering the dummy, a member of the editorial collegium gives his verdict on the previous issue. (Any journalist may express his views on the contents and layout at these *letuchkas* and also at fortnightly editorial conferences.) The editor-in-chief then informs the staff about the latest tasks in connection with reporting and propaganda. Special editorial conferences and meetings or meetings of the party organisation of journalists are arranged *ad hoc* to discuss important questions. Such meetings are also attended by correspondents from the regions.

The editorial collegium and the secretariat have recently been paying great attention to the 'face' of the paper: the layout, presentation of news, articles, features and pictures. Readers like plenty of photographs and drawings (as described in the chapter on changes in the press after 1953, *Rudé právo* now prints up to sixteen photographs per issue of four to six pages), and headlines in colour on the front page. They prefer their favourite columns and sections to be always in the same position. The paper therefore has a permanent place in its layout for every regular section. The aim is to present a lively, attractive layout, with interesting but politically militant contents.

Working with the *aktiv* of contributors—worker and farmer

correspondents, non-professional departments, consulting specialists and contributing scientists—is considered by the collegium to be of the utmost importance. It is not considered wise to rely on occasional, haphazard contacts and contributions. The editors must work systematically with the collaborators, invite them to the editorial office, talk to them, inform them about editorial plans and exploit their experience.

Rudé právo, as the article maintains, is working with the *aktiv* in such a systematic way. Individual departments are organising regular discussion meetings which yield, from the communist propaganda viewpoint, interesting material. Thus the department of industry and transport organised in its editorial rooms a discussion with members of the 'brigades of socialist work' movement; 'it brought to the surface serious problems and on its conclusions the department wrote an interesting article'. In the same way another department conducted a discussion with local administrative workers on their experiences and problems.

The editorial collegium is now developing new ways of guiding the *aktiv* of contributors such as meetings with workers in factories to discuss problems not only of production but also of 'cultural life', to establish closer relations with readers, and 'attract them to active participation in the work of the newspaper'.

The paper tried also to enlist leading Czechoslovak writers for collaboration. It organised a discussion, offered them free visits to factories, collective farms and construction sites to write feuilletons and reportages. The response was, however, weak in quality and in quantity. A similar meeting was also organised with young poets.

The 'science and technique' department has not yet been established. Instead, the paper is trying to form a 'scientific council' which should help the editors in spreading atheistic propaganda.

The department for readers' letters is considered of the utmost importance. The paper receives some 2,300 letters monthly and sometimes prints letters with illustrations over an entire page. Experience shows that the more often letters are published the greater is their influx.

Pravda

Pravda, the organ of the Communist Party of the Soviet Union, has a handsome, seven-floor, 'thirties-style glass-and-

concrete building in Pravda Street in north-west Moscow. The
building has long, straight corridors, large and airy rooms,
but no large newsrooms on the editorial floors. Instead each
editorial section has one, two or more rooms.

The newspaper is managed by an editorial collegium of
the same composition as in *Rudé právo*. All its members are
appointed by the party presidium. The collegium meets daily
between 14.00 and 15.00 hours and there is also the daily
letuchka with the same proceedings as mentioned in the case of
Rudé právo.[2]

The newspaper is divided into two main editorial departments—home and foreign—with many sections in each. The
home department occupies the entire fourth floor and has the
following main sections: party life, propaganda of marxism-
leninism, agriculture, industry, information, literature and the
arts, science, feuilleton, readers' letters, sport etc. There are
130 people employed in the home department (excluding correspondents outside Moscow). Fifty of this number are in the
readers' letters section, five in the photographic section.

Journalists working in sections like agriculture and industry
are mostly specialists with university or technical school
diplomas. They spend most of their time in the field, visiting
factories, collective and state farms and construction sites.
(Short-term assignments for newsmen outside the capital are
called *komandirovka*.) In the feuilleton department there are
specialist journalists: feature writers, feuilletonists and columnists. *Pravda* employs many known Soviet writers for these
purposes as external contributors.

The newspaper has a wide network of its own correspondents, and offices over the entire vast territory of the Soviet
Union—altogether forty-five 'correspondent points' in union
republics and major industrial and agricultural centres. Their
work is directed by the information (news) department. In the
union republics, correspondents are chosen from the 'national
cadres'. Dispatches of news and information from correspondents—called correspondence—are marked in the paper as
'From *Pravda*'s own correspondent'. Correspondents have also
to write features and feuilletons and to work with the local *aktiv*
of contributors. They must work systematically with readers'
letters, too.

All journalists working on *Pravda*'s staff—called *pravdisti*
—must possess high ideological rather than professional quali-

ties. They are 'passionate party journalists to whom everything is "near and dear". Their weapons are not pen, ink, paper, but the ideas of the party, the mind of the party, the word of the party.'[3]

The greater part of *Pravda's* staff start work at 10 a.m., other journalists and technical staff arrive at 2 p.m. and remain on duty until the final production stages of the paper.

The busiest section in the early morning is that for readers' letters. More than a thousand letters arrive each day. They have to be sorted, recorded, part of them sent to central offices or organisations for clarification, part distributed to individual editorial sections, or prepared for the daily editorial meeting to be printed in the current issue.

The daily work in the home editorial sections usually begins with seeing callers. Many readers of *Pravda*—workers, farmers, engineers, scientists, writers, poets—visit the office, either invited or on their own initiative. Some bring articles, features or poems; others bring suggestions for articles or just want advice on various problems.

The foreign department, with its four sections, occupies almost the whole of the third floor. Except for most actual news and some routine reporting, *Pravda* now tries to rely for foreign coverage on its own correspondents who are spread in some twenty places in almost all major countries in the Americas, Europe, Asia and Africa. A good foreign correspondent of *Pravda* is an 'informed, well-educated man, approaching everything from the party's standpoint, speaking one foreign language (and not rarely several of them), able promptly to write compact and politically incisive comments and news'.[4]

The vastness of the Soviet Union poses serious production problems for *Pravda*. Only a third of the total circulation was printed in Moscow in 1962: the rest in twenty-six cities in all important places in the European part of the Union and in such distant places as Omsk, Alma Ata, Tashkent, Novosibirsk, Irkutsk and Khabarovsk. In 1963 new printing centres were planned in Zaporozhie, Tselinograd (Kazakhstan) and Vladivostok.[5]* Simultaneous editions are printed from matrices flown from Moscow by specially chartered planes. But even

---

* *Izvestia* printed about 1·6 million copies in Moscow and the rest in twenty-seven cities, *Komsomolskaya pravda* in nineteen, *Selskaya zhizn* in fourteen, *Trud* in ten, *Sovietskaya Rossia* in nine, *Literaturnaya gazeta* and *Sovietsky sport* in five.

with the fastest jet planes in service, the provincial editions cannot give the latest news since there are enormous physical distances and considerable differences in local times; Khabarovsk, for instance, is seven hours ahead of Moscow, yet its subscribers receive *Pravda* on the same day as those in Moscow. Editorial deadline for some of the provincial editions is around 15.00 hours, for most of them around 19.00 hours so that their news is very stale. This is a great disadvantage for propaganda particularly as far as foreign news is concerned. The last, Moscow edition of *Pravda* is run off the stone at 2 a.m.

The only good solution to the problem of simultaneous production of *Pravda* and other major central newspapers in the Soviet Union would be the introduction of teletypesetting. The next state economic plan, after 1965, may well contain provisions of this kind for gradual introduction of a similar system.*

★

The function of the editorial secretary in a communist newspaper is not quite the same as that of the managing editor in the western press. A good discription of his key position is contained in a summary of his powers and duties which was printed in the authoritative organ of the Soviet journalists, *Sovietskaya pechat*, in reply to inquiries of several secretaries of regional newspapers.[6]

The editorial secretary, says the article, is sometimes called 'head of staff', 'chief engineer' or 'conductor of the newspaper orchestra'. There is part truth in each of these 'titles'. In essence they characterise the secretary as organiser, as one of the leaders of the editorial *kolektiv*. The secretary, under the leadership of the editor-in-chief, organises the production of the paper. To begin with, he checks up on how the departments have fulfilled the editorial plan, and co-ordinates their work. He prepares the make-up (an extremely easy job for newspapers serving the republics and the regions since the contents are, even today, basically decided many days ahead). His task is to make

* On 28 January 1964, TASS announced that 'Soviet scientists and engineers have worked out a method for the photo-telegraphic transmission of newspaper pages, and that the first Soviet-built apparatus for this purpose has made its appearance'. The report also said that, during the first half of 1964, regular transmissions would start between Moscow and Leningrad, and 'in the near future tests would be made between Moscow and Novosibirsk'.

sure that leading articles, editorial commentaries, articles and features on important political questions of the day are included. He has wide powers, can refuse to accept articles and give instructions on how to rewrite them. He helps the departments to improve their organisation and working methods.

Hungary

A deputy editor-in-chief of the Hungarian communist organ wrote in *Sovietskaya pechat*[7] that his paper's entire work, political line, perspective and operative plans are based on decisions of the party congresses, conferences, meetings of the Central Committee, and government. 'Thumbing through several issues of our paper shows that leaders, articles, reportages, interviews, commentaries and news deal with the most important questions of public life, party work and socialist construction in general.' Yet the editorial collegium is not satisfied since 'relatively few articles are published on ideological themes or propagandist theses'. The paper suffers also from 'campaign-illness' (as all other communist newspapers do), that is the bad habit of formally fulfilling the task of propagating some production innovation or other similar campaign in a few issues immediately after the decision of the party on that matter, then dropping it entirely soon after.

'To strengthen ties with the people', the paper organises meetings with readers. Prominent representatives of the party and government, specialists and experienced workers here discuss problems of party propaganda, industry and agriculture. The paper also organises regular exchanges of experience among workers, and literary competitions.

Poland

A Polish journalist gives the following picture of how the Polish papers work.[8] The most important person, in his view, is the editorial secretary. In most cases he is an experienced and highly qualified journalist, a party member, in his late forties or early fifties. He runs the paper and is in charge of the technical side of editing and publishing; decides what and where contributions should be printed. He is in close contact with the editor-in-chief, and gives special assignments to newsmen. He also represents the paper on the Union of Journalists.

Members of the editorial collegium are the editor-in-chief, his deputies, heads of departments and three or four leading journalists elected yearly by the editorial staff. In this respect the Polish practice differs from other communist countries.

Polish papers usually have the following main departments (their number varying according to the size of the paper): economic, foreign, information, women's interests, science, sport, and (in party organs) party life. The number of journalists in each department varies: from fourteen at the news desk to six in the economic department, five in the foreign and one in the science departments.

The information or news department is a recent development and, due to specific Polish conditions, its work differs in many respects from that of papers in other communist countries. Previously each department covered events in its sphere. *Życie Warszawy* has, for example, about seven reporters in its news department who also help other departments in case of need. Division of work between this department and other departments is elastic. The competitive spirit existing in news reporting among Polish newspapers is evident in keen rivalry between the news and other departments and between journalists on the staff of the paper in general because there is a distribution of premiums for efficiency. A good Polish newsman has his established contacts and sources which he tries to maintain by careful reporting. News conferences were frequent in the period 1956-9 and are still held by various government organs, more so than in any other country of the Soviet bloc.

The newspapers in Poland (and also in other countries like Czechoslovakia, East Germany and Hungary) are nowadays not generally dependent on the official news agencies. Their own reporters cover important events, celebrations, press conferences, arrivals and departures of foreign delegations etc., and each paper tries to boost its prestige by adding to the dateline 'From our own correspondent' or 'Our own report'. But important speeches, documents etc., may only be printed in official versions supplied by the agency.

In Poland the press, until 1962, was still able to cover independently sessions of parliament and even the congresses of the party. In the best years of news freedom, Polish newspapers and newsmen were even able to make their own investigations into corruption in high places, expose them, and also to criticise the government's actions and decisions. Newsmen with good contacts in ministries were able to get confidential information on political and economic matters, on the future plans of individual ministries and to publish them. The decree of 1963, mentioned in the previous chapter on the communist conception of news, will undoubtedly have an adverse effect on news reporting, and the news departments in Polish editorial offices will lose their significance and also some of their staff.

Yugoslavia

In Yugoslavia the system of management of newspapers was reorganised in line with the Yugoslav conception of the application of marxism through the ownership and management of enterprises by 'society'. Each newspaper has two organs: a 'workers' council', elected by the employees, and a 'publishing council' appointed by the publisher, which may be a state institution, political party, trade union or social group.

In the leading Yugoslav newspaper *Politika*, which formally is an independent and not a party organ, the employees elect, for instance, a workers' council of twenty-five which in its turn elects an executive committee of five, including the editor-in-chief and the editorial secretary.

The executive committee deals with all administrative and editorial matters. It refers matters of special importance to the council which also has to approve in principle the work of the committee. The council meets approximately once or twice in a month, while the committee meets at least once a week. In cases of differences between the executive committee and the council, the committee of the trade union organisation acts as arbitrator.

The publishing council of *Politika* consists of nine persons, and the editor-in-chief and editorial secretary are again included. The other members are prominent personalities in public life. But again it is the party which suggests the names of suitable personalities for the council. Thus the communist party, or more precisely the Socialist Alliance of the Working People of Yugoslavia, exercises behind-the-scenes control over *Politika* in particular and over the press in general.

READERS' LETTERS AND NON-PROFESSIONAL WRITERS

Material from non-professional writers features prominently in every issue in wide variety. Communist editors are proud that more than half the contents of their newspapers (apart from news) consists of material contributed by, or solicited from, readers and non-staff writers.

Such participation of the 'working people' in the work of the paper is considered to be a proof of the democratisation of the press in fulfilment of Lenin's dreams. Lenin said that the communist newspaper would be 'lively and vigorous only when for every five journalists there are five hundred or five thousand non-professional collaborators'.

A considerable proportion of matter published in a communist newspaper comes from experts—scientists, engineers, economists—who are regular contributors used by the paper for its ideological, technical and scientific propaganda. Yet this 'authors' *aktiv*' does not represent the true participation of the masses. The true participation, and sign of good mass political work, is reflected in critical, positive and also negative contributions of the workers themselves on important aspects of contemporary life.

This participation of the 'masses' has undergone, and is still undergoing, significant changes and is taking a wide variety of forms. These can be summed up in the following scale indicating progress from the simplest to the latest, politically highly developed form:

> Readers' letters
> Worker and farmer correspondents
> Permanent control posts of correspondents
> Brigades of correspondents and journalists
> Councils of non-staff (editorial) workers.

All these forms help the press to fulfil the functions assigned to it by Lenin, namely those of public agitator, propagandist, organiser, critic or controller. As explained in the chapter on the functions of the press, they are supposed to help establish a channel conveying the views of the masses to the party leadership.

Readers' letters are an important institution and every newspaper has its separate department or section to deal with an influx varying from a dozen to a hundred or a thousand each day, according to the level and importance of the paper. *Pravda* receives about 1,000 letters a day, and *Izvestia* almost the same number. *Rudé právo* in Czechoslovakia (a country with 13·5 million inhabitants) receives 2,300 letters monthly. The Hungarian *Népszabadság* received 30,000 letters in 1960.

Readers' letters may complain about short supplies and delays in distribution of consumer goods or food, criticise the work of local and higher authorities, write about negative or positive events, and suggest improvements. They may also criticise social or legal injustice, ask questions about political and ideological problems or the international situation. In general, readers in the communist countries write to the newspapers because there are no other places where they can publicly air complaints or obtain help. In a system favourable for bureaucratic, political and administrative oppression, a letter to the newspaper has become a substitute for those institutions which in a democratic regime give the citizen protection and help against injustice from organs of local or state administrations. Readers' letter also in many ways fulfil the role performed in democratic society by a free press with its open investigations and reports: a role which the communist press is not yet allowed to perform.

Thus, in a letter to the editor of *Izvestia*,[9] a 'legal worker' (a member of the court or an attorney) from a Soviet town, Belgorod, drew attention to a decision of the local court which had sentenced an innocent citizen to death on fabricated evidence and extorted a confession of murder. Only after the intervention of *Izvestia* did the authorities order a retrial, where the court acquitted the accused and severely punished members of the militia, procurators and judges who had conspired in covering up a group who were the real murderers.

Izvestia tried by this example to show the effectiveness of its intervention and how democratic was the practice of publishing readers' letters. But, in fact, it shows the inadequacy of the Soviet legal system which did not give the accused a fair chance of defence or appeal. It shows the inability of 'legal workers', who knew about the frame-up, to take any effective steps within the system. And it also shows that the editor of the local newspaper, though he knew the inside story, could not expose it since he was forbidden to do so by the local party leaders.

The department of readers' letters in *Izvestia* has a large staff of about fifty, mostly women, to deal with the increasing flow. Letters are sorted early in the morning. If an interesting letter is found, it is immediately forwarded to the appropriate editorial department with a note saying: 'Attention! Interesting letter! Special control!' The editorial secretary is notified and a card (cards have different colours for each month for reference purposes) is put on the file.[10]

The department by various means brings the attention of journalists of all departments to incoming letters. It organises on Wednesdays 'Hours of interesting letters' which are attended 'by those who wish'. At these meetings letters are read which have previously been sent to departments, and the journalists discuss whether the themes have 'social importance' and in what form they should be published. Here it is also decided whether more precise information and more facts are needed, or whether a special correspondent should be sent to investigate. Generally, however, the 'literary worker', that is the journalist, has an 'automatic permission' to go wherever he wants when he finds a suitable letter, and he can himself decide whether to use it for writing a report, article, feature or a feuilleton.

Otherwise the most important letters are selected daily and passed to the editor-in-chief or his deputy; all new, controversial material is submitted for discussion at meetings of the editorial collegium. The editor-in-chief usually reads outstanding letters at the daily 'planning meetings' and there it is decided how to deal with them. The local correspondents of *Izvestia* also participate in editorial work with the letters.

The tide of letters into the editorial offices has its ebbs and flows. The number increases before important political events and anniversaries, during campaigns and discussions conducted by papers in connection with elections, party congresses, flights of astronauts etc. The highest number of letters received by *Izvestia* was 65,830 in 1956. Then a decline set in; in 1957 57,688 were received, in 1958: 52,522 and in the first half of 1959 only 27,000 letters. In May, the Central Committee, alarmed by this development and by the paper's falling circulation, decided to improve the paper and appointed a new editor-in-chief, A. Adzhubei.

The new management decided to attract readers to 'active participation' and with the help of party organisations throughout the country, letters began to arrive in growing quantity. In the second half of 1959, 54,000 letters were received; in 1960, 211,379; and in the first eight months of 1961, 180,000. The total for the whole of 1961 was expected to be well over 300,000.

Readers of *Izvestia* raise many themes in their letters. Thousands poured in, and hundreds were printed when the paper started a discussion under the slogan ' "Soviet" equals

"Excellent" '. Another discussion, started by a critical letter on the low level of literary language in the Russian press and in public speeches, attracted 3,000 letters. An unusual response came to a reader's letter about the fate of an invalid war veteran, deserted by his family and cared for with love by strangers. Five thousand readers wrote, offering sympathy and help, and showing indignation at the behaviour of the invalid's family and quoted similar bad and good examples from their own experience.

To *Izvestia*'s department for readers' letters is attached the 'reception room' (all major Soviet newspapers have one). Besides writing letters, readers often decide to visit editors and complain or discuss their problems with them personally. In 1960, about 40,000 people came to the 'reception' and editorial departments of *Izvestia*. The staff of 'reception' deals with every visitor individually.

Visitors generally bring the same complaints as writers of letters. An analysis in *Izvestia* showed that they mostly ask help in legal, labour and pension difficulties or complain about bad medical and communal services. To deal effectively with the growing number of complaints, the paper has asked the Ministries of Health and Social Services, the High Court and the Office of the Republican Procurator to assign specialists once or twice a week to give advice direct to the readers in the editorial reception rooms.

Communist newspapers now admit that they receive anonymous letters from readers who, afraid of persecution, decline to sign their complaints about the misdeeds of officials. There are also 'slanderous' letters, unsigned, or signed with the names of real people—usually party and administrative officials —who did not write them. Such letters 'slander' the work of the communist party, its institutions and leaders.*

* The Czechoslovak journalist and writer, Ladislav Mňačko, admitted in *Literární noviny* (11 January 1964) that people very often do not sign letters to the press for fear of reprisals. 'The citizen', he wrote, ' "taught" by the earlier and not so recent past, has given up many of the manly virtues. I have drawers full of letters proving this—anonymous and signed.' The anonymous letters, Mňačko says, show that people are still afraid that writing a letter criticising aspects of communist rule will be 'dangerous for them and their children'. 'And surely this is true. To express openly one's true views is still often risky. It brings trouble—and reprisals. This was the case until now, and it is still often the case even now.' This testimony comes from Czechoslovakia, where the situation in 1963 and previously was much better than in the Soviet Union.

Communist newspapers have quite a serious problem to know how to use all the letters and to know what to do with those which are unused. They introduce various columns based on readers' material. In 1961, *Izvestia*, for instance, ran the following columns: 'Letters with a comment'; 'Letters from the editorial mail'; 'Reflections on some letters'; '*Kommandirovka* (journalistic assignment) at readers' request'.

But only a small fraction of letters can be published. Thus *Izvestia* published 4,568 letters from a total of over 211,000 received in 1960; *Népszabadság* published about 1,300 from 30,000. *Izvestia* has a column called 'Though the letter was not published', in which the editors try as far as possible to account for letters which were not printed. About fifty per cent of such letters are sent to party, administrative or trade union organs with a request to verify them, to give more facts or to answer them.

Readers' letters, though welcomed and viewed seriously by the communist press, have one great disadvantage: they are rambling, arrive haphazardly, and are mostly only about what interests their writers. Letters do not always touch upon 'important social themes', that is themes which would suit the requirements of political and economic propaganda.

The Soviet press therefore began, under the direction of the communist party, from its earliest years to 'cultivate' certain writers of letters who criticised the misdeeds of management, administrative and party officials in factories and villages. Party leaders recognised that in such writers, sincerely indignant and moved by the desire to remove shortcomings and social vices, they had natural allies. Such writers, living among the masses and knowing their life intimately and familiar with every detail in the management of factories or villages, could also be useful in informing the authorities about enemies of the regime and provide the state organs with grounds and evidence for arrest.

The original spontaneity was very soon transformed into an organised movement of worker and farmer correspondents, known as the *rabselkor* movement (from *rabochy korrespondent*—worker correspondent, and *selsky korrespondent*—peasant correspondent). Every paper tried to build up an *aktiv* of such correspondents, at first only teaching them the simple principles of writing a letter or 'correspondence' for publication, but later

P

also systematically directing their activities through 'seminars', conferences and circular letters about what and how to write so that it suited the needs of party propaganda.

Individual enthusiasts or idealists were mostly replaced by a bureaucratised movement. A former Soviet journalist, A. Kotlyar, who experienced the transformation, gives in his recollections[11] a vivid account of the gradual decline. The population, originally co-operating with these correspondents, gradually cooled towards them, seeing that they were becoming agents of the authorities and in many cases nothing but informers.

In Stalinist days the *rabselkor* movement was very far from an expression of the 'democratisation of the press'. How it was run can be seen from admissions printed in 1955–7 in east European journalistic publications. The satellite countries took over the system of the *rabselkor* movement from the Soviet Union and transformed it into an identical movement of informers serving party organs.

The journal of the Czechoslovak journalists[12] admitted in 1955 that the number of correspondents was grossly exaggerated and included people who only wrote one letter to the newspaper or even those who actually never wrote at all, and that the editors who were pressed by the party to show the growth of the movement bribed workers in factories and peasants in villages to act as 'correspondents'. In many cases their names were attached to reports which had been written by staff reporters.

Two years later the journal again wrote,[13] in an analysis of past defects, that the correspondents' movement was 'over-organised' and that a wrong concept of the function of the movement was prevalent. The editors thought every letter received was a contribution from a 'worker' or 'farmer' correspondent. The correspondents were (wrongly, it was now said) given 'concrete tasks as if they were permanent correspondents of the paper', and the attitude toward them was bureaucratic. Serious mistakes were made in recruitment. In some places correspondents were even 'elected' (that is appointed) by the party primary organisations. The hard-pressed editors tried to win over the few active worker correspondents by offering them high rewards.

Such practices and the common knowledge that in most cases the reports sent in by correspondents were used by the police, so thoroughly discredited the whole movement by the end of the stalinist period that in the subsequent 'thaw' editors ignored it almost completely. The journal of the Czechoslovak journalists complained that editors

> ... wrongly held that the correspondents had nothing to say to the reader, that they did not know what and how to say it, and that the only person who had the right and ability to speak interestingly to the reader was the journalist. Such views were supported by the claim that when editors started to reject contributions from correspondents and began to fill the pages with articles and features written by journalists, the newspapers began to be read by the people and their circulations began to rise. ... The view of some editors was that the journalists could well do without the worker and farmer correspondents.[14]

This negative attitude to the 'people's correspondents', as they were also called, was widespread not only in the satellite countries but also in the Soviet Union. The Central Committee of the Soviet party was alarmed about the development and issued in August 1958 a decree 'On the improvement of the guidance of the mass movement of the worker and farmer correspondents in the Soviet press'.

The decree ordered not only the press to reorganise its work with correspondents, but also the party organs on all levels, down to the primary organisation, to 'encourage' workers to take up the function of correspondents, and urged party members in general to write letters to the press. The decline in readers' letters (and also in circulation) which was shown by the example of *Izvestia* was halted in 1959 and eventually reversed by intensive political work. The organisations of the party had to establish special commissions for 'work with the press' to help increase the general interest of the population in the press and its circulation. The number of correspondents began to rise and in 1960, according to *Sovietskaya pechat*, there were 'five million workers, farmers, and intellectuals who actively took part in the work of the press, radio and television'.[15]

The press in the Soviet Union and later also in other communist countries worked with the correspondents in many ways. The old approach of using them individually more and more gave way to a collective form of work. 'Standing watchposts' of correspondents in factories, *kolkhozes* or *sovkhozes* were established in increasing numbers. They had to watch and report collectively developments and important political or economic events in their areas. Another favoured form was that of 'correspondents' brigades' or mixed 'brigades of correspondents and reporters' appointed *ad hoc* for inquiries into economic problems of individual plants, industrial branches or districts.

But after 1958 a new practice of working with non-professional collaborators was evolved in the Soviet press. It was linked with the new party drive for wider 'public participation' in all spheres and affairs of political and economic life.

In June 1960 the Central Committee of the Communist Party of the Soviet Union gave official support to the new trend in a decree 'On the further development of the public foundations of the Soviet press and radio'. The decree approved the practice of organising so-called non-staff or non-professional departments (*neshtatnye otdely*), councils of worker and farmer correspondents and author-specialists attached to editorial departments of the newspapers and radio, and working 'strictly on a public basis'.[16]

Members of these non-staff departments are supposed to be 'volunteers who offer their help to the press organs to spread all that is new and progressive in Soviet reality, to fight with all the power of the printed word against shortcomings, stagnation, sluggishness and conservatism'.[17] To what extent the new form is voluntary and a spontaneous expression, can be seen from the fact that the decree of the Central Committee of the CPSU 'recommended the central committees in the union republics and the committees in *krays* and *oblasts to designate* (author's italics), for work in the non-staff departments, prominent workers and *kolkhozniks*, representatives of the intelligentsia and of party, trade union and *komsomol* organisations'.[18]

Non-staff or non-professional departments, which are regarded as a higher form of the *rabselkor* movement, organise their work as any other editorial department. They have their own operative and perspective plans and their members not only write for their newspaper but also, on instructions from the editorial collegium, work with authors of articles and try to win over for collaboration with their paper a wide circle of new correspondents. Being not only writers of 'correspondence' but also in a sense assistants to the editors, the members of the non-professional departments had to receive special schooling in seminars. The courses organised previously for ordinary people's correspondents proved to be inadequate.

Following the decree, non-professional departments were quickly established not only in the central Soviet newspapers but also in the provinces. By the end of 1960, for instance, 50 out of the 68 city and *rayon* newspapers in Altai already had their non-professional departments which, they claimed, were working regularly. The remaining 18 papers were preparing to establish such departments.[19]

The criticising and controlling function of the press is, however, not measured only by the number of letters sent in by correspondents and published in the pages of the newspaper; a decisive factor is the effectiveness of press criticism. In this respect the situation in the Soviet Union and in other communist countries is far from satisfactory.

Of course, the authority of such organs as *Pravda* or *Izvestia* is in most cases sufficient to induce the criticised organs and officials to take hasty steps and improve their work or behaviour, though even they sometimes experience difficulties. But the difficulties of other organs are very considerable. In general, the lower the level or authority of the newspaper, the less the effectiveness of its critical material. The Central Committee was well aware of this shortcoming and insisted in many decrees on the necessity for heeding the voice of the public. The decree on the improvement of the *rabselkor* movement, issued in 1958, advised party and state administrative organisations to discuss regularly reports of their organs on measures taken after the press had criticised their work. The decree instructed editors to keep a systematic check on readers' and correspondents' material which could not be published, and to notify their findings to the appropriate party, state or trade union organs.

After a short spell of activity and enthusiasm in 1958–9 the party and government organs again, as in the past, neglected press criticism. The Central Committee therefore had to issue a new decree in September 1962 'On the improvement of the effectiveness of press criticism'.

The decree, as *Sovietskaya pechat* reported[20], deplored the fact that there were many cases where the criticism voiced by the press was not supported by party organs, ministries and authorities in general. There were even cases where the officials of some organisations and some authorities tried to deny the criticism. Also, it often happened that the authorities did not reply to critical reports. Thus *Trud*, the central organ of the trade union movement, in the first six months of 1962 published 218 items criticising shortcomings in the work of trade union and economic organisations and industrial enterprises. But it received only 129 letters announcing what measures had been taken to deal with the complaints. Over 200 officials of party and governmental organisations and construction enterprises did not reply to criticisms in *Stroitelnaya gazeta* (Builders' Gazette); and the newspaper of the transport workers, *Gudok* (The Whistle), waited vainly for replies in seventy-four cases. Far worse was the situation in small regional newspapers. Thus *Priirtyshskaya pravda*, in Kazakhstan, in 1960 sent 800 letters from readers to various offices and organs with a request to reply to criticisms, but only twenty replies were received.

The Central Committee of the CPSU also reproached some newspapers for their unenthusiastic and unsystematic attitude and lack of fighting spirit in enforcing the effectiveness of criticism. It also had some sharp words for those papers which were publishing unfounded, unjust and unverified criticism and were allegedly confounding the need for a bold and insistent criticism with irresponsible exaggeration and sensationalism.

The Central Committee instructed the committees of organisations at the republic, *kray*, *oblast*, district and city levels to ensure that the press should more effectively help in the economic, cultural and social transformation of society. The most important critical reports of the press were to be discussed at committee and plenary meetings of the organisations concerned, and party organs were to make sure that those who tried to suppress criticism should be punished. The editorial collegiums of newspapers and periodicals were instructed to attract more citizens 'for the fight to increase the effectiveness of the public's criticism', to make better use for these purposes of the authors' *aktivs*, worker and peasant correspondents, *rabselkor* posts and non-professional departments.

FINANCING, CIRCULATION, SUBSCRIPTION METHODS

In most communist countries, with the exception of Yugoslavia, Poland and China, newspapers are not run on a

business-like basis. They are considered as purely political
instruments with many specialised tasks other than informing
or entertaining the reader, and as such they are subsidised
from state funds according to decisions of the party.

In an effort to spread newspapers as carriers of propaganda among the masses, their price is kept artificially low. In
Czechoslovakia, for instance, the price is the same as before the
war although production costs have gone up by about 300 per
cent to 400 per cent. Moreover, the central Czechoslovak newspapers today have practically no income from advertising and
their editorial staff, compared with pre-war, is much larger. But
even the provincial or the 'bourgeois' papers which do carry a
varying amount of advertisements, could not be self-supporting.

The party organs control circulation through the allocation of funds and newsprint. In east European countries, for
instance, the papers published by the party have much higher
quotas of newsprint than the papers published by the 'bourgeois'
parties or national fronts. The circulations of the latter are
deliberately kept well below the level of demand so that people
are forced to buy the party papers.

The circulation of the party press is artificially increased
by different methods of subscription-campaign organised by
party organisations. It is more or less obligatory for party
members to subscribe to the organs of the party, be it on the
central, republic or lower level. In the Soviet Union, where there
are no 'bourgeois' papers and the whole press is regarded as
communist, campaigns for subscriptions are conducted regularly, especially at the end of the year. Such campaigns are
a highly political affair in which party, *komsomol* and trade
union organisations participate and help the official organisation, Soyuzpechat (Union Press), in increasing circulation.
Party organisations are now obliged to form 'public councils'
charged with the task of supporting the press in every way. In
such subscription-campaigns groups of agitators visit families
and persuade them to subscribe to several publications.

The elaborate political system of subscription-campaigns
was well illustrated by Moscow *Pravda*. In 1962 it printed under
an agitational headline 'Newspapers and periodicals in every
family' a report from its Leningrad correspondent which said:

The campaign for subscriptions to newspapers and
periodicals for the new year 1963 is in full swing. What

is being done to secure that newspapers and periodicals reach every family? How do the public organisations and the organs of Soyuzpechat participate in this important political work? How do the party organisations direct their efforts? To discuss these questions, a conference of the *aktiv* of party workers, workers of Soyuzpechat, collaborators of the newspapers and periodicals, radio and television from Leningrad and the Leningrad *oblast* was organised in Smolny.

The head of the department of propaganda and agitation of the Leningrad *oblast* committee of the CPSU, S.A. Malinin, gave an address. The following participated in the discussion: B.A. Miloradov, secretary of the Tikhvinsk city committee of the CPSU; M.A. Sedov, chairman of the public council for co-operation in the dissemination of the press, attached to the party committee of the factory organisation in the construction enterprise; M.A. Popov, head of the Lomonosovsky *rayon* department for the dissemination of the press, and others.

Both in the address and in participants' contributions to the discussion, it was emphasised that there were still many shortcomings in the organisation of press subscriptions and distribution. . . . Measures were outlined for improving the propagation of the party press and of technical publications, and for improving the work of party organisations, all communists and *komsomols* in the dissemination of newspapers and periodicals.[21]

Apart from this effective political support, the circulation of the party press is also kept artificially high by the practice of government offices, industrial and other economic enterprises, institutes, and party, youth and trade union organisations subscribing to very large numbers of copies of certain publications. The above mentioned report in *Pravda* criticised one enterprise in Leningrad which was buying in bulk 400 copies of the periodical 'The Construction Sites of Russia'. If the vast number of agitational institutions, *agitpunkts*, 'red corners' and reading rooms in factories and villages is added, it becomes clear that a very considerable part of printed copies are not bought by ordinary readers.

The fight against such 'official' subscriptions, as they are called, is now widespread. *Sovietskaya pechat* stressed in

an article[22] on the problems of newspaper distribution that in
1962 'measures were taken to decrease "official" and to increase
individual subscriptions. Thus a large quantity of copies of
newspapers and journals were saved for individual subscription.'

The same article also gave a detailed picture of the methods
applied in the subscription-campaigns. It said that Soyuzpechat, the official distribution agency, was using about
700,000 'public spreaders' of the press. In 1962 thousands of
new 'points' for subscription were working in the factories
and offices, enterprises, *kolkhozes*, *sovkhozes*, teaching institutions, various state and public organisations, on construction
sites and on large housing estates. 'Public spreaders' had organised canvassing in large housing estates and in the flats in the
older parts of the cities, to acquaint the population with brochures and sample copies. In many cities the campaign was
actively supported by the 'councils for the propagation and
dissemination of the press', created on a public basis.

Soyuzpechat and other publishing houses had prepared
publicity matter for this campaign. Thus Soyuzpechat, alone,
published and distributed over 2 million copies of catalogues,
about 3 million multicolour posters and a large quantity of
other advertising material. The advertising campaign for
subscriptions was also conducted in the central and local
press, on television and radio.

Such a large-scale campaign, in which the participation
of party and *komsomol* organisations and members predominates,
inevitably leads to political and social pressures on the ordinary
citizen, and every year yields better results. According to the
article in *Sovietskaya pechat*, the subscription campaign in
1962 brought in twice as many subscriptions as in 1961. Thus
the figures obtained for *Pravda* and *Izvestia* were respectively
4·4 millions, and 4·3 millions subscriptions; for *Komsomolskaya
pravda* over 3 millions; for *Selskaya zhizn* 2 millions; for the
journal *Politicheskoye samoobrazovanie* (Political Self-Education), 570,000 subscriptions.

In fact, most of the circulation of the press in the Soviet
Union and in other communist countries is sold on the basis of
subscriptions and only a small part of it sold individually in the
streets or news kiosk. The total proportion of copies of all
Soviet newspapers and periodicals sold by subscription was
about 75 per cent in 1961. In the first ten months of the same

year sales of all publications totalled 384·4 million roubles (£150 million or $384·4 million), while direct sales to readers brought in 'a disappointing sum' of only 99·4 million roubles (£38 million or $99·4 million). The rest, 285 million roubles (£112 million or $285 million), came from subscriptions.[23]

The reliance on the subscription system, though it has undoubtedly many economic advantages, proves to be in some respects a brake on the better distribution of the papers. The reason is the inefficient bureaucratic system of the distributing organisation, Soyuzpechat. It has been frequently criticised in the press, yet its bureaucratic ways have not changed. An article in the Soviet journalists' review complained in 1961 that if the offices of Soyuzpechat take a subscription, say, on the 5 June, daily, delivery does not start until 15 August. Subscribers, well knowing its bureaucratic ways, demanded the delivery at least from the 15 July. But the workers of the organisation replied that thirty-five days would not be enough for the transaction of all the office work involved, and justified themselves with the simple statement: 'Such is our method of work.' The same applies to direct sales; if a citizen wants to buy his paper regularly at a kiosk or papershop in the street, he has to place the order in May in order to get his paper from July onwards.[24]

The amount of paper work involved in the subscription procedure may be seen from the fact that the organisation 'improved' its work, without any visible results, by changes in order forms which saved more than ten tons of paper a year. But these ten tons—a review article remarked dryly—give only a very feeble notion of the masses of paper in which the offices of all levels concerned with subscriptions are inundated.

Increased circulation of newspapers and periodicals in the Soviet Union and other communist countries is also hampered by chronic and acute shortage of printing paper in general and newsprint in particular. In the Soviet Union, improvements are planned so that, compared with 1958, production of paper should increase by 260 per cent in 1965 and of newsprint by 270 per cent and thus reach the level of one million tons a year.[25] Large new plants are being built in Siberia and many existing plants are being radically reconstructed.

But in 1963 the newsprint supply was still lagging far behind demand and the printing industry was complaining of irregular supplies and varying quality. One day the central newspapers, including *Pravda*, appear on good quality, smooth paper, and the following day on the worst possible quality newsprint which makes printing, and especially the reproduction of photographs, a nightmare.

Yet despite all these difficulties the total circulation of newspapers and periodicals in the Soviet Union is rising. The circulation is still far from saturation point and very much below the level of other industrially developed countries. With the spread of education and changes for the better in the press after 1956, hunger for the printed word is conspicuous. Compared with 1956, the one-issue circulation of newspapers increased by 15 million copies in 1961 and that of periodicals by 20·5 millions.[26]

The circulation of the Soviet press is bound to grow for some time even without political and social pressures. There is great scope for increase in the number of publications of general interest, magazines, and also of specialised periodicals. The central party press is apparently near its maximum circulation and any future growth can only be small compared with the rise in the last ten or twenty years. Soviet readers seem now to turn more and more to the non-party daily press which is more vivid, less verbose and nearer to life. The quick and successful establishment of *Sovietskaya Rossia* as a very popular daily with over 2 million circulation, and the rapid growth of *Izvestia* which (as subscription figures suggest), in 1963 almost equalled *Pravda's* circulation, are a clear pointer in this direction.

The growth of some representative publications is shown in the following comparison of circulations in 1940, 1956 and 1961:[27]

	1940	1956	1961
	(in millions of copies)		
Pravda	2.0	5.4	6.0
Izvestia	1.6	1.6	4.1
Ogonyok	0.3	1.0	1.8
Rabotnica	0.4	1.2	2.5
Krestyanka	0.3	0.8	2.2
Krokodil	0.3	0.7	1.5

The scope for considerable expansion of magazine circulations is suggested by the fact that for 1963 it was planned to print 4 million copies of *Rabotnica* and 3·2 million of *Krestyanka* per issue.

However great in absolute figures the rise in the circulation of Soviet newspapers may appear, a comparison of statistics for the circulation of daily newspapers and consumption of newsprint in relation to the size of population in the Soviet Union and east European countries and in the leading countries of the world shows convincingly the backwardness of the former and the long way they have yet to go to reach world standards.

NUMBER OF COPIES OF DAILY NEWSPAPERS PER 1,000 POPULATION

East Germany	456	United Kingdom	506
Czechoslovakia	269	Sweden	477
Bulgaria	200	Iceland	450
USSR	181	Luxembourg	445
Rumania	161	Bermuda	419
Hungary	152	Japan	416
Yugoslavia	66	Norway	384
Albania	47	New Zealand	383

Figures are for 1961 with the exception of East Germany (1959), Albania (1960), Luxembourg (1960). For the USA the figure in 1960 was 326 per 1,000.

CONSUMPTION OF NEWSPRINT PER CAPITA IN KILOGRAMMES

Hungary	4.8	USA	36.3
East Germany	4.4	Australia	34.5
Yugoslavia	2.6	New Zealand	29.7
Czechoslovakia	2.4	Canada	24.5
Rumania	2.3	United Kingdom	24.1
Bulgaria	1.9	Sweden	23.6
USSR	1.7	Finland	21.7
Albania	not available	Switzerland	19.8

Figures are for 1961, except East Germany (1960), USSR (1960) and Sweden (1960).
Both tables are based on *UN Statistical Yearbook*, 1962, published in New York, 1963.

In east European countries the circulation position differs in many aspects from that in the Soviet Union. The party press can maintain its artificially high circulation only by limiting its rivals, the 'non-political' or 'bourgeois' newspapers, and by exerting sales pressure upon the population through its primary organisations.

Experience shows that whenever and wherever the party lost prestige and influence, the circulation of its papers fell considerably while that of others, freed from limitations, rose in the same proportion. In Yugoslavia the circulation of the official communist organ *Borba* went down from 500,000 to 250,000 in the period 1950–5 after the management of the national press had been put on a purely commercial basis. The same happened in Poland in 1956. There *Trybuna ludu* and other party newspapers and magazines suffered heavy losses while many popular papers and magazines, despite largely increased circulations, still could not satisfy demand. The Polish journalistic review *Prasa Polska* revealed that, between December 1956 and May 1957, subscriptions to party papers declined by 51 per cent, from 936,000 to 457,000 copies.[28]

In the short spell of 'liberalisation' in 1955–7 when the local communist parties to some extent lost their control, the circulation of communist publications fell in Czechoslovakia, Rumania and Bulgaria. Subsequently renewed party controls and campaigns for more or less obligatory subscription to the party press not only for party members but also for others who 'want to get ahead', helped to raise the circulation to previous and—with refined methods of social pressure—to higher levels.

The Soviet system of subsidising the press from state funds was modified in satellite countries; party organs have their own publishing houses and from their profits production losses are partially recovered. But even then the press is financially dependent on party and state. This system was changed in many aspects in Yugoslavia and Poland (and also in China).

In Yugoslavia the management of the press was put on a commercial basis by the system of self-administration applied to the press by a law of 1956, though it had been practised for some years previously. The system of state subsidies was not totally abolished but the majority of newspapers now balance their budgets with revenue from circulation and advertising. The need to increase revenue has led to the 'westernisation' of the Yugoslav press both in contents and lay-out. Several papers went further than just printing interesting—sometimes even sensational—stories, cartoon strips, detective and crime stories. They began to introduce prize-competitions. Yet despite all efforts the Yugoslav press is in a bad financial situation. Several publications, especially cultural magazines, had to close in 1959–63 and the large national dailies were suffering substantial financial losses. In 1963 the government was therefore considering the reintroduction of effective state subsidisation of the press.*

* In early February 1964, the Cultural-Educational Council of the Jugoslav Federal Assembly discussed the economic position of newspaper-publishing bodies. It was pointed out that many enterprises would experience great difficulties if they had to continue to work on a commercial basis. Preferential treatment and subsidies, it was argued, should be permanently applied. The circulation of daily newspapers was too small in relation to the population. It was decided that a report on the position of the press should be presented to the Council at its next meeting.

Very similar developments took place in the Polish press after 1956. The party and government, moved more by economic than political considerations, decided to reduce the subsidies to some newspapers and to deny them to others. The result was a very sharp competition for readers, reflected in changed contents (as described in chapter 7) and the introduction of advertising on a scale hitherto unknown in the press modelled on the Soviet example.

ADVERTISING

Up to 1953, and even as late as 1956, advertising—except for classified advertisements of a personal character in some east European newspapers—was almost non-existent in the communist press. The official attitude to it was negative; it was maintained that advertising was 'parasitic', 'non-productive', and that it was a characteristic phenomenon of decadent capitalist society.

Since 1956 a slow but persistent change in this attitude has been noticeable throughout the Soviet bloc. This is the result, on the one side of a general improvement in the production and supply of goods which have sometimes even to seek buyers and the need to attract visitors to cultural events, and, on the other side, of the greater adaptation of communist society and its economic life to the ways and levels of western countries. Advertisements now appear more often and in (relatively) larger extent. Thus revenue from advertising is becoming a constant, though still a small, part of the budget of a large section of the press.

As advertising slowly took a permanent place in communist society, efforts were made to find its 'social justification'. Illustrative of the new approach was an article in the Polish journalistic review *Prasa Polska* which—at that time—still had to defend advertising against the 'remnants of stalinist thinking'. It said:

> Following the downfall of false timidity concerning advertising in the years of 'petrified speech', arguments in favour of healthy good sense are once again being heard, and the newspaper advertisement is regaining its citizenship rights. . . . One may defend the opinion that a good advertisement has much of the propaganda element in it and there-

fore is a natural enough part of journalists' professional activities. . . . Particularly in our type of planned economy . . . the advertisement does away with the role played by the host of greedy agents and second-hand dealers. Their fees have now ceased to burden the price of advertised merchandise.[29]

At the end of 1957, for the first time, an All-Socialist Advertising Conference was held in Prague which fully endorsed and justified advertising by declaring that it is necessary both for the consumer and trade, that it is a service which speeds up the sale of goods and thus increases the turnover of capital, informs consumers of new and more economic products and of their quality, increases the efficiency of distribution and lowers its costs and in this way benefits the consumer.

With the development of advertising, special monopolistic state advertising agencies were established in all communist countries. They are concerned with the design and placing of display advertisements in the press (also on television and radio in some countries). The post of the advertising manager in communist newspapers, due to the over-riding role of these agencies, has not the same significance as in the western press, and is hardly more than a clerical job.

In the Soviet Union, the press of the 1920s, and especially during the NEP period, carried advertisements and private notices about births, marriages, losses of articles and the like. Publishing houses had special agents to solicit advertisements from trade organisations. With the arrival of the First Five-Year Plan, its emphasis on heavy industry and the resulting scarcity of consumer goods, trade organisations lost interest in advertising and it disappeared from the press. Classified advertisements and private notices continued for a time; in the early 'thirties the secret police (GPU) began to suspect that they might be used by groups of 'class enemies' for communication, and they were therefore suppressed completely.

After 1956, and more markedly after 1958-9, when the supply of some goods such as watches, radio sets, canned food etc. improved and in some areas even exceeded demand, advertisements began to appear in the provincial press and also in some newspapers at republic level. The advertisements, still published irregularly and at long intervals, were mostly straightforward announcements of sales, state lotteries, films, theatrical plays, concerts, exhibitions and sporting events. They were dull, old-fashioned in copy and layout, of very poor typographical style, without eye-appeal. The central Soviet newspapers still do not carry advertisements and even in the provincial press revenue from advertising is negligible.*

In east European countries with higher living and press standards and with old traditions still well ingrained, advertising is becoming a constant feature of certain types of newspapers and is improving in effectiveness and in graphic quality. Prominent in this respect are Poland and particularly Czechoslovakia, with the highest living standards and more consumer goods than anywhere else in the communist orbit. Hungary, with its new liberalising tendencies and rapidly improving supply of consumer goods, and East Germany are paying greater attention to advertising. Some display advertisements are comparable in technique and style with western advertising. (Advertising films, especially in Czechoslovakia, are of high quality.) The tendency towards improved graphic design is, however, confined mainly to magazines. In provincial newspapers the advertisements are usually presented with little imagination, and are lumped together in unsightly pages or half-pages. Classified announcements inserted by individuals still take the greater part of the space reserved for advertising.

The extent of advertising in the press of various east European countries was partially dealt with in previous chapters

* Better understanding and greater consideration is shown towards advertising in technical and commercial journals which regularly print a relatively large number of advertisements, many from foreign firms. Advertising by foreign firms in such Soviet journals is officially encouraged both for its revenue in valued foreign currencies and because of the need to bring to the technical staff in factories the latest knowledge of machinery and products from the west.

Foreign advertising in the Soviet press is handled by a special agency, Vneshtorgizdat (Foreign Trade Publishing House). In 1963 it had, according to a statement by its chairman, A. V. Vasiliev, a staff of 1,212 employed in writing advertisement copy for 150 all-union specialised technical and trade journals with a combined circulation of over 6 million and for ten newspapers with a circulation over 2·5 million copies, for radio and television in Moscow and other cities. It also organises 'public relations' for foreign customers.

The growing interest of communist countries in advertising and contacts with foreign advertisers was also shown in May 1963 when the Soviet Union, Poland and Czechoslovakia for the first time sent observers to the International Advertising Association's world congress in Stockholm.

in a different connection. A brief survey by countries will complete the picture and bring their different attitudes to the fore.

In Poland, the press is—apart from Yugoslavia—well ahead of all other communist countries in the allocation of space to commercial and personal advertising. In the popular daily *Życie Warszawy* advertisements occupy an average of 30 per cent and in the two evening papers, *Express wieczorny* and *Kurier Polski*, 25 per cent of the column space. Provincial papers and magazines carry advertisements over about 15–20 per cent of their space. Even the party organ *Trybuna ludu* prints them, though only on about 3–5 per cent of its space; among them are display advertisements and many of a personal character: announcements of death, condolences, etc. For some newspapers advertisement-revenue is an important element in their finances, but still small in comparison with revenue from subscriptions and direct sales.

In Yugoslavia, where, even more than in Poland, the press is self-supporting, almost all newspapers and magazines print advertisements; their extent varies from 10–25 per cent of their space according to the type of newspaper. It must, however, be pointed out that the Yugoslav press has on average twice as many pages as the other east European press, and thus revenue from advertising is of much greater importance in its budget.

In East Germany the practice in 1963 did not differ much from the findings of the *Infratest* research quoted on p. 106. The amount of advertising varies from 3–4 per cent in the central party organ *Neues Deutschland* or youth paper *Junge Welt*, to 25 per cent in the 'bourgeois' papers.

In Czechoslovakia, press advertising is less widespread and is irregular. Some provincial newspapers give on occasions up to 15 per cent, usually about 8–10 per cent, and some magazines about 5 per cent, of their columns to advertising. 'Bourgeois' newspapers allocate about 10–12 per cent of their space to advertisements, mostly personal classified announcements; but display advertisements have been increasing since 1963.

In Hungary, classified advertisements also usually outnumber display advertising in the daily press where they fill one or two pages. Weeklies and magazines carry varying quantities of display advertisements. The party organ *Népszabadság* prints a relatively high amount of both classified and display advertisements—on average 10 per cent of its space, more on Sundays; other central newspapers 15 per cent. Surprisingly, the evening

Q

newspaper *Esti Hírlap* prints fewer advertisements than other newspapers, which is in contrast to the general practice in communist countries.

In Rumania, Bulgaria and Albania, advertising in the press is negligible or non-existent, due to lower economic development and the scarcity of consumer goods. The Bulgarian evening paper *Vecherni novini* is an exception with 5–10 per cent space allocated to advertisements.

In general, advertising—like neon lights, trade fairs and various other means of sales promotion—is regarded today in industrially and culturally more advanced communist countries as necessary both for trade and consumer. With the increasing volume of production and widening variety of consumer goods and with the enlarged newspapers which may come in the next years, advertising will undoubtedly increase and influence the present system of financing the press.

JOURNALISTS IN THE COMMUNIST SOCIETY

THE OLD SOVIET SLOGAN of the 'thirties: 'The cadres are the all-decisive force', certainly applies in its fullest sense to the work of the communist press. 'Cadres' are those who possess high political and class consciousness, understand the political line of the party, accept it as their own, are able to put it into practice and are capable of answering for it, defending it and fighting for it, and able to align themselves correctly in any situation.

These, indeed, are the qualities which the communist party requires from its journalists as leading propagandists. It cannot, as Khrushchev said, 'put the press in unreliable hands. It must be in the hands of the most faithful, most trustworthy, most politically steadfast people devoted to its cause.'[1]

The party reserves for itself, therefore, the right to appoint the staff of newspapers and periodicals. The rules of the Communist Party of the Soviet Union contained up to 1961 paragraphs explicitly stating this right. Thus the rules approved at the Nineteenth Congress in 1952 and confirmed again by the Twentieth Congress in 1956 said in paragraph 36 that the Central Committee nominates the editorial staff of the central organs working under its control, and approves the appointment of the editorial staff of party organs in large local organisations. Paragraph 43 stipulated the same for the editorial staff of newspapers and periodicals working under the control of the republic, *kray* and *oblast* committees, and paragraph 51 for *rayon* and city papers.[2]

The latest rules approved by the Twenty-second Congress in October 1961 do not explicitly stipulate such procedure, but only state that the Central Committee of the all-union party and other committees at all lower levels direct and control the work of newspapers and periodicals in their sphere. The practice of appointing the staff by the party organs has, however, been retained without any change.

To maintain the closest links between the party and its press, the editors-in-chief of party organs are usually members of the corresponding committees. Thus *Pravda*'s editor-in-chief is a member of the Central Committee of the CPSU; the editor of a republic organ is a member of the republic's party committee and so on. The system, which has been in operation since 1930 and was sanctioned formally by a decision of the Central Committee in 1937, proves very effective in transmitting policy decisions of the committees to their newspapers and maintaining control over them. The editors-in-chief have to submit regular reports on the work of their papers to the committees. These in turn discuss the report and give instructions about further work. The system of nominating editors-in-chief to the executive bodies has later been applied also to the press of trade unions and other public organisations.

The party approaches the problem of selecting suitable candidates for journalism and their training from the same political aspect. From the 'twenties up to the 'fifties, the Soviet communist party preferred to recruit prospective journalists from among those with 'working class' background, that is from worker and poor farmer families, all too often at the expense of educational and professional qualifications. In the 'twenties the stress on working class background led to numerous allocations to party journalistic courses of illiterate people who had first to be taught to read and write.

East European communist countries were pursuing a similar policy in the late 'forties and early 'fifties. In Czechoslovakia and East Germany, for instance, the parties tried, in 1948–51, to replace the old 'bourgeois' journalists with 'workers' cadres' who were 'delegated' by party organisations to the staffs of newspapers, or selected by the editors from worker correspondents. The whole campaign was a failure and only a very few worker correspondents were retained. After the establishment of journalistic institutes and faculties at the universities, students from worker and farmer families had a quota of up to 60–70 per cent. But it was never filled and thus the communist parties had reluctantly to admit students of 'bourgeois' or middle class origin.

THE TRAINING OF JOURNALISTS

The communists always regarded the journalistic profession as a political function, a party assignment, and this was reflected also in their approach to the training of journalists. From the earliest days of its rule, the Soviet communist party took their training into its own hands, shaped it to its propagandist and agitational needs and filled the curriculum with the necessary ideology and party decisions, tossing practical aspects of journalism aside as unnecessary 'bourgeois' technicality.

Already in 1919, during the civil war, the party organised short courses in journalism and attached them to Agit-Rosta. In 1921 the Moscow Institute of Journalism was established. Its task was to prepare journalists selected from among the worker and peasant correspondents. By the end of 1923 the Institute was reorganised into a higher school (of university level) with three-year and later four-year courses. At that time the party began also to found numerous 'newspaper technical schools' and short courses for future journalists. It also paid greater attention to the preparation of worker and peasant correspondents among the non-Russian nationalities for permanent work on newspapers. Journalistic sections were established at the Communist Workers' University of the Far East (KUTV), at the Communist University of the Peoples of the Western Territories (KUNZ), and at other higher schools.

In November 1930 the Central Committee of the then All-Union Communist Party (of bolsheviks), VKP(b), issued an important decree 'On the cadres of journalistic workers'. On its instructions a new network of communist institutes of journalism was established at *kray* and *oblast* communist universities. Evening institutes for journalism were organised in many cities. The students of the Institute of Red Professorship (Institut Krasnoy Professury) in Moscow, and also students of the Moscow and Leningrad Institutes of Journalism could—after submission of theses—obtain academic degrees in journalism. Besides this, short courses were also organised for the improvement of the qualifications of editors and other leading newspapermen.

During the war years 1941-5, the training of journalists was concentrated mainly in the central journalistic course, attached to the all-union Central Committee, and in short-term courses organised by the committees in the republics, *krays* and *oblasts*. After the war, the network of journalistic schools and courses was re-established. The High Party School (university level) attached to the Central Committee of the VKP(b), the party schools in republics and large *oblasts*, and also the Central Komsomol School had all established journalistic departments to train new journalists and to improve the qualifications of older journalists by refresher courses.[3]

As can be seen from this short review, the communist party concentrated in its hands the education of journalists, especially of 'leading cadres', editors-in-chief, editors and heads of departments, who usually went through courses organised directly by the Central Committee. All the above mentioned 'universities' and 'institutes' were party institutions where the stress was always on marxism-leninism and party policy documents. Training in professional skill was, after the late 'twenties, more and more neglected, to the detriment of Soviet journalism.

This basic attitude to the training of journalists, which concentrated exclusively on theory to the neglect of practice, remained unchanged in the Soviet Union throughout the 'thirties and 'forties. A. Kotlyar, who was working in the 'twenties on the staff of several Soviet newspapers and in the 'thirties was lecturing on western literature at the Ukrainian Institute of Journalism, describes the system in the following way:

> In the 'twenties instruction in journalism still consisted, apart from the study of marxism-leninism, to a considerable extent of analysing and classifying various methods of the craft of journalism. Despite some shortcomings at least it gave the grounding of a good working knowledge of journalism. Since the 'thirties this approach to the teaching of journalism was considered a formalist heresy, a deviation into 'bourgeois technicalities'. According to the new theory, the journalist had, first of all, to know what to write about, not how to write. For if he knew the former, the latter would take care of itself. ... Elucidation of journalism was reduced to restating Lenin's pronouncements on the press, and later also Stalin's statement that the press is the instrument with the help of which the party maintains constant contact with the masses. This was presented as the 'science of the press'. Practical journalistic training and the study of various forms of journalistic expression hardly found a place in the curriculum, 95 per cent of which was taken up by marxism-leninism-stalinism.[4]

From 1946 onwards, the training of journalists was conducted by universities of ordinary type in many cities such as Leningrad, Kiev, Minsk, Lvov, Sverdlovsk, Riga, Tashkent and Alma-Ata, usually in departments or under chairs attached to philological or philosophical faculties. Moscow University established a special faculty of journalism in 1952. Universities and party institutes of all kinds, which are still continuing their activities, were turning out journalists on a comparatively large scale. From Moscow University 1,765 journalists graduated in the years 1952–61, and in 1962 there were altogether 8,000 persons working in the press who had graduated from some type of high journalistic school.[5]

But even the introduction of journalistic education to universities did not alter the fact that professional preparation was of a very low standard. Theory of marxism-leninism, history of the communist party and of the workers' movement, political and economic decisions of the congresses and central committees still take up the greater part of the teaching program. The remainder of the program is still 'divorced from practice' as was pointed out in a critical article in *Sovietskaya pechat* in 1962, which analysed the shortcomings of the instruction of journalism at Soviet universities.[6]

The article did not deal, of course, with the ideological contents of the curriculum. But it pointed out that the shortcomings in practical training stem from the fact that the Ministry of Special Education insists that the education of journalists must be based on philological foundations. This leads to overcrowding the curriculum with too many philological lectures unnecessary to journalists, such as 'Introduction to the science of linguistics', 'Contemporary Russian language with elements of the theory and history of language', 'History of the Russian literary language', 'Practical stylistics of the Russian language', and so on.

The staff of journalistic chairs or faculties, deans and lecturers, are almost without exception people who have no journalistic experience. They insist that the faculties should give the students general education and not 'narrow' professional specialisation. The students cannot, therefore, in their five years of study gain any practical preparation and experience since they are not even permitted to participate in the production of 'study newspapers' published by the faculties or chairs of journalism. The only time they can learn anything of the practical side of journalism is during their practice in the editorial offices of local newspapers during vacations after the third and fourth year.

A detailed picture of the curriculum of a typical communist journalistic faculty or chair can be seen in the example of Bucharest University. The university had a faculty of journalism modelled entirely on the Moscow University faculty. Due to low standards and lack of lecturers, the faculty was incorporated in 1956 into the philosophical faculty as an independent chair. The curriculum was taken over from Moscow University, the only change being the substitution of the word 'Rumanian' for 'Russian' when necessary. It provides the following lectures:

Political economy	Theory and practice of
Dialectical materialism	journalism
Logic	Typographic technology
History of philosophy	Rumanian language
Geography	Russian language
General history	One foreign language
Rumanian history	History of Rumanian
Marxist esthetics	literature
History of art	History of world literature
History of the Soviet	History of Russian and
press	Soviet literature

The curriculum also included: organisational foundations of Rumanian industry; agriculture; culture; and physical training. The student could choose one specialised subject from: news reporting; economics of publishing; international relations; radio broadcasting.[7]

In some communist countries the Soviet model was not followed so blindly. The ideological basis of journalistic training and its preponderance in the curriculum was retained, but more attention was given to the practical side. In East Germany, for instance, an Institute for Publicistics and Press Science was opened at Leipzig University in 1951, changing in 1954 into the Faculty for Journalism and Press Science. The course originally took three years, later it was extended to five years. The curriculum is divided into four main groups, namely:

1   Social sciences (marxism-leninism and its application to social sciences)
2   The science of publicistics and journalism
3   One specialised subject according to student's choice
4   Languages: German, Russian and another foreign language for those specialising in foreign affairs.

The students spend much more time than their Soviet colleagues working in printing plants and in editorial offices to acquire the necessary technical skill. In 1955 the faculty also opened a separate department for radio journalism.

The Institute tried to enroll mainly students of working class background, but without much success and students from 'bourgeois' families had to be admitted. Even in 1952, when efforts to attract 'workers' cadres' were greatest, the 'bourgeois' students formed the majority, and since then their proportion has been increasing. The profession of journalism, with its total political subservience to the party, became so discredited in East Germany that the Institute and later the faculty could not find enough students to fill its planned quota of 270 students each year.[8]

The same position also arose in the Soviet Union where the status of journalist was very low during the stalinist period. Since then the situation has somewhat improved but in 1961 and 1962 *Sovietskaya pechat* was still complaining that too few able students were enrolling outside Moscow. Very often students 'who were refused access to other faculties and who looked down at the journalist's profession' chose the study of journalism as a last resort, and the faculties, in order to fill their quotas, accepted them without testing their qualifications or interest.

A different situation arose in Poland. There the status of journalism has been high since 1945. The names of many journalists were well known throughout the country, and the voice of the press in general was in the years 1945–9, and again after 1955, strong enough to exercise influence. Journalists were the leading force in the political ferment and changes of 1955–7. Furthermore the profession offered such attractions as high salaries and, above all, the much coveted chance of travelling abroad.

In such circumstances, the department of journalism at Warsaw University—the only institution providing journalistic education in Poland—was always flooded with applications. Usually about 1,500 students from the high schools applied for enrolment but only a small number could be accepted: in 1953 about 185, in 1954, 175. The planners in the years 1950–3 grossly overestimated the potential increase in demand for graduates of journalism and thus the intake of new students had to be gradually reduced after 1954, while in 1957–9 no new students were admitted because there were no vacancies for the former graduates and because at that time the government was cutting down subsidies and many publications were closing due to financial difficulties.

But this development was not without its beneficial result. Students were very carefully selected in a series of written and oral examinations lasting almost two weeks. Demands on students during their study years were more exacting, and thus the level of young journalists in general is today much higher in Poland than in any other communist country.

Until 1955 the curriculum closely followed the Soviet pattern; then the stress on practical training became much greater. A Polish journalist described study in the journalistic department thus: during the first year, students attend seminars on the theory and practice of journalism where the different forms of journalistic expression are explained; the students have to write letters to the editor, describe accidents, street scenes, student life, and learn the technique of interviewing.

In the second year students are asked to write more sophisticated items such as book or film reviews, commentaries on current events and reports of important meetings. In the third year the student chooses his specialist course and accordingly selects his final thesis. He also decides on the form of journalistic expression that suits him best: rural or industrial reportage, news commentary, book, film or theatre review, or feuilleton. Practical training is supported throughout his studies by many specialised seminars conducted by leading Polish journalists from the newspapers, news agency and radio.

Each year the student spends one month working on the staff of a newspaper. Freshmen are sent to small provincial newspapers and radio stations. They do only simple jobs: proof-reading, sub-editing readers' letters, preparing simple agency news items for press, etc. In the second practice period, a student will start to work at the news desk, and gather news on his own. The third stage gives him opportunities to show his ability in reporting and writing on assignments for different sections of the newspaper.[9]

In the Soviet Union and in most other communist countries students of journalism are, after graduation, assigned posts to newspapers according to the plan of a special commission. Salaries of journalists are fixed by the government after consultation with the union of journalists. There are several grades in the pay scale, usually four or five. The basic salary in the highest grade is generally twice as high as that for the lowest; the latter is slightly over the national average of industrial wages. Journalists receive, however, on top of the basic salary special bonuses according to the number and quality of written or published articles. But even with bonuses the salary of a journalist, whether in the Soviet Union or elsewhere, is hardly ever more than twice as high than the lowest grade or average industrial wage, and only a very few journalists earn that much. Salaries of editors and editors-in-chief are outside the scale and can be higher than the salaries in the top grade with bonuses. Soviet journalists on central (Moscow) newspapers are better paid than in other east European countries.

An important role in the continuous ideological education of journalists is played by the unions. In east European countries the unions of journalists were used from the very beginning in the fight against the 'class enemy' among the journalists; they organised purges of the adversaries of communism or politically 'indifferent' journalists, and also initiated courses for the ideological reorientation and re-education of those former 'bourgeois' journalists who were retained. They 'fight' constantly against so-called 'mere-journalism', that is, the tendency to regard journalism only as a profession or trade and not as a party assignment. The journals of the unions are fully used for this purpose; they contain articles discussing all aspects of journalistic work from the ideological standpoint.

The unions are, without exception, subordinated to the propaganda departments of the Central Committee which directs their work. Their subordination to the party's political aims and their political and ideological tasks are explicitly stated in the rules or resolutions adopted as guidance for their work.

The rules of the Union of the Soviet Journalists state, for instance, that its aims are:

1 To encourage the maximum participation of Soviet journalists in the mobilisation of the workers in their determined struggle for the victory of communism in the USSR.
2 To raise the ideological standards and professional skills of Soviet journalists.
3 To train journalists in a spirit of loyalty to the country and to the communist party.[10]

The Journalists' Union in East Germany, according to a resolution adopted at one of its plenary meetings, 'has eminently important tasks to fulfil in the fight for peace, for the broadening of the National Front of Democratic Germany, for the democratic construction of the German Democratic Republic'. The resolution further said that the union has '. . . the duty to uphold the cleanliness and dignity of the German democratic press, and to fight energetically against the ideas and influences of Americanism and cosmopolitanism. This includes also the protection of the democratic press from spies, foreign agents and bribable "mere-journalists".'[11]

The Union of Czechoslovak Journalists has the same ideological and political tasks and its rules oblige it to improve constantly the ideological level of its members. The union does not conceal the fact that it is subordinated to and directly supervised by party organs; on the contrary, it is proud of the fact and admits it publicly. Acting in the spirit of its rules the union, in 1962, took measures to increase the political consciousness of its members. Editorial boards of newspapers and periodicals, as well as the Czechoslovak News Agency, the Czechoslovak Radio and Television Corporations, have worked out a survey of the educational background and activities of journalists. The following items were inquired into: social origin, school background, linguistic knowledge, length of employment in the press, and public activities in mass organisations and outside the editorial offices in general. The survey embraced 2,984 journalists out of the total number of 3,400 in the country.

The statistical data were then discussed in commissions and at a meeting of the central committee of the union. The meeting drew several conclusions about the education of journalists: every journalist should display deep communist consciousness and possess political experience and a profound general knowledge, as well as the required journalist qualifications and professional skill in his particular field, and finally he should be sufficiently trained in newspaper style.

The committee did not hide its dissatisfaction with the low level of political consciousness of Czechoslovak journalists and their political inertia or unwillingness to take up political and lecturing propagandist functions in mass organisations. It therefore ordered a campaign to improve the general level of 'journalistic cadres'. It stated in an adopted resolution that journalists 'should be given the opportunity constantly to educate themselves'. Individual study controlled by editorial boards should be the main way towards this aim. Educational plans and courses should be launched for this purpose. Newspapermen from the provincial press should be guided in the campaign by the Journalists' Union under the direct supervision of communist party organs.[12]

JOURNALISTS AND THE LIMITATIONS OF THE COMMUNIST PRESS

The whole press system with its thorough ideological indoctrination of journalists, its clearly stipulated methods of writing and reacting to events both great and small, has one objective: to teach the journalist that he must express, not his own views, but only the party policy. The journalist is taught to adapt himself so that his words are always in line with the will of the party.

But do the communist journalists accept this interpretation of their profession today as they did before 1953 or 1956?

The deep ideological and social upheavals which the communist movement has been undergoing in the last ten years; new currents of thinking and ferment among the intellectuals, and the discrediting of communist propaganda after the popular uprisings and riots in East Germany, Poland and Hungary; the unilateral resumption of nuclear tests by the Soviet Union and its Cuban adventure in brinkmanship—these things have, without doubt, affected journalists.

The old attitude of the communist party to the press before 1953 proved ineffective. The grey, uniform, uninspiring press of the Soviet Union and of the new communist countries had little influence and was discredited in the eyes of the masses. Journalists themselves lost courage and initiative, and instead of conducting active, inspiring propaganda, they just repeated official slogans and safe phrases. Fear of deviation or of disapproval by high party officials suppressed all originality and all freshness of approach to real problems of society. The prestige and status of journalism sank low.

The new leadership in the Soviet Union has been trying since Stalin's death to improve the situation in the press and especially to increase the prestige of journalism. N. S. Khrushchev on many occasions has extolled the role of journalists, stressing that they occupy a 'place of honour in the great cause of building communism', and that they are 'faithful helpers' and 'the most faithful transmission belt' of the party. Five leading Soviet journalists have been nominated by the party as candidates and elected as deputies of the Supreme Soviet of the USSR. Some of them have been awarded the highest Soviet order. *Pravda* and *Izvestia* have introduced a new phenomenon in the press: the so-called independent political commentators who are said to have complete freedom to express their own opinions on international political matters. Editors-in-chief have been given, compared with the pre-1953 period, considerable freedom to introduce new forms of journalistic expression and change the face of their newspapers.

Yet neither in the printed opinions of the 'independent commentators' nor in the newspapers of the 'freed' editors can the observer see any signs of independence or freedom from the official party line. Certainly there is more freedom for the press than there was in Stalin's days to discuss aspects of contemporary cultural, social and economic life. But partly free discussion is still possible only in cases where the official policy is still fluid, and not yet decided by the leaders themselves, or within the narrow margin of liberty permitted and tolerated by the leadership as a stimulus or safety valve. Thus all the new 'freedoms' granted by the communist regime to journalists are only marginal. They do not touch the core of real freedom of the press.

But even after these small changes the question must be asked: Do the communist journalists want to be only 'faithful transmission belts', instruments and passive servants of the party? Or do they want to serve their people and not the party or its leadership when the latter's policies are in conflict with the national interest, as was so often the case in the past and may be today?

Among Soviet journalists, there is, as yet, no sign of changed attitudes. Their initiative has been suppressed by the rigid system of party supervision and direction to such an extent that they had to be pushed, as we have seen, even into the small, politically safe, technical changes and marginal liberties offered by the party itself in its drive to increase the effectiveness of the press. Soviet journalists are no rebels yet, only faithful servants of the party. The ferment through which certain sections of Soviet artists, poets and writers have been going since the Twenty-second Congress, has not yet reached the editorial offices of newspapers and magazines, except the few literary ones. And even there it has only slightly rippled the surface.

But in east European countries the desire for truth, freedom from party dictate, and for real improvement of the press is strong. Not only journalists in rebellious Hungary and Poland, but lately also in Czechoslovakia, regarded as the most 'stalinist' stronghold, now defend more and more persistently the theory that the press has a social responsibility to reflect truthfully and to shape actively and positively public opinion and the development of society. Though proclaiming their faith in, and allegiance to, the cause of communism, they are demanding the right to discharge their newly discovered social responsibility in their own way, to probe into the past, to learn from it, and to act in future only according to their conscience, and not to follow blindly the instructions of the authorities.

It is difficult to estimate how widely such views are spread among communist journalists since they only rarely reach the pages of newspapers or magazines. But their existence is confirmed by renewed and strong attacks by the party, published at the end of 1962 and in 1963 in many east European reviews, against the influences of 'bourgeois conceptions' of the press. Any new ideological or political upheavals are bound to bring to the fore such tendencies, as was shown again in Czechoslovakia during 1963.

In Hungary, the desire for truth and freedom of the press was openly proclaimed in 1956. The executive committee of the Federation of Hungarian Journalists, headed by communists, adopted a resolution on 6 October, saying: 'We will never in future permit the press to abandon its role of defending truth by becoming an instrument for slandering and prosecuting innocent people.'[13]

The committee also decided to convene a general assembly on 28 October with a view to standing up against 'the system which hitherto has been based upon lies' and to 'take account of this crime committed against the people'.[14] But the revolution which broke out several days before that date prevented discussion of the motion.

Arrests and long prison or even death sentences passed on journalists, as well as exclusion of some 150 Hungarian journalists from their federation and thus from their profession, could not suppress such tendencies, which are still noticeable beneath the apparently quiet surface calmed by the officially conducted 'liberalisation'.

An unsigned editorial in the Hungarian party's central

organ, *Népszabadság*, on 8 December 1963 sharply attacked two provincial literary journals for 'their harmful petty-bourgeois views'. *Alföld*, the monthly literary review published in Debrecen, and *Jelenkor* (the Present Time), published in Pécs, were both accused of voicing 'hostile and harmful' opinions. According to the party daily, several articles, studies and critical pieces appeared in the two magazines that were at obvious variance with marxism-leninism, with the tenets of marxist aesthetics and with the party line and its ideological pronouncements. *Népszabadság* asserted that these articles were not simply mistakes of well-intentioned ignorance. Many of the articles in the papers criticised were trying to 'subject marxism to a bourgeois revision' and proclaim a bourgeois ideology. The editorial demanded to know why the editors published such reprehensible material in the first place, and why they did not at least challenge such harmful views.

Alföld was found especially guilty in that its editors had already been warned several times. As for *Jelenkor*, its editors were charged with accepting poems and short stories which had been turned down elsewhere. 'These are warning symptoms', *Népszabadság* says, 'pointing to the erroneous views which crop up among intellectuals, in artistic life as well as in other fields'.[15]

In Rumania, the newspaper *Informatia Bucurestiului* was severely reprimanded by the party leadership in January 1964 for publishing 'pro-western pronouncements' and 'unchecked' news which conflict with the party policy. Two of the paper's editors were dismissed.

Even in Bulgaria—the most quiet communist country—some journalists are trying to express their independent views. Such journalists were reprimanded in May 1963 at the congress of the Journalists' Union by Mitko Grigorov, a member of the Politburo. He charged them with 'deviating' from socialist ideology and 'making compromises with bourgeois ideology', and complained that 'ideological life' in the editorial offices was very low.

The same tendencies are noticeable also in the Polish press. According to a statement made by the head of the party's press department, Artur Starewicz, in July 1963 the press of Poland is still infected by 'the remnants of false views on the role of the press, which should allegedly be independent and whose main mission should allegedly consist not in the shaping of public opinion [i.e., according to the official image—Author], but in "reflecting it", and in exerting pressure on the government.'[16]

In Czechoslovakia, the demands both for truth and for independence from the party or from the discredited party leadership were made openly by leading communist journalists during 1963. The already mentioned congresses of journalists and writers in Prague and Bratislava provided a suitable platform. One of the rebellious communist journalists, Miro Hysko, spoke for all of them when he declared:

> The most urgent struggle for us today is to gain the right to express and publish correct, i.e. marxist-leninist views, even if they clash with the subjective views of even (high) official functionaries. . . . If a journalist cannot fulfil his duty towards the deceived public, the shame and responsibility for this falls on those who prevent him from doing so. . . . In the present struggle against the consequences of the cult of personality, the issue is not merely the period of the infamous political trials, but also the period after the Twentieth CPSU Congress. And what is involved is not only the responsibility for the continuation of the methods of the cult of personality. . . . The damage done by us through our journalistic activity at that time consists in our having helped to create an atmosphere of distrust and suspicion and in our having killed every endeavour for the assertion of sound judgment, thus preparing the ground for the suppression of fundamental civil rights, as well as for reprisals against many courageous people, communists and non-communists alike. . . .[17]

This attitude was widely held among Czechoslovak journalists. Antonín Novotný, the First Secretary of the Communist Party and President of the Republic, who initiated a counterattack by the party apparatus, admitted that there were journalists 'who would like, in the name of some cultural and journalistic freedom, to deny the leading role of the communist party and who do not recognise this formative principle in the life of our socialist society. Some individuals in various articles even belittle the principles and organisation of the socialist state, society and communist party.'[18]

Experiences of the last ten years thus clearly show that communist journalists, despite careful selection and ideological training, at certain critical times make a stand not only against

R

the policies of the communist party, but even against the party itself, against the communist system and ideology.

The desire of journalists for a truthful, independent and effective press thus comes into direct conflict with the party and its leadership. The conflict is, however, much deeper than even the rebellious communist journalists realise. The party can make concessions only in marginal, harmless areas of press activities. It cannot afford to relax its control and direction because this would lead inevitably to inquiries, first into connections between the present leadership and past crimes or 'mistakes', then into the role of the party, and finally it would lay open to question the whole political and ideological system of communism. As Lenin stated forty-five years ago, granting full freedom to journalists would mean committing suicide. And for the same reason Khrushchev declared in discussion with writers and artists in March 1963 that press, literature and the arts cannot be free, either now, in the transition period, or in communism itself.

The attitude creates an insoluble contradiction for the communist regime. How can journalists, fettered by ideological training and orthodoxy, by the necessity to adhere to the rigid official propaganda line and a policy which is too often in collision with the views and interests of the people, display truly persuasive and convincing powers?

Defects and weaknesses of the communist press are inherent in its system. By insisting on the subordination of the press to the dictate of the party, on the priority of ideological and economic propaganda, on the uniform treatment of all aspects of life, on the subjugation of the journalist's mind to rigid doctrine, the communist regime deprives itself of the many-sided, human, inconspicuous and therefore truly effective ways of influencing the masses.

The pernicious effects of such enslavement of the human mind and the press were aptly described by Karl Marx himself when, as a liberally minded young man in 1843, he attacked the Prussian press censorship. At that time he could not, of course, realise that his theories and doctrines would be used to create the very prototype of such enslaved press as he described. Relevant passages from his two articles on this subject[19] make a fitting conclusion to our book:

You admire the charming variety, the inexhaustible riches

of nature. You do not demand from the rose that it should have the same scent as the violet. But the richest thing in the world, the human mind, must only be allowed to exist in one kind. I am humorous, but the law prescribes that I should write seriously. I am bold, but the law commands that my style should be unassuming. The greyest of grey is the only permitted colour of freedom. Every dewdrop, into which the sun shines, glistens with an inexhaustible play of colours. But the intellectual sun, in however many individuals and objects it is reflected, must be allowed to produce only the official colour.

The censored press has a demoralising effect. The archvice, hypocrisy, is inseparable from it, and from this, its basic vice, stem all its other weaknesses which indeed lack any disposition to virtue, its vices of passivity which even from an esthetic standpoint are detestable. The government only hears its own voice, knows that it only hears its own voice, yet acts under the illusion that it hears the voice of the people, and demands from the people to accept this illusion as true. So the people for their part sink partly into political superstitution, partly into political disbelief or withdraw completely from civic life and become a rabble interested only in its own affairs.

Since the people must look upon free writings as illegal, they get used to consider what is illegal as free, freedom as illegal, and what is legal as unfree. Thus the censorship kills civic spirit.

APPENDICES

I

NEWS AGENCIES IN EAST EUROPEAN COUNTRIES AND THE SOVIET UNION

ADN   *Allgemeiner Deutscher Nachrichtendienst* (General German News Service): official news agency of the German Democratic Republic. Founded 1946.

APN   *Agentstvo pechati Novosti* (Press Agency Novosti/News/), generally known as Novosti. Founded in 1961 as an unofficial agency intended to provide information, features and pictures on Soviet life.

Agerpres   *Agentie de informatii telegrafice* (Telegraph Information Agency): official news agency of Rumania. Founded 1949; generally known under its logotype or as Rumanian News Agency.

ATA   *Agjensia telegrafike Shqipetare* (ATS: Albanian Telegraph Agency): official news agency of Albania. Founded 1945; its logotype ATA, used internationally, is derived from the initials of its French name *Agence Télégraphique Albanaise.*

BTA   *Bulgarska telegrafna agentsia* (Bulgarian Telegraph Agency): official news agency of Bulgaria. Founded 1898.

ČTK   *Československá tisková kancelář* (Czechoslovak Press Bureau), known also as CETEKA: official news agency of Czechoslovakia. Founded 1918.

MTI   *Magyar távirati iroda* (Hungarian Telegraph Bureau): official news agency of Hungary. Founded 1881.

PAP   *Polska agencia prasowa* (Polish Press Agency): official news agency of Poland. Founded 1944.

Tanyug   *Telegrafska agencija Nova Jugoslavia* (Telegraph Agency New Yugoslavia): official news agency of Yugoslavia. Founded 1943.

TASS   *Telegrafnoye agentstvo Sovietskovo Soyuza* (Telegraph Agency of the Soviet Union): official news agency of the USSR and also of the Russian Federal Republic. Founded 1925.

News agencies of the Soviet Union Republics:

Armentag—Armenia	Kirtag—Kirghizia
Aztag—Azerbaidzhan	Leta—Latvia
Belta—Byelorussia	Moldtag—Moldavia
Eta—Estonia	Tadzhikta—Tadzhikistan
Elta—Lithuania	Turkmentag—Turkmenistan
Gruztag—Georgia	Ratau—Ukraina
Kaztag—Kazakstan	Uztag—Uzbekistan

II

NEWSPAPERS AND PERIODICALS IN EAST EUROPEAN COUNTRIES AND THE SOVIET UNION

The lists below give a selection of the most important and best known newspapers and periodicals in each country. The circulation figures, where they could be obtained, refer mostly to the period 1961–2

ALBANIA

Population (1960): 1,625,000

All newspapers and periodicals cited here are published in Tirana.

I NEWSPAPERS

Bashqimi (Unity): daily; organ of the Democratic Front. Founded 1943.

Puna (Labour): weekly; organ of the Central Council of the Trade Unions. Founded 1945.

Zeri i Popullit (People's Voice): daily; organ of the Central Committee of the Labour (Communist) Party. Circulation: 55,000. Founded 1942.

Zeri i Rinisë (The Voice of Youth): twice weekly; organ of the Central Committee of the Youth Union. Founded 1945.

II PERIODICALS

Drita (The Light): literary and artistic journal; organ of the Union of Artists and Writers. Founded 1960.

10 *Korriku* (10th July): weekly; published by the Ministry of Defence for the Armed Forces. Founded 1946.

Ekonomia Popullore (People's Economy): economic monthly; published by the State Planning Commission. Founded 1954.

Hosteni (Goad): satirical and humorous journal; published by the Union of Journalists.

Kultura Popullore (People's Culture): cultural monthly review; published by the Ministry of Culture and Education. Founded 1958.

Letërsia Jonë (Our Literature): literary monthly review; published by the Union of Artists and Writers.

Luftëtari (The Warrior): journal for the Armed Forces; published by the Ministry of Defence. Founded 1945.

Nëndori (November): literary quarterly review printing new short stories, essays, poems, etc.; published by the Union of Artists and Writers. Founded 1954.

BULGARIA

Population (1961): 8,000,000

All newspapers and periodicals cited here are published in Sofia.

I NEWSPAPERS

Kooperativno selo (The Co-operative Village): daily; published by the Ministry of Agriculture. Circulation: 100,000.

Naroden sport (People's Sport): published every second day.

Narodna armiya (People's Army): daily paper for the armed forces; published by the Ministry of Defence. Founded 1944.

Narodna mladezh (People's Youth): daily paper for young people; published by the Central Committee of the Dimitrov Communist Youth Union. Circulation: 200,000. Founded 1948.

Otechestven front (Fatherland Front): daily; organ of the Presidium and National Council of the Fatherland Front. Circulation: 200,000. Founded 1942.

Rabotnichesko delo (Workers' Cause): daily; organ of the Central Committee of the Bulgarian Communist Party. Circulation: 500,000. Founded 1947.

Trud (Labour): daily; organ of the Central Council of the Trade Unions. Circulation: 130,000. Founded 1946.

Vecherni novini (Evening Gazette): popular daily for the population of Sofia; published by the City Committee of the CP. Circulation: 110,000. Founded 1951.

Zemedelsko zname (Agrarian Banner): daily; organ of the Agrarian People's Party. Circulation: 125,000.

II PERIODICALS

Bulgarski zhurnalist (Bulgarian Journalist): monthly journalistic review; published by the Union of Journalists.

Ikonomicheska misal (Economic Thought): monthly economic journal. Circulation: 3,000.

Iskustvo (The Arts): monthly review for culture and arts; published by the Ministry of Culture and Union of Painters. Circulation: 3,000. Founded 1949.

Literaturen front (Literary Front): weekly for literature, arts and politics; published by the Union of Writers.

Literaturna misal (Literary Thought): bi-monthly review for literary-criticism and history; organ of the Institute for Bulgarian Literature at the Academy of Sciences. Circulation: 7,000.

Literaturni novini (Literary Gazette): journal for literature; published fortnightly.

Narodna kultura (People's Culture): weekly journal for culture; published by the Ministry of Culture. Circulation: 42,000.

Novo vreme (New Times): monthly theoretical organ of the Central Committee of the CP. Circulation: 25,000.

Partien zhivot (Party Life): journal for party activists, dealing with practical, organisational and theoretical party problems; published twice monthly by the Central Committee of the CP.

Plamak (Flame): monthly review for literature and arts; published by the Union of Writers. Circulation: 15,000.

Sturshel (Gadfly): satirical and humorous weekly.

Zhenata dnes (Woman of Today): monthly illustrated magazine; published by the Committee of Bulgarian Women. Circulation: 310,000.

CZECHOSLOVAKIA
Population (1961): 13,776,000

All newspapers and periodicals cited here are published in Prague, except for the Slovak publications which are published in Bratislava.

I NEWSPAPERS

Československý sport (Czechoslovak Sport): popular sport newspaper; published five times a week by the Organisation for Physical Culture.

Lidová demokracie (People's Democracy): daily central organ of the People's Party. Circulation: 130,000. Founded 1945.

Mladá fronta (The Young Front): daily organ of the Czechoslovak Youth Organisation. Circulation: 250,000. Founded 1945.

L'ud (The People): daily central organ of the Slovak Revival Party; it deals especially with agricultural problems.

Práca (Labour): daily central organ (in Slovak) of the Revolutionary Trade Union Movement. Circulation: 125,000.

Práce (Labour): daily central organ (in Czech) of the Revolutionary Trade Union Movement. Circulation: 250,000. Founded 1945.

Pravda (Truth): daily central organ of the Slovak Communist Party. Circulation: 267,000. Founded 1920.

Smena (Shift): daily organ of the Slovak section of the Czechoslovak Youth Organisation. Circulation: 120,000. Founded 1947.

Svobodné slovo (The Free Word): daily central organ of the Socialist Party. Circulation: 134,000. Founded 1907.

Rudé právo (The Red Right): daily central organ of the Central Committee of the Communist Party. Circulation: 1 million. Founded 1920.

Večerní Praha (Evening Prague): popular evening paper published by the City Committee of the Communist Party in Prague. Circulation: 120,000.

Večerník (Evening Paper): popular evening paper published by the City Committee of the Slovak Communist Party in Bratislava.

II PERIODICALS

Československý novinář (Czechoslovak Journalist): monthly organ of the Union of Journalists. Founded 1949.

Dikobraz (The Porcupine): satirical illustrated weekly.

Hospodářské noviny (The Economic Gazette): weekly paper on economic and technical problems.

Host do domu (Guest in the House): monthly review for literature, arts and literary criticism.

Katolické noviny (Catholic Gazette): popular religious paper for catholics; published by the governmental Office for Religious Affairs.

Kulturní tvorba (Cultural Creation): weekly paper for cultural, artistic and political problems. Founded 1963.

Kultúrny život (Cultural Life): cultural and political weekly paper; Organ of the Slovak Union of Writers.

Květy (Flowers): popular illustrated weekly magazine; published by the Central Committee of the Communist Party. Circulation: 140,000.

Literární noviny (Literary Gazette): weekly cultural-political organ of the Czechoslovak Union of Writers. Circulation: 125,000.

Nová mysl (New Mind): theoretical monthly organ of the Central Committee of the Communist Party for ideological, philosophical and social problems. Circulation: 80,000.

Novinářský sborník (Journalistic Review): quarterly theoretical journal dealing with journalistic problems 'from the marxist-leninist aspect'; published by the Union of Journalists.

Plamen (The Flame): literary monthly journal presenting essays, short stories, poems, literary criticism; published by the Union of Writers. Founded 1959.

Roháč (Stag-Beetle): illustrated satirical and humorous Slovak weekly; published in Bratislava.

Sloboda (Freedom): weekly organ of the Freedom Party (in Slovakia) dealing with general political and economic problems; published in Bratislava.

Slovenka (Slovak Woman): popular illustrated weekly for women; published in Bratislava.

Svět v obrazech (The World in Pictures): illustrated weekly magazine. Circulation: 80,000. Founded 1945.

Vlasta: illustrated popular weekly magazine; published by the Committee of Czechoslovak Women. Circulation: 545,000.

GERMAN DEMOCRATIC REPUBLIC

Population (1961): 17,079,000

All newspapers and periodicals cited here are published in East Berlin, unless otherwise stated. Circulation figures are for 1960.

I NEWSPAPERS

Bauern-Echo (Farmers' Echo): daily; organ of the German Democratic Farmers' Party. Circulation: 150,000.

Berliner Zeitung (Berlin Gazette): 'independent' daily. Circulation: 500,000. Founded 1945.

Bz am Abend (Bz in the Evening): evening edition of the *Berliner Zeitung.*

Deutsches Sportecho (German Sport Echo): popular general sport newspaper; published three times weekly.

Junge Welt (The Young World): daily; organ of the Central Council of the Free German Youth Organisation.

Der Morgen (The Morning): daily; organ of the German Liberal Democratic Party. Circulation: 50,000. Founded 1945.

National-Zeitung (National Gazette): daily; organ of the National Democratic Party. Circulation: 50,000.

Neue Zeit (New Times): daily; organ of the Christian Democratic Union. Circulation: 50,000.

Neues Deutschland (New Germany): daily; organ of the Central Committee of the (Communist) SED Party. Circulation: 800,000. Founded 1945.

Tribüne (Tribune): daily; organ of the Central Council of the Trade Unions.

Die Volksarmee (The People's Army): paper for the Armed Forces; published three times weekly by the Ministry of Defence.

In some provincial towns the district committees of the SED publish mass circulation dailies, for example: *Leipziger Volkszeitung* (Leipzig People's Newspaper) in Leipzig (350,000); *Freiheit* (Freedom) in Halle (360,000); *Ostsee-Zeitung* in Rostock (260,000).

II PERIODICALS

Deutsche Aussenpolitik (German Foreign Policy): monthly review for international affairs.

Einheit (Unity): theoretical monthly of the Central Committee of the SED for ideological, philosophical and social problems.

Eulenspiegel: satirical and humorous illustrated weekly.

Frau von heute (Woman of Today): illustrated weekly magazine for women.

Freie Welt (Free World): large illustrated weekly magazine.

Neue Deutsche Literatur (New German Literature): monthly literary review.

Neue Deutsche Presse (New German Press): monthly organ of the Union of Journalists dealing with journalistic problems.

Neue Berliner Illustrierte (New Berlin Illustrated): popular illustrated weekly magazine. Founded 1946.

Neuer Weg (New Way): journal for practical problems of party life; published twice monthly for party activists by the Central Committee of the SED.

Sinn und Form (Content and Form): bi-monthly review for literature and arts.

Sonntag (Sunday): popular entertainment weekly paper.

Die Weltbühne (The World Scene): weekly journal for politics, economics, arts, literature and culture. Founded 1904.

Die Wirtschaft (Economy): weekly journal for economic, technical and political problems.

Wochenpost (Weekly Post): popular illustrated weekly.

Zeit im Bild (Time in Pictures): illustrated weekly magazine.

HUNGARY

Population (1961): 10,065,000

All newspapers and periodicals cited here are published in Budapest.

I NEWSPAPERS

Esti Hírlap (Evening Newspaper): popular evening newspaper. Circulation: 120,000.

Hétföi Hirek (Monday News): general newspaper published on Mondays when other newspapers do not appear.

Magyar Honvéd (Hungarian Fatherland Defender): daily for the Armed Forces; published by the Ministry of Defence.

Magyar Ifjuság (Hungarian Youth): weekly paper for the young people; published by the Socialist Union of Youth.

Magyar Nemzet (Hungarian Nation): daily; organ of the People's Patriotic Front. Circulation: 80,000.

Népsport (People's Sport): popular sport newspaper, five times weekly.

Népszabadság (People's Freedom): daily; organ of the Central Committee of the Hungarian Socialist Workers' (Communist) Party. Founded 1942. Circulation: 650,000.

Népszava (People's Word): daily; organ of the Trade Union Movement. Founded 1872. Circulation: 200,000.

II PERIODICALS

Élet is Irodalom (Life and Literature): weekly journal for literature and politics.

Élet is Tudomány (Life and Science): popular weekly science magazine. Circulation: 180,000.

Figyelö (Observer): economic weekly.

Film, Színház, Muzsika (Film, Theatre, Music): weekly journal for cultural, artistic, film, theatre and musical interests.

Képes Ujság (Illustrated Newspaper): popular weekly magazine.

Közgazdasági Szemle (Economic Review): monthly economic review; published by the Institute of Economics.

Ludas Matyi (Matyi the Gooseboy): satirical and humorous weekly.

Nemzetközi Szemle (International Review): monthly international affairs review.

Nök Lapja (Women's Paper): popular illustrated weekly magazine.

Társadalmi Szemle (Social Review): monthly journal for political, ideological and social problems; published by the Central Committee of the Hungarian Socialist Workers (Communist Party).

POLAND
Population (1961): 30,133,000

All newspapers and periodicals cited here are, unless otherwise stated, published in Warsaw.

I NEWSPAPERS

Dziennik ludowy (People's Daily): daily; organ of the United Peasant Party.

Express ilustrowany (Illustrated Express): popular afternoon newspaper.

Express wieczorny (Evening Express): popular evening paper. Circulation: 500,000. Founded 1946.

Glos pracy (Labour's Voice): daily; organ of the Central Council of the Trade Unions. Circulation: 50,000. Founded 1951.

Gromada-Rolnik Polski (Community-Polish Farmer): three times weekly; popular newspaper for the rural population. Circulation: 600,000. Founded 1947.

Kurier Polski (Polish Courier): daily; organ of the Democratic Party. Circulation: 150,000. Founded 1957.

Slowo powszechne (General Word): daily; published by the pro-communist catholic organisation *Pax*. Circulation: 100,000. Founded 1947.

Sport: popular sport newspaper; published in Katowice three times weekly. Circulation: 140,000.

Sztandar mlodych (The Banner of the Youth): daily paper for young people; organ of the Socialist Youth Union. Circulation: 100,000. Founded 1951.

Trybuna ludu (People's Tribune): daily; organ of the Central Committee of the Polish United Workers' (Communist) Party. Circulation: 210,000. Founded 1948.

Żolnierz wolności (Soldier of Freedom): daily newspaper for the Armed Forces; published by the Ministry of Defence. Circulation: 57,000. Founded 1950.

Życie Warszawy (Warsaw Life): popular 'independent' daily newspaper. Circulation: 300,000. Founded 1944.

In addition to central newspapers, there are also in Poland numerous and in many cases large daily newspapers in provincial cities like Bydgoścz, Gdansk, Kraków, Lodź, and Wroclaw with circulations ranging from 100,000 to 350,000. Largest of these papers is *Trybuna robotnicza* (Workers' Tribune) in Katowice with a circulation of some 350,000.

II PERIODICALS

Dookola świata (Around the World): popular illustrated weekly magazine; published by the Socialist Youth Union. Circulation: 250,000.

Film: illustrated weekly film magazine. Circulation 180,000.

Karuzela: humorous and satirical magazine; published twice weekly in Lodz. In 1957 it had a circulation of 350,000.

Kierunki (Trends): weekly of the 'progressive' catholic movement for cultural and social problems. Founded 1956.

Kobieta i życie (Woman and Life): popular illustrated weekly magazine for women. Circulation: 550,000. Founded 1946.

Kulisy (Scene): popular Sunday newspaper. Circulation: 260,000.

Kultura (Culture): political-cultural weekly. Founded 1963 replacing two previous 'revisionist' or independent cultural weeklies: *Nowa kultura* (New Culture) and *Przeglad kulturalny* (Cultural Review).

Nowa wieś (New Village): illustrated weekly magazine for young readers. Circulation: 260,000.

Nowe drogi (New Ways): theoretical and political monthly organ of the Central Committee of the Polish United Workers' (Communist) Party. Founded 1947.

Panorama: popular illustrated weekly magazine for Silesia. Published in Katowice. Circulation: 355,000.

Polityka (Politics): political-cultural weekly. Founded 1947.

Prasa Polska (Polish Press): monthly review for journalistic problems; published by the Union of Journalists.

Przekrój (Cross-section): popular illustrated weekly magazine. Circulation: 450,000. Founded 1945.

Przyjaciólka (Friend): popular illustrated women's weekly magazine. Circulation: 1,990,000. Founded 1948.

Radar: illustrated popular monthly magazine for youth.

Świat (World): general illustrated weekly magazine. Circulation: 200,000.

Szpilki (Beans): satirical and humorous weekly. Circulation: 105,000.

Twórczość (Creativity): literary monthly.

Tygodnik powszechny (General Weekly): weekly for catholic intelligentsia; published in Cracow by the catholic authorities.

Więź (Link): political-cultural monthly published by the Catholic Intelligentsia Club.

Znak (Sign): political-cultural monthly journal for catholic intelligentsia.

Życie gospodarcze (Economic Life): general economic weekly journal. Circulation: 17,000.

Życie literackie (Literary Life): weekly for culture, literature, arts and politics. Circulation: 15,000.

Życie partii (Party Life): monthly journal for practical problems of party life; published for the party activists by the Central Committee of the Polish United Workers' (Communist) Party.

RUMANIA

Population (1961): 18,566,000

All newspapers and periodicals cited here are, unless otherwise stated, published in Bucharest.

I NEWSPAPERS

Agricultura noua (The New Agriculture): newspaper for the rural population; published by the Ministry of Agriculture twice weekly.

Aparare patriei (Fatherland's Wings): daily newspaper for the Armed Forces; published by the Ministry of Defence. Founded 1945.

Informatia Bucurestiului (Bucharest Information): daily evening newspaper; published by the City Committee of the Rumanian Workers' Party (Communist) and Bucharest People's Council. Founded 1952.

Munca (Labour): daily; organ of the Central Council of Trade Unions.

Rominia libera (Free Rumania): daily; organ of the People's Councils (Government).

Scinteia (The Spark): daily; organ of the Central Committee of the Rumanian Workers' Party (Communist). Circulation 1 million.

Scinteia tineretului (The Youth Spark): daily; organ of the Union of Working Youth.

Sportul popular (People's Sport): popular sport newspaper published four times weekly.

Steagul rosu (The Red Flag): daily organ of the Bucharest Region Committee of the Rumanian Workers' Party (Communist) and of the People's Council of the Bucharest Region.

II PERIODICALS

Contemporanul (The Contemporary): political, cultural and social weekly paper.

Femeia (Woman): monthly journal for women.

Flacara (The Flame): illustrated weekly literary and arts review.

Gazeta literara (Literary Gazette): weekly journal on literary and cultural problems; published by the Union of Writers.

Luceafarul (The Evening Star): bi-weekly review for literature, arts and literary crticicism.

Lupta de clasa (Class Struggle): theoretical and political monthly organ of the Central Committee of the Rumanian Workers' Party (Communist).

Presa noastra (Our Press): monthly journalistic review; published by the Union of Journalists.

Viaia militara (Military Life): illustrated monthly review for soldiers; published by the Ministry of Defence.

Viaia romineasca (Rumanian Life): monthly review for literature and literary criticism; organ of the Union of Writers.

Urzica (The Stinging Nettle): satirical and humorous bi-weekly.

SOVIET UNION
Population (1961): 219,745,000

All central newspapers and periodicals cited here are published in Moscow, unless otherwise stated.

I UNION AND RUSSIAN FEDERAL REPUBLIC NEWSPAPERS

Gudok (Whistle): daily paper for the railwaymen; published jointly by the Ministry of Transport and Union of Railwaymen. Founded 1918.

Ekonomicheskaya gazeta (Economic Gazette): daily paper for economic, industrial and technical problems. Circulation: 300,000.

Izvestia (News); full title: *Izvestia sovietov deputatov trudyashchikhsa SSSR* (News of the Councils of Workers' Deputies of the USSR): daily; organ of the Government. Circulation: 4,100,000. Founded 1917.

Komsomolskaya pravda (Komsomol Truth): daily paper for young people; organ of the Central Council of the Lenin Communist Youth Union. Circulation: 3,350,000. Founded 1925.

Krasnaya zvezda (Red Star): daily paper for the Armed Forces; published by the Ministry of Defence. Founded 1925.

Literaturnaya gazeta (Literary Gazette): literary newspaper; published three times weekly by the Union of Writers. Circulation: 620,000.

Pionierskaya pravda (Pioneer Truth): newspaper for children; published by the Komsomol organisation twice weekly. Circulation: 4,050,000.

Pravda (Truth): daily; organ of the Central Committee of the CPSU. Founded 1912. Circulation: 6,000,000.

Selskaya zhizn (Rural Life): daily; published by the party for the rural population. Circulation: 900,000.

Sovietskaya Rossiya (Soviet Russia): daily newspaper for the Russian Federal Republic. Circulation: 2,000,000. Founded 1956.

Sovietskaya kultura (Soviet Culture): cultural paper; published three times weekly by the Ministry of Culture and Union of Cultural Workers.

Sovietsky flot (Soviet Navy): paper for the Navy; published by the Ministry of Defence.

Sovietsky sport (Soviet Sport): daily; published by the governmental Committee for Sport. Circulation: 850,000.

Stroitelnaya gazeta (Builders' Gazette): newspaper for workers in the construction industry; published three times weekly by the governmental Committee for Construction.

Trud (Labour): daily; published by the Central Council of the Trade Unions. Circulation: 1,540,000. Founded 1921.

Uchitelskaya gazeta (Teachers' Gazette): newspaper for the teachers; published three times weekly by the Ministry of Education and Union of Teachers. Circulation: 600,000.

Vechernaya Moskva (Evening Moscow): evening newspaper for Moscow. Circulation: 350,000.

II PERIODICALS

Agitator: journal for the party agitators; published by the Central Committee of the CPSU twice monthly. Circulation: 500,000.

Don (The River Don): literary monthly.

Iskustvo (Arts): artistic monthly.

Kommunist: theoretical organ of the Central Committee of the CPSU; eighteen issues a year. Circulation: 500,000.

Komsomolskaya zhizn (Komsomol Life): theoretical journal of the Komsomol organisation; published twice monthly.

Krestyanka (The Peasant Woman): monthly illustrated magazine for rural women. Circulation: 2,200,000.

Krokodil (Crocodile): satirical and humorous journal; published every ten days. Circulation: 1,500,000.

Mezhdunarodnaya zhizn (International Life): monthly review of international affairs.

Nash sovremennik (Our Contemporary): literary bi-monthly. Founded 1963.

Nedelya (Week): weekly magazine edition of *Izvestia*.

Neva (The River Neva): literary monthly; published in Leningrad.

Novoye vremya (New Times): journal for international affairs; published weekly (also in numerous foreign languages).

Novy mir (New World): literary monthly; published by *Pravda*.

Ogonyok (Small Fire): illustrated weekly magazine. Circulation: 1,800,000.

Oktyabr (October): literary monthly.

Partiynaya zhizn (Party Life): journal on theoretical and organisational problems of party life; published twice monthly for party activists by the Central Committee of the CPSU. Circulation: 500,000.

Politicheskoye samoobrazovanie (Political Self-Education): monthly journal for political, ideological and economic questions. Circulation: 600,000.

Problemy mira i socializma (Problems of Peace and Socialism): joint monthly theoretical organ of communist countries. English edition appears under the title *Marxist Review*.

Rabotnica (Woman Worker): illustrated monthly magazine for women. Circulation: 2,500,000.

Rasprostrannenie pechati (Dissemination of the Press): monthly journal for the workers of Soyuzpechat, the organisation for the distribution and dissemination of the press.

Sovietskaya pechat (Soviet Press): monthly review on journalism; published by the Union of Journalists.

Za rubezhom (Abroad): weekly journal of international affairs.

Znamya (Banner): literary monthly.

Zvezda (Star): literary monthly.

III OFFICIAL NEWSPAPERS OF THE UNION REPUBLICS

Official newspapers of the union republics are mostly joint daily organs of the Central Committee of the Communist Party in each republic, the Supreme Soviet and the Council of Ministers. They are published in the local vernacular and in Russian; in the following list, the vernacular publication is cited first.

Armenia:
Sovetakan Aistan (Soviet Armenia)
Kommunist

Azerbaidzhan:
Kommunist
Bakinskiy rabochiy (The Baku Worker)

Byelorussia:
Zvezda (Star)
Sovietskaya Byelorussia (Soviet Byelorussia)

Estonia:
Rahva Hääl (People's Voice)
Sovietskaya Estonia (Soviet Estonia)

Georgia:
Kommunisti
Zarya vostoka (Eastern Dawn)

Kazakhstan:
Socialistik Kazakhstan (Socialist Kazakhstan)
Kazakhstanskaya pravda (Kazakhstan Truth)

Kirghizistan:
Sovietik Kyrgyzstan (Soviet Kirghizstan)
Sovietskaya Kirgizia (Soviet Kirghizstan)

Latvia:
Cina (Fight)
Sovietskaya Latviya (Soviet Latvia)

Lithuania:
Tiesa (Truth)
Sovietskaya Litva (Soviet Lithuania)

Moldavia:
Moldova sochialiste (Socialist Moldavia)
Sovietskaya Moldavia (Soviet Moldavia)

Tadzhikistan:
Sovet Tochikistoni (Soviet Tadzhikistan)
Kommunist Tadzhikistana (Tadzhikistan Communist)

Turkmenistan:
Sovet Turkmenistany (Soviet Turkmenistan)
Turkmenskaya iskra (Turkmen Spark)

Ukraine:
Radyanska Ukraina (Soviet Ukraina)
Pravda Ukrainy (Ukrainian Truth)

Uzbekistan:
Kyzyl Uzbekistan (Red Uzbekistan)
Pravda vostoka (Truth of the East)

S

YUGOSLAVIA

Population (1961): 18,549,000

I NEWSPAPERS

Borba (Fight): official daily; organ of the Socialist Alliance of Working People. Published in the Cyrillic alphabet in Belgrade and in Latin characters in Zagreb. Circulation: 250,000. Founded 1922.

Delo (Cause): daily; published in Ljublijana in Slovenian. Circulation: 80,000.

Dnevnik (Daily): daily newspaper for the province of Vojvodina.

Nova Makedonija (New Macedonia): daily; organ of the Socialist Alliance in Macedonia. Circulation: 28,000.

Oslobodenje (Liberation): daily; organ of the Socialist Alliance in Bosnia and Herzegovina. Circulation: 65,000.

Politika: non-party daily; published in Belgrade. Circulation: 350,000. Founded 1904.

Sport: popular sport daily published in Belgrade. Circulation: 55,000.

Večernje novosti (Evening News): daily; published by *Borba* in Belgrade. Circulation: 150,000.

Vjesnik (Gazette): daily; organ of the Socialist Alliance of Croatia; published in Zagreb.

II PERIODICALS

Danas (Today): literary bi-weekly; published in Belgrade.

Duga (Rainbow): weekly illustrated general magazine; published in Belgrade.

Ekonomska politika (Economic Policy): general economic weekly; published in Belgrade by *Borba*.

Ilustrovana Politika (Politika Illustrated): weekly illustrated review; published by *Politika* in Belgrade.

Komunist: weekly organ of the Central Committee of the League of Communists; published in Belgrade. Circulation: 240,000.

Književne novine (Cultural News): bi-weekly for cultural, artistic and social questions; published in Belgrade.

Medunarodna politika (International Politics): review of international affairs; published twice monthly in Belgrade.

Narodna armija (People's Army): weekly paper for the Armed Forces; published by the Ministry of Defence in Belgrade.

Naša stvarnost (Our Reality): monthly review for social, cultural and political problems; published in Belgrade.

Politikin zabavnik (Politika's Entertainment Magazine): popular illustrated weekly paper with comics; published by *Politika* in Belgrade. Circulation: 170,000.

Praktyčna žena (Practical Woman): popular illustrated journal for women; published twice monthly in Belgrade.

Pregled (Review): monthly review for social and cultural problems; published in Sarajevo (Bosnia and Herzegovina).

Rad (Labour): weekly paper of the Trade Unions; lavishly illustrated; published in Belgrade. Circulation: 110,000.

Svijet (World): weekly illustrated magazine; published in Sarajevo. Circulation: 75,000.

NOTES

Chapter 1   INTRODUCTION: THE PRESS AS A POLITICAL INSTRUMENT

1 Rudolf Herrnstadt, editor-in-chief of the communist organ *Neues Deutschland*, declared at a press conference in East Berlin in 1950: 'Our newspapers are not being published to entertain people or to make a financial profit, but to make political propaganda. They are a political institution which for purposes of efficiency (only) bear the character of newspapers.' Quoted from Richert, Ernst, *Agitation und Propaganda, Ein System der publizistischen Massenführung* (Agitation and Propaganda, A system of Publicist Guidance of the Masses), Berlin, 1958. Later referred to as Richert, E., *Agitation and Propaganda*.

Chapter 2   MARXISM-LENINISM, PROPAGANDA AND THE PRESS

1 *Bolshaya Sovietskaya Entsiklopedia* (The Large Soviet Encyclopedia), Moscow, second edition, vol. 26, 1952, p. 323. Later referred to as LSE.
2 Lenin, *Sochinenia* (Collected Works), Moscow, fourth edition, vol. 5, pp. 41–2. Later referred to as Lenin, *Soch.*
3 Lenin, *Soch.*, vol. 7, p. 383.
4 Stalin, *Sochinenia* (Collected Works), Moscow, vol. 6, p. 114. Later referred to as Stalin, *Soch.*
5 Stalin, *Soch.*, vol. 31, p. 27.
6 *Materially XXII syezda KPSS* (Documents of the Twenty-second Congress of the CPSU), Moscow, 1961; section: Program of the CPSU, pp. 323–428. Later referred to as *Doc. 22nd Cong.*
7 See for example Inkeles, Alex, *Public Opinion in Soviet Russia— A Study in Mass Persuasion*, Cambridge, Mass., 1950, p. 38.
8 *Encyclopaedia Britannica*, London, 1961, vol. 18, pp. 580–3.
9 *Der Grosse Brockhaus*, Wiesbaden, vol. 1, 1952, p. 91.
10 ibid., vol. 9, 1956, p. 417.
11 *Encyclopaedia Americana*, Chicago, vol. 22, 1957, pp. 658–9.
12 LSE, vol. 1, 1952, pp. 292–305, entry *Agitatsia;* vol. 35, 1955, pp. 70–4, entry *Propaganda.*
13 Lenin, *Selected Works*, 2 vols., Moscow, 1953, vol. 1, pp. 273–4.
14 ibid.
15 *Spravochnik sekretarya pervichnoy partiynoy organizatsii* (Handbook for Secretaries of Primary Party Organisation); section: Propaganda. Moscow, 1960.
16 *Lenin o propagande i agitatsii* (Lenin on Propaganda and Agitation), Moscow, 1956, p. 25.
17 Doc. Twenty-second Congress, section: Party Rules, pp. 429–48.
18 ibid.
19 Kalnins, Bruno, *Der sowjetische Propagandastaat* (The Soviet Propaganda State), Stockholm, 1956, pp. 38–9.

Chapter 3   THE FUNCTIONS OF THE COMMUNIST PRESS

1 *Novinářský sborník* (Journalistic Review), Prague, 1957, No. 4, p. 445.
2 Lenin, *Selected Works*, vol. 1, pp. 389–90.
3 Stalin, *Soch.*, vol. 5, p. 204.
4 LSE, vol. 10, 1952, p. 8.
5 *Novinářský sborník*, 1957, No. 4, p. 445.
6 LSE, vol. 5, 1952, p. 515.
7 Stalin, *Soch.*, vol. 11, p. 129.
8 LSE, vol. 5, 1952, p. 532.
9 ibid., p. 533.
10 In November-December 1959 the United Nations Organisation discussed problems of freedom of information. A draft resolution was submitted by journalistic and other interested bodies stating, in the preamble, that news should be accurate, objective and comprehensive.
11 International Press Institute Survey, *The Press in Authoritarian Countries*, Zurich, 1959, p. 21. Later referred to as IPI Survey.

Chapter 4   CHARACTERISTICS OF THE COMMUNIST PRESS

1 See for example LSE, vol. 17, 1952, pp. 326–7, entry *Newspapers*.
2 ibid., vol. 32, 1955, pp. 170–2.
3 Lenin, *Soch.*, vol. 1, pp. 380–1.
4 ibid.
5 ibid., vol. 10, p. 61.
6 *Novinářský sborník*, 1957, No. 4, p. 453.
7 ibid.
8 ibid., p. 454.
9 ibid.
10 LSE, vol. 38, 1955, p. 266.
11 ibid.
12 Lenin, *Soch.*, vol. 28, p. 439.
13 ibid.
14 LSE, entry *Freedom of the Press*, vol. 38, 1955, p. 267.
15 Quoted from IPI Survey, p. 14.
16 ibid., p. 13.

Chapter 5   DIFFERENTIATION IN THE STRUCTURE OF THE PRESS

1 LSE, vol. 5, 1952, p. 7.
2 *VKP (b) v rezolyutsiakh i resheniakh* (The All-Union Communist Party/of Bolsheviks/in resolutions and decisions), Moscow, sixth edition, part I, p. 312.
3 ibid., p. 235.
4 ibid., p. 509.
5 ibid., pp. 509–10.

6 *Sovietskaya pechat* (The Soviet Press), Moscow, 1961, No. 10, pp. 10–23.
7 ibid., 1962, No. 5, pp. 16–18.
8 ibid., 1961, No. 10, pp. 10–23.
9 ibid.
10 ibid., 1962, No. 5, pp. 16–18.
11 *Statistický obzor* (Statistical Horizon), Prague, 1961
12 LSE, vol. 16, 1952, pp. 248–57, entry *Journals*.
13 ibid.
14 ibid.
15 ibid.
16 ibid.
17 ibid.
18 *Sovietskaya pechat*, 1961, No. 10, pp. 10–23.
19 ibid., 1962, No. 5, pp. 16–18.
20 ibid., 1961, No. 10, pp. 10–23.

Chapter 6   DIFFERENTIATION IN THE CONTENTS OF THE SOVIET PRESS

1 Inkeles, A., op. cit., p. 162.
2 ibid.
3 ibid., p. 163.
4 *Novinářský sborník*, 1957, No. 4, pp. 446–7.
5 IPI Survey, p. 15.
6 ibid.
7 N. S. Khrushchev in a speech to Soviet journalists. Quoted from *Sovietskaya pechat dolzhna byt samoy silnoy i samoy boyevoy* (The Soviet Press Must Be the Strongest and Most Militant Instrument), Moscow, 1959, p. 13.

Chapter 7   DIFFERENTIATION IN THE CONTENTS OF THE EAST
                               EUROPEAN PRESS

1 For a detailed account of changes and general developments in the Polish and other east European press see numerous articles in the monthly review *East Europe*, 1955–63, and relevant passages in the IPI Survey.
2 *Trybuna ludu*, Warsaw, 12 July 1963. Quoted from *East Europe*, New York, September 1963, pp. 22–4.
3 IPI Survey, p. 96.
4 The review is based on an article in *Sovietskaya pechat*, 1961, No. 9, pp. 52–4. The article was written by the deputy chief-editor of *Népszabadság* (People's Freedom).
5 ibid.
6 *Lidová demokracie*, Prague, 22 April, 1961.
7 ibid., 17 June, 1962.
8 *Pravda*, Bratislava, 3 June, 1963.

9 *Rudé právo*, Prague, 21 September, 1963.
10 ibid., 23 September, 1963.
11 Details taken from an article, '*Contents Analysis of the Press in the German Republic*' by Viggo Graf Bluecher in *Gazette*, Leyden, 1961, No. 1, pp. 89–107.
12 A comprehensive review of developments in the Yugoslav press is given in IPI Survey, pp. 121–33.
13 Quoted from IPI Survey, p. 129.
14 *Review of International Affairs*, Belgrade, 20 February, 1963.

Chapter 8   DIRECTION AND SUPERVISION OF THE PRESS

1 *Novinářský sborník*, 1957, No. 4, p. 445.
2 *Sovietskaya pechat v dokumentakh* (The Soviet Press in Documents), Moscow, 1961.
3 Kotlyar, A., *Newspapers in the USSR: Recollections and Observations of a Soviet Journalist*, published by Research Program on the USSR, New York City, 1955.
4 ibid., p. 12.
5 ibid., p. 13.
6 Richert, E., *Agitation and Propaganda*.
7 ibid., p. 126.
8 ibid., p. 127.
9 ibid., p. 128.
10 *Novinářský sborník*, 1957, No. 4, p. 448.
11 Bluecher, V. G., op. cit.
12 *Novinářský sborník*, 1957, No. 4, p. 453.

Chapter 9   CENSORSHIP

1 *Times*, London, 1 September, 1962.
2 BUP report quoted by the *Guardian*, London, 1 September, 1962.
3 *Guardian*, London, 11 October, 1962.
4 IPI Survey, pp. 75–6.
5 *Sunday Times*, London, 2 December, 1962.
6 *Times*, London, 26 October, 1962.
7 Gayev, A., *Tsenzura sovietskoy pechati* (Censorship of the Soviet Press), published by the Institute for the Study of History and Culture of the USSR, Munich, 1955.
8 IPI Survey, pp. 36–7.
9 *Journalism Quarterly*, Iowa City, Summer 1961.
10 IPI Survey, p. 106.
11 ibid., p. 107.
12 ibid., pp. 107–8.
13 ibid., p. 108.
14 ibid.

15 *Prasa Polska* (The Polish Press), Warsaw, March 1961. Quoted from *East Europe*, 1961, No. 9, p. 23.
16 ibid.
17 *Novinářský sborník*, 1962, No. 3.

Chapter 10   THE IMAGE OF LIFE IN THE COMMUNIST PRESS
1 Kotlyar, A., op cit., p. 63.
2 *Public Opinion Quarterly*, Princeton, Spring 1947; Dallin, Alexander, 'America through Soviet Eyes', pp. 26–39.
3 ibid., Davison, W. Phillips, 'An Analysis of the Soviet Controlled Press', pp. 40–57.
4 ibid.
5 Bluecher, V. G., op. cit.
6 ibid.
7 ibid.
8 Richert, E., *Agitation and Propaganda*, pp. 129–30.

Chapter 11   THE COMMUNIST CONCEPT OF NEWS
1 *Novinářský sborník*, 1957, No. 4, p. 451.
2 *Sovietskaya pechat*, 1958, No. 9, pp. 42–6.
3 Quoted from *Novinářský sborník*, 1957, No. 4, p. 448.
4 ibid.
5 IPI Survey, p. 23.
6 Palgunov, N. G., *Osnovy informatsii v gazetakh*; *TASS i yevo rol* (Principles of Information in the Newspapers; TASS and its Role), Moscow, 1955, passim. Later referred to as Palgunov, Tass.
7 ibid., passim.
8 *Novinářský sborník*, 1957, No. 4, p. 457.
9 IPI Survey, pp. 23–4.
10 *Rudé právo*, Prague, 16 November, 1960.
11 Quoted from *East Europe*, 1960, No. 2, p. 33.
12 *Presa Noastra* (Our Press), Bucharest, May–June, 1958. Quoted from *East Europe*, 1960, No. 2, p. 33.
13 Quoted from Paul, H. W., *Propaganda in the East German Democratic Republic: The Development of Means and the Apparatus*, in *Gazette*, Leyden, 1959, No. 1, pp. 57–86.
14 ibid.
15 ibid.
16 IPI Survey, p. 102.
17 ibid., pp. 102–3.
18 *New York Times*, 19 February, 1963.
19 IPI Survey, p. 75.
20 *Novinářský sborník*, 1957, No. 4, p. 450.
21 ibid.
22 *Literární noviny* (Literary Gazette), Prague, 19 June, 1963.

Chapter 12   THE COMMUNIST NEWS AGENCY
Information in this chapter on the Soviet agency TASS is based,
unless otherwise stated, either on the author's personal knowledge
of the agency's work, or on Palgunov's *Tass and its role*. Information
about the Czechoslovak News Agency is based on the author's
personal knowledge of its affairs.
A detailed study of the Soviet agency's operations is contained in
The Two Faces of TASS by T. E. Kruglak, Minneapolis, 1962.

1 Article 'Principles of News Broadcasts' in *Novinářský sborník*,
  1957, No. 4, p. 481.
2 *Novy mir*, 1958, No. 8. Quoted from *East Europe*, 1959, No. 2,
  p. 45.
3 *Sovietskaya pechat*, 1961, No. 1, p. 36.
4 ibid., No. 3, pp. 49–52.
5 ibid., No. 7, p. 29.
6 Quoted from *East Europe*, 1958, No. 11, p. 29.
7 *Communist Propaganda Around the World: Apparatus and
  Activities*, US Information Agency, Washington, 1962, passim.
8 *Sovietskaya pechat*, 1963, No. 6, pp. 26–9.

Chapter 13   HOW THE COMMUNIST NEWSPAPERS WORK

1 Vacík, Miloš, 'In Czech and Slovak', *Sovietskaya pechat*, 1960,
  No. 2, pp. 49–52.
2 Makarenko, Yuri, 'An ordinary day on Pravda', *Sovietskaya
  pechat*, 1962, No. 5, pp. 21–8.
3 ibid.
4 ibid.
5 *Sovietskaya pechat*, 1963, No. 4, pp. 23–6.
6 'The Editorial Secretary of a Rayon Paper', *Sovietskaya pechat*,
  1960, No. 8, 42–4.
7 Szántó, Jenö, 'Népszabadság', *Sovietskaya pechat*, 1961, No. 9,
  pp. 52–4.
8 Schindzielorz, Karol, 'Becoming a Journalist in Poland', *Journalism Quarterly*, Iowa City, Autumn 1959, pp. 460–8.
9 Yastrebov, Y., 'Author, Letter, Newspaper: From the Practice
  of *Izvestia*', *Sovietskaya pechat*, 1961, No. 9, pp. 14–19.
10 ibid.
11 Kotlyar, op. cit., passim.
12 *Bulletin of the Journalistic Research Institute*, Prague, 1955,
  No. 17, p. 522.
13 *Novinářský sborník*, 1957, No. 4, pp. 459–60.
14 ibid.
15 *Sovietskaya pechat*, 1960, No. 7, p. 1.
16 ibid.
17 ibid., 1960, No. 8, pp. 7–9.
18 ibid., 1960, No. 7, p. 1.

19 *Sovietskaya pechat*, 1961, No. 1.
20 ibid., 1962, No. 9, pp. 1–3.
21 *Pravda*, Moscow, 20 October, 1962.
22 *Sovietskaya pechat*, 1962, No. 12, pp. 43–4.
23 *Razprostrannenie pechati* (Dissemination of the Press), Moscow, 19 October, 1961, p. 11.
24 *Sovietskaya pechat*, 1961, No. 7, p. 44.
25 ibid., 1961, No. 6, p. 44.
26 ibid.
27 ibid.
28 IPI Survey, p. 112 and 125.
29 *Prasa Polska*, June 1958. Quoted from *East Europe*, 1959, No. 9.

Chapter 14   JOURNALISTS IN THE COMMUNIST SOCIETY

1 N. S. Khrushchev in a speech to Soviet writers in 1957. Quoted from *Sovietskaya pechat*, 1957, No. 9, p. 1.
2 *Ustav KPSS* (Rules of the CPSU), Moscow, 1958.
3 LSE, entry 'Journalistic Education', in vol. 16, 1952, p. 243.
4 Kotlyar, op. cit., passim.
5 *Sovietskaya pechat*, 1962, No. 1, pp. 36–42.
6 ibid.
7 Sylla, Jiří, 'The Periodical Press in Rumania', *Gazette*, Leyden, 1962, No. 2.
8 Richert, E., *Agitation and Propaganda*.
9 Schindzielorz, op. cit.
10 IPI Survey, pp. 19–20.
11 Paul, H. W., op. cit.
12 *Československý novinář* (The Czechoslovak Journalist), Prague, 1962, No. 4.
13 IPI Survey, p. 96.
14 ibid.
15 Quoted from *East Europe*, January, 1964, p. 43.
16 *Trybuna ludu*, Warsaw, 12 July, 1963.
17 *Pravda*, Bratislava, 3 June, 1963.
18 *Rudé právo*, Prague, 23 September, 1963.
19 *Gesammelte Schriften von Karl Marx und Friedrich Engels, 1841 bis 1850* (Collected works of K. Marx and F. Engels 1841–50), vol. I, pp. 145, 242–3.

INDEX